DAILY BIBLE READINGS THAT CONNECT WITH YOUR LIFE

ENGAGE 365

BEGINNINGS AND ENDINGS

Engage 365: Beginnings and Endings
© The Good Book Company, 2020

Published by:
The Good Book Company

thegoodbook.com | thegoodbook.co.uk
thegoodbook.com.au | thegoodbook.co.nz | thegoodbook.co.in

A CIP catalogue record for this book is available from the British Library.

The notes for this volume of *Engage 365* have been edited by Alison Mitchell.
Based on *Engage* notes mainly written by Martin Cole, with extra material from Cassie Martin, Roger Fawcett, Chris Jennings, Jim Overton, Jill Silverthorne, Fiona Simmons, Sarah Smart, Adrian Taylor-Weekes and Helen Thorne.

ISBN: 9781784984496 | Printed in India

Design by André Parker

Contents

INTRODUCTION

Time to Engage

HOW TO USE ENGAGE 365

1 Set a time when you can read the Bible every day.

2 Find a place where you can be quiet and think.

3 Grab your Bible and a pen.

4 Ask God to help you understand what you read.

5 Read the day's verses with *Engage 365* taking time to think about it.

6 Pray about what you have read.

BIBLE STUFF

We use the NIV Bible version, so you might find it's the best one to use with *Engage 365*. But any modern Bible version will be fine.

If the notes say "Read Genesis 1 v 1–2"... look up Genesis in the contents page at the front of your Bible. It'll tell you which page Genesis starts on. Find chapter 1 of Genesis, and then verse 1 of chapter 1 (the verse numbers are the tiny ones). Then start reading. Simple.

GET GOING

Each day's page throws you into the Bible, to get you handling, questioning and exploring God's message to you — encouraging you to act on it and talk to God more in prayer. And there's space along the side of each page to jot down what our great God is showing you.

And whenever you start a new book of the Bible, or a new section within it, there'll be a page introducing that book or section.

ENGAGE 365 CHART

There are many ways you can use *Engage 365*. If you'd like to read the Bible for a year, starting in January, the chart below gives dates to follow. Or you can start on any date you like by beginning with Day 1. Or just search for a Bible book you'd like to explore, and jump right in. However you use it, *Engage 365* will help you to dig in to God's great word for yourself.

DAY	PAGE	DATE	BIBLE PASSAGE	DAY	PAGE	DATE	BIBLE PASSAGE
1	13–14	Jan 1	**GENESIS** 1 v 1–2	24	38	Jan 24	Luke 4 v 1–13
2	15	Jan 2	Genesis 1 v 3–13	25	39	Jan 25	Luke 4 v 14–30
3	16	Jan 3	Genesis 1 v 14–23	26	40	Jan 26	Luke 4 v 31–37
4	17	Jan 4	Genesis 1 v 24–31	27	41	Jan 27	Luke 4 v 38–44
5	18	Jan 5	Genesis 2 v 1–3	28	42	Jan 28	Luke 5 v 1–11
6	19	Jan 6	Genesis 2 v 4–7	29	43	Jan 29	Luke 5 v 12–16
7	20	Jan 7	Genesis 2 v 8–17	30	44	Jan 30	Luke 5 v 17–26
8	21	Jan 8	Genesis 2 v 18–25	31	45	Jan 31	Luke 5 v 27–32
9	22	Jan 9	Genesis 3 v 1–13	32	46	Feb 1	Luke 5 v 33–39
10	23	Jan 10	Genesis 3 v 14–19	33	47–48	Feb 2	**COLOSSIANS** 1 v 1–8
11	24	Jan 11	Genesis 3 v 20–24	34	49	Feb 3	Colossians 1 v 9–14
12	25	Jan 12	Genesis 4 v 1–16	35	50	Feb 4	Colossians 1 v 15–20
13	26	Jan 13	Genesis 4 v 17–26	36	51	Feb 5	Colossians 1 v 21–23
14	27–28	Jan 14	**LUKE** 1 v 1–25	37	52	Feb 6	Colossians 1 v 24–29
15	29	Jan 15	Luke 1 v 26–38	38	53	Feb 7	Colossians 2 v 1–7
16	30	Jan 16	Luke 1 v 39–56	39	54	Feb 8	Colossians 2 v 8–12
17	31	Jan 17	Luke 1 v 57–80	40	55	Feb 9	Colossians 2 v 13–15
18	32	Jan 18	Luke 2 v 1–20	41	56	Feb 10	Colossians 2 v 16–23
19	33	Jan 19	Luke 2 v 21–40	42	57–58	Feb 11	**PSALM** 1
20	34	Jan 20	Luke 2 v 41–52	43	59	Feb 12	Psalm 2
21	35	Jan 21	Luke 3 v 1–14	44	60	Feb 13	Psalm 3
22	36	Jan 22	Luke 3 v 15–20	45	61	Feb 14	**GENESIS** 5 v 1–32
23	37	Jan 23	Luke 3 v 21–38	46	62	Feb 15	Genesis 6 v 1–8

DAY	PAGE	DATE	BIBLE PASSAGE
47	63	Feb 16	Genesis 6 v 8–22
48	64	Feb 17	Genesis 7 v 1–24
49	65	Feb 18	Genesis 8 v 1–14
50	66	Feb 19	Genesis 8 v 15–22
51	67	Feb 20	Genesis 9 v 1–7
52	68	Feb 21	Genesis 9 v 8–17
53	69	Feb 22	Genesis 9 v 18–29
54	70	Feb 23	Genesis 10 v 1–32
55	71	Feb 24	Genesis 11 v 1–9
56	72	Feb 25	Genesis 11 v 10–32
57	73–74	Feb 26	**LUKE** 6 v 1–11
58	75	Feb 27	Luke 6 v 12–26
59	76	Feb 28	Luke 6 v 27–36
60	77	Mar 1	Luke 6 v 37–42
61	78	Mar 2	Luke 6 v 43–49
62	79	Mar 3	Luke 7 v 1–10
63	80	Mar 4	Luke 7 v 11–17
64	81	Mar 5	Luke 7 v 18–35
65	82	Mar 6	Luke 7 v 36–50
66	83	Mar 7	Luke 8 v 1–15
67	84	Mar 8	Luke 8 v 16–21
68	85	Mar 9	Luke 8 v 22–25
69	86	Mar 10	Luke 8 v 26–39
70	87	Mar 11	Luke 8 v 40–56
71	88	Mar 12	**COLOSSIANS** 3 v 1–4
72	89	Mar 13	Colossians 3 v 5–11
73	90	Mar 14	Colossians 3 v 12–14
74	91	Mar 15	Colossians 3 v 15–17
75	92	Mar 16	Colossians 3 v 18–21
76	93	Mar 17	Colossians 3 v 22 – 4 v 1
77	94	Mar 18	Colossians 4 v 2–4
78	95	Mar 19	Colossians 4 v 5–6
79	96	Mar 20	Colossians 4 v 7–18
80	97	Mar 21	**PSALM** 4
81	98	Mar 22	Psalm 5
82	99–100	Mar 23	**GENESIS** 12 v 1–9
83	101	Mar 24	Genesis 12 v 10–20
84	102	Mar 25	Genesis 13 v 1–13
85	103	Mar 26	Genesis 13 v 14–18
86	104	Mar 27	Genesis 14 v 1–16
87	105	Mar 28	Genesis 14 v 17–24
88	106	Mar 29	Genesis 15 v 1–21
89	107	Mar 30	Genesis 16 v 1–16
90	108	Mar 31	Genesis 17 v 1–14
91	109	Apr 1	Genesis 17 v 15–27
92	110	Apr 2	**LUKE** 9 v 1–9
93	111	Apr 3	Luke 9 v 10–17
94	112	Apr 4	Luke 9 v 18–22
95	113	Apr 5	Luke 9 v 23–27
96	114	Apr 6	Luke 9 v 28–36
97	115	Apr 7	Luke 9 v 37–45
98	116	Apr 8	Luke 9 v 46–50
99	117	Apr 9	Luke 9 v 51–62
100	118	Apr 10	Luke 10 v 1–16
101	119	Apr 11	Luke 10 v 17–24
102	120	Apr 12	Luke 10 v 25–37
103	121	Apr 13	Luke 10 v 38–42
104	122	Apr 14	Luke 11 v 1–4
105	123	Apr 15	Luke 11 v 5–10
106	124	Apr 16	Luke 11 v 14–28
107	125	Apr 17	Luke 11 v 29–36
108	126	Apr 18	Luke 11 v 37–54
109	127–128	Apr 19	**ACTS** 1 v 1–11
110	129	Apr 20	Acts 1 v 12–26

DAY	PAGE	DATE	BIBLE PASSAGE
111	130	Apr 21	Acts 2 v 1–13
112	131	Apr 22	Acts 2 v 13–28
113	132	Apr 23	Acts 2 v 25–41
114	133	Apr 24	Acts 2 v 42–47
115	134	Apr 25	Acts 3 v 1–12
116	135	Apr 26	Acts 3 v 11 – 4 v 4
117	136	Apr 27	Acts 4 v 5–22
118	137	Apr 28	Acts 4 v 23–31
119	138	Apr 29	Acts 4 v 32 – 5 v 11
120	139	Apr 30	**PSALM** 6
121	140	May 1	Psalm 7
122	141	May 2	Psalm 8
123	142	May 3	Psalm 9
124	143	May 4	**GENESIS** 18 v 1–15
125	144	May 5	Genesis 18 v 16–33
126	145	May 6	Genesis 19 v 1–11
127	146	May 7	Genesis 19 v 12–29
128	147	May 8	Genesis 19 v 30–38
129	148	May 9	Genesis 20 v 1–18
130	149	May 10	Genesis 21 v 1–7
131	150	May 11	Genesis 21 v 8–21
132	151	May 12	Genesis 21 v 22–34
133	152	May 13	Genesis 22 v 1–10
134	153	May 14	Genesis 22 v 9–19
135	154	May 15	Genesis 23 v 1–20
136	155	May 16	Genesis 24 v 1–16
137	156	May 17	Genesis 24 v 15–54
138	157	May 18	Genesis 24 v 54–67
139	158	May 19	Genesis 25 v 1–11
140	159–160	May 20	**LUKE** 12 v 1–12
141	161	May 21	Luke 12 v 13–21
142	162	May 22	Luke 12 v 22–34

DAY	PAGE	DATE	BIBLE PASSAGE
143	163	May 23	Luke 12 v 35–48
144	164	May 24	Luke 12 v 49–59
145	165	May 25	Luke 13 v 1–9
146	166	May 26	Luke 13 v 10–21
147	167	May 27	Luke 13 v 22–30
148	168	May 28	Luke 13 v 31–35
149	169	May 29	Luke 14 v 1–14
150	170	May 30	Luke 14 v 15–24
151	171	May 31	**ACTS** 5 v 12–27
152	172	Jun 1	Acts 5 v 27–42
153	173	Jun 2	Acts 6 v 1–7
154	174	Jun 3	Acts 6 v 8–15
155	175	Jun 4	Acts 7 v 1–16, 44–50
156	176	Jun 5	Acts 7 v 17–43
157	177	Jun 6	Acts 7 v 51–53
158	178	Jun 7	Acts 7 v 51–60
159	179	Jun 8	Acts 8 v 4–25
160	180	Jun 9	Acts 8 v 26–40
161	181	Jun 10	**PSALM** 10
162	182	Jun 11	Psalm 11
163	183-184	Jun 12	**GENESIS** 25 v 19–34
164	185	Jun 13	Genesis 26 v 1–11
165	186	Jun 14	Genesis 26 v 12–35
166	187	Jun 15	Genesis 27 v 1–29
167	188	Jun 16	Genesis 27 v 30 – 28 v 9
168	189	Jun 17	Genesis 28 v 10–22
169	190	Jun 18	Genesis 29 v 1–30
170	191	Jun 19	Genesis 29 v 31 – 30 v 24
171	192	Jun 20	Genesis 30 v 25 – 31 v 21
172	193	Jun 21	Genesis 31 v 22–55
173	194	Jun 22	Genesis 32 v 1–21
174	195	Jun 23	Genesis 32 v 22–32

DAY	PAGE	DATE	BIBLE PASSAGE
175	196	Jun 24	Genesis 33 v 1–20
176	197	Jun 25	Genesis 34 v 1–31
177	198	Jun 26	Genesis 35 v 1–15
178	199	Jun 27	Genesis 35 v 16 – 36 v 8
179	200	Jun 28	**LUKE** 14 v 25–35
180	201	Jun 29	Luke 15 v 1–10
181	202	Jun 30	Luke 15 v 11–32
182	203	Jul 1	Luke 15 v 11–32 again
183	204	Jul 2	Luke 16 v 1–15
184	205	Jul 3	Luke 16 v 19–31
185	206	Jul 4	Luke 17 v 1–4
186	207	Jul 5	Luke 17 v 5–10
187	208	Jul 6	Luke 17 v 11–19
188	209	Jul 7	Luke 17 v 20–37
189	210	Jul 8	Luke 18 v 1–8
190	211	Jul 9	Luke 18 v 9–17
191	212	Jul 10	Luke 18 v 18–30
192	213	Jul 11	Luke 18 v 31–43
193	214	Jul 12	**PSALM** 12
194	215	Jul 13	Psalm 13
195	216	Jul 14	Psalm 14
196	217–218	Jul 15	**ACTS** 9 v 1–19
197	219	Jul 16	Acts 9 v 19–31
198	220	Jul 17	Acts 9 v 32–43
199	221	Jul 18	Acts 10 v 1–23
200	222	Jul 19	Acts 10 v 23–35
201	223	Jul 20	Acts 10 v 34–48
202	224	Jul 21	Acts 11 v 1–18
203	225	Jul 22	Acts 11 v 19–30
204	226	Jul 23	Acts 12 v 1–19
205	227	Jul 24	Acts 12 v 19–24
206	228	Jul 25	**GENESIS** 37 v 1–11

DAY	PAGE	DATE	BIBLE PASSAGE
207	229	Jul 26	Genesis 37 v 12–36
208	230	Jul 27	Genesis 38 v 1–30
209	231	Jul 28	Genesis 39 v 1–23
210	232	Jul 29	Genesis 40 v 1–23
211	233	Jul 30	Genesis 41 v 1–57
212	234	Jul 31	Genesis 42 v 1–38
213	235	Aug 1	Genesis 43 v 1–34
214	236	Aug 2	Genesis 44 v 1–34
215	237	Aug 3	Genesis 45 v 1–28
216	238	Aug 4	Genesis 46 v 1 – 47 v 12
217	239	Aug 5	Genesis 47 v 13–31
218	240	Aug 6	Genesis 48 v 1–22
219	241	Aug 7	Genesis 49 v 1–12
220	242	Aug 8	Genesis 49 v 13–28
221	243	Aug 9	Genesis 49 v 29 – 50 v 14
222	244	Aug 10	Genesis 50 v 15–26
223	245–246	Aug 11	**LUKE** 19 v 1–10
224	247	Aug 12	Luke 19 v 11–27
225	248	Aug 13	Luke 19 v 28–44
226	249	Aug 14	Luke 19 v 45 – 20 v 8
227	250	Aug 15	Luke 20 v 9–19
228	251	Aug 16	Luke 20 v 20–40
229	252	Aug 17	Luke 20 v 41–47
230	253	Aug 18	Luke 21 v 1–4
231	254	Aug 19	Luke 21 v 5–11
232	255	Aug 20	Luke 21 v 12–19
233	256	Aug 21	Luke 21 v 20–38
234	257	Aug 22	**ACTS** 13 v 1–12
235	258	Aug 23	Acts 13 v 13–31
236	259	Aug 24	Acts 13 v 32–41
237	260	Aug 25	Acts 13 v 42–52
238	261	Aug 26	Acts 14 v 1–7

DAY	PAGE	DATE	BIBLE PASSAGE
239	262	Aug 27	Acts 14 v 8–20
240	263	Aug 28	Acts 14 v 21–28
241	264	Aug 29	Acts 15 v 1–11
242	265	Aug 30	Acts 15 v 12–35
243	266	Aug 31	Acts 15 v 36–41
244	267	Sep 1	**PSALM** 15
245	268	Sep 2	Psalm 16
246	269–270	Sep 3	**EXODUS** 1 v 1–22
247	271	Sep 4	Exodus 2 v 1–10
248	272	Sep 5	Exodus 2 v 11–22
249	273	Sep 6	Exodus 2 v 23–25
250	274	Sep 7	Exodus 3 v 1–10
251	275	Sep 8	Exodus 3 v 11–15
252	276	Sep 9	Exodus 3 v 16–22
253	277	Sep 10	Exodus 4 v 1–17
254	278	Sep 11	Exodus 4 v 18–31
255	279	Sep 12	Exodus 5 v 1–21
256	280	Sep 13	Exodus 5 v 22 – 6 v 12
257	281	Sep 14	Exodus 6 v 13 – 7 v 7
258	282	Sep 15	Exodus 7 v 8–25
259	283	Sep 16	Exodus 8 v 1–15
260	284	Sep 17	Exodus 8 v 16–32
261	285	Sep 18	Exodus 9 v 1–12
262	286	Sep 19	**LUKE** 22 v 1–23
263	287	Sep 20	Luke 22 v 24–30
264	288	Sep 21	Luke 22 v 31–38
265	289	Sep 22	Luke 22 v 39–46
266	290	Sep 23	Luke 22 v 47–62
267	291	Sep 24	Luke 22 v 63 – 23 v 25
268	292	Sep 25	Luke 23 v 26–34
269	293	Sep 26	Luke 23 v 35–43
270	294	Sep 27	Luke 23 v 44–49

DAY	PAGE	DATE	BIBLE PASSAGE
271	295	Sep 28	Luke 23 v 50–56
272	296	Sep 29	Luke 24 v 1–12
273	297	Sep 30	Luke 24 v 13–35
274	298	Oct 1	Luke 24 v 36–53
275	299–300	Oct 2	**ACTS** 16 v 1–10
276	301	Oct 3	Acts 16 v 11–15
277	302	Oct 4	Acts 16 v 16–40
278	303	Oct 5	Acts 17 v 1–15
279	304	Oct 6	Acts 17 v 16–21
280	305	Oct 7	Acts 17 v 22–28
281	306	Oct 8	Acts 17 v 29–34
282	307	Oct 9	Acts 18 v 1–4
283	308	Oct 10	Acts 18 v 5–17
284	309	Oct 11	Acts 18 v 18–28
285	310	Oct 12	**PSALM** 17
286	311	Oct 13	Psalm 18
287	312	Oct 14	**EXODUS** 9 v 13–35
288	313	Oct 15	Exodus 10 v 1–20
289	314	Oct 16	Exodus 10 v 21–29
290	315	Oct 17	Exodus 11 v 1–10
291	316	Oct 18	Exodus 12 v 1–13
292	317	Oct 19	Exodus 12 v 14–28
293	318	Oct 20	Exodus 12 v 29–42
294	319	Oct 21	Exodus 12 v 43–51
295	320	Oct 22	Exodus 13 v 1–16
296	321	Oct 23	Exodus 13 v 17–22
297	322	Oct 24	Exodus 14 v 1–14
298	323	Oct 25	Exodus 14 v 15–31
299	324	Oct 26	Exodus 15 v 1–12
300	325	Oct 27	Exodus 15 v 13–21
301	326	Oct 28	Exodus 15 v 22–27
302	327–328	Oct 29	**REVELATION** 1 v 1–8

DAY	PAGE	DATE	BIBLE PASSAGE
303	329	Oct 30	Revelation 1 v 9–20
304	330	Oct 31	Revelation 2 v 1–11
305	331	Nov 1	Revelation 2 v 12–29
306	332	Nov 2	Revelation 3 v 1–13
307	333	Nov 3	Revelation 3 v 14–22
308	334	Nov 4	Revelation 4 v 1–11
309	335	Nov 5	Revelation 5 v 1–14
310	336	Nov 6	Revelation 6 v 1–17
311	337	Nov 7	Revelation 7 v 1–17
312	338	Nov 8	Revelation 8 v 1–13
313	339	Nov 9	Revelation 9 v 1–21
314	340	Nov 10	Revelation 10 v 1–11
315	341	Nov 11	Revelation 11 v 1–19
316	342	Nov 12	**ACTS** 19 v 1–10
317	343	Nov 13	Acts 19 v 11–22
318	344	Nov 14	Acts 19 v 23–41
319	345	Nov 15	Acts 20 v 1–12
320	346	Nov 16	Acts 20 v 13–21
321	347	Nov 17	Acts 20 v 22–24
322	348	Nov 18	Acts 20 v 25–31
323	349	Nov 19	Acts 20 v 32–38
324	350	Nov 20	**PSALM** 19
325	351	Nov 21	Psalm 20
326	352	Nov 22	Psalm 21
327	353–354	Nov 23	**EXODUS** 16 v 1–12
328	355	Nov 24	Exodus 16 v 13–36
329	356	Nov 25	Exodus 17 v 1–7
330	357	Nov 26	Exodus 17 v 8–16
331	358	Nov 27	Exodus 18 v 1–27
332	359	Nov 28	Exodus 19 v 1–25
333	360	Nov 29	Exodus 20 v 1–6
334	361	Nov 30	Exodus 20 v 7–11

DAY	PAGE	DATE	BIBLE PASSAGE
335	362	Dec 1	Exodus 20 v 12–17
336	363	Dec 2	Exodus 20 v 18–26
337	364	Dec 3	**REVELATION** 12 v 1–17
338	365	Dec 4	Revelation 13 v 1–18
339	366	Dec 5	Revelation 14 v 1–13
340	367	Dec 6	Revelation 14 v 14 – 15 v 4
341	368	Dec 7	Revelation 15 v 5 – 16 v 21
342	369	Dec 8	Revelation 17 v 1–18
343	370	Dec 9	Revelation 18 v 1–24
344	371	Dec 10	Revelation 19 v 1–10
345	372	Dec 11	Revelation 19 v 11–21
346	373	Dec 12	Revelation 20 v 1–15
347	374	Dec 13	Revelation 21 v 1–8
348	375	Dec 14	Revelation 21 v 9 – 22 v 5
349	376	Dec 15	Revelation 22 v 6–21
350	377–378	Dec 16	**ACTS** 21 v 1–16
351	379	Dec 17	Acts 21 v 17–36
352	380	Dec 18	Acts 21 v 37 – 22 v 21
353	381	Dec 19	Acts 22 v 21 – 23 v 11
354	382	Dec 20	Acts 23 v 12–35
355	383	Dec 21	Acts 24 v 1–27
356	384	Dec 22	Acts 25 v 1–22
357	385	Dec 23	Acts 25 v 23 – 26 v 23
358	386	Dec 24	Acts 26 v 19–32
359	387	Dec 25	Acts 27 v 1–26
360	388	Dec 26	Acts 27 v 27–44
361	389	Dec 27	Acts 28 v 1–10
362	390	Dec 28	Acts 28 v 11–16
363	391	Dec 29	Acts 28 v 17–31
364	392	Dec 30	**PSALM** 22
365	393	Dec 31	Psalm 23

GENESIS

In the beginning

Once upon a time...

The Bible doesn't quite start like that. Genesis is not a fairy tale for one thing. Neither is it a science textbook. Nor is it a DIY "How to create the universe" instruction manual. It's a book about God.

Genesis is also a book about beginnings — in fact, that's what the word "genesis" means.

The beginning of the world, the beginning of life, the beginning of the human race, the beginning of a big problem and the beginning of God's rescue plan.

WHO WROTE IT?

Genesis was written by Moses, probably just before God's people entered the promised land. Its purpose was to remind the Israelites where they came from and all that God had done for their ancestors.

WHERE'S THE T-REX?

You won't find much about dinosaurs. In fact, you won't find anything about dinosaurs — try *Jurassic Park* for that. You also won't find answers to those tricky questions like: *Did Adam and Eve have belly buttons?*

What you will discover is loads about God — who He is, why He created the world and why He made us. And the meaning of life.

Shall we start at the beginning?

Before the beginning

Genesis. The beginning. The start of something. Birth, origin, source or foundation. But God was there before the beginning! In the beginning God...

👁 Read Genesis 1 v 1–2

ENGAGE YOUR BRAIN

▷ *Who was involved in the creation of the heavens and the earth?*

Dumb question? Look carefully at verse 2 and then read Colossians 1 v 15–17.

God — Father, Son and Holy Spirit — was fully involved in creating everything.

▷ *So who do the heavens and earth belong to?*

▷ *What are the implications of that for us and everyone else?*

▷ *Why do you think people have such a problem with accepting that God created the world?*

SHARE IT

Why not challenge a friend or relative today? You could ask them: *Just suppose that God really did create the world and made you. How would it change the way you look at yourself? Would it change the way you live?*

PRAY ABOUT IT

Take time out to really think about verse 1. We think our world and our lives are so important and significant, but God was there before it all.

If you're a Christian, the Bible says that God chose you in Christ "before the creation of the world to be holy and blameless in his sight" (Ephesians 1 v 4). Thank God for who He is.

THE BOTTOM LINE

In the beginning: God.

2 | Filling the void

There's something very appealing about a blank sheet of paper, or snow that no one else has trodden on. There's so much potential. Here we see God starting to make something of the "formless and empty" earth.

👁 Read Genesis 1 v 3–13

ENGAGE YOUR BRAIN

▶ *What is the first thing God says?*

In the Bible, darkness = evil. By starting things off like this, we see that God is the complete opposite. Elsewhere in the Bible it says: "God is light; in him there is no darkness at all" (1 John 1 v 5).

▶ *How does God bring things into existence?*

▶ *What does that tell us about Him?*

▶ *Fill in the grid below for the first three days.*

DAY	What does God create?
1	
2	
3	

▶ *What is God's verdict on what He has created? (v4, v10, v12)*

It can be hard to believe that the world was created to be good when we watch the news or read the papers or internet. But it was good, and one day it will be again.

PRAY ABOUT IT

Go outside, or look out of your window at some of the amazing things God has created: the stars, plants, animals, EVERYTHING.

Spend time praising God that He merely spoke and these things were created. Thank Him that we can talk with such a powerful, awesome God!

THE BOTTOM LINE

God is so powerful that He spoke the world into existence.

What a wonderful world

**What do you like about the world you live in?
What in nature really blows your mind or makes you smile?**

👁 **Read Genesis 1 v 14–23**

ENGAGE YOUR BRAIN

▷ *Carry on filling in the grid for days 4 and 5. Can you spot a pattern?*

DAY	What does God create?
1	Light & dark
2	Sky & water
3	Dry land & plants etc
4	
5	

▷ *Have you noticed any words or phrases that are repeated?*

▷ *What do they tell us about God?*

God's creation is a carefully planned and ordered place. But it's also teeming with life and amazing diversity. Check out verses 12 and 21.

Also look at verse 24. God is fantastically creative and fun. He must have a sense of humour — just look in the mirror! Think of some of the incredible animals He created.

SHARE IT

Some people think God is boring. What can you point out to them in creation to show them that God is amazingly creative, with a sense of humour? Think of creative ways you can share how exciting God is with people you know.

PRAY ABOUT IT

Thank God for all the incredible things He has made. Pick three that really blow your mind.

4 Creating an image

"Aww, look at him, he's so human." No, he's not. He's a cat wearing a vest. However lovely Mr Tibbles or Fluffy might be, there is a big difference between humans and animals. Let's see why in the next few verses of Genesis 1.

 Read Genesis 1 v 24–31

ENGAGE YOUR BRAIN

Let's recap where we've got to:

DAY	What does God create?
1	Light & dark
2	Sky & water
3	Dry land & plants etc
4	Sun, moon & stars
5	Birds & sea creatures
6	

▷ *What is the big difference between human beings and animals (v26)?*

God made the world and He is the supreme ruler. We are like Him, made in His image, and we are supposed to rule the world under Him.

▷ *What are humankind's two big tasks? (v28)*

PRAY ABOUT IT

Look at how God blesses human beings (v28–30). The world richly provides all we need to live. There's enough food in the world that no one needs to starve, but greed and war leave millions starving. Thank God for giving us what we need to live, and pray for those who are suffering because of war or corruption.

▷ *What is God's final verdict on creation (v31)?*

THE BOTTOM LINE

You are made in God's image. Yes, you!

5 Under a rest

Saturday mornings, the end of the school year, getting up at noon. Mmmm, lovely rest. Roll on day seven!

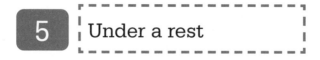 **Read Genesis 2 v 1–3**

ENGAGE YOUR BRAIN

▶ *How did God view the world after the first six days were over? (Genesis 1 v 31)*

▶ *Can you spot any difference between day seven and the days that went before?*

Has God given up on the world then? Just wound it up like a watch and let it run itself? No, verse 3 says He rested from His work of creation, not that He stopped caring for what He made.

This tells us two things about God:

1. God works
For six days, God worked, and what breathtaking work He did — creating the universe, the world we live in and all its stunning variety.

2. God rests
At the end of six days of work, God was happy with all He'd created, so He rested.

GET ON WITH IT

So if God both works and rests, guess what that means for us…

1. We work
There's no excuse for laziness and looking for an easy life. God commanded us to work and we should throw ourselves into it, serving Him in all our work and studies. Being lazy reflects badly on the God we live for.

2. We rest
Some people are workaholics: they just don't stop. Or they never stop studying. Our work or studies are not the most important thing! Yes, we should work hard for God, but we should also take time to rest and enjoy the great world He's given us.

PRAY ABOUT IT

Anything you want to say to God?

6 Extreme close-up

We've seen the big picture — God's people (1 v 26–31) in God's place (1 v 1–25) enjoying God's blessing (2 v 1–3). So let's zoom in for a close-up. An extreme close-up. Zooming all the way up someone's nostrils…

👁 Read Genesis 2 v 4–7

ENGAGE YOUR BRAIN

▷ *What was the man made from?*

▷ *How did the man become a living being?*

We are dependent on God for every breath we take. The tragedy is that we often forget this. Imagine an astronaut bad-mouthing his oxygen tanks or a deep-sea diver telling everyone he was perfectly able to breathe on his own underwater, thank you very much…

We are totally dependent on God and to forget or ignore that is just as stupid, ungrateful and dangerous.

PRAY ABOUT IT

Thank God for giving you life.

Ask Him to help you remember that you are totally dependent on Him.

GET ON WITH IT

If human life is a gift from God, think how important that makes your own life! God created you! Try to remember that fact the next time you look in the mirror and don't like what you see. Even when you're feeling down about yourself, God cares for you. Our lives are important. Not to be thrown away in suicide or regret. God breathes life into us!

If God is the one who gives life, what implications does this have for genetic engineering? Should parents be able to choose the gender or appearance of their babies? We don't know all the answers to these questions, but they're worth thinking about. Why not ask your Christian friends what their views are.

THE BOTTOM LINE

Life is a gift from God.

7 Garden party

Mowing the grass. Pruning the roses. Weeding the flowerbeds. Yawn. But God's garden was not about boring, grubby, hard work.

👁 Read Genesis 2 v 8–17

ENGAGE YOUR BRAIN

▶ What was in God's garden?

▶ What does God's garden show us about God?

God didn't just give Adam and Eve boring, basic food. He gave them loads of good plants for food and made His garden beautiful. He wanted them to enjoy being in it with Him for ever; that's why the tree of life was there.

▶ What was God's one rule?

▶ Does He give a reason or is He just being unreasonable?

TALK IT THROUGH

▶ If God has given humankind the job of taking care of His creation, what should we be doing about looking after the planet?

Why not discuss this with other Christians at church or youth group?

GET ON WITH IT

▶ Does this passage change the way you think about work?

Today, try to see your work as a gift from God and to work hard.

PRAY ABOUT IT

Praise God for the superb kingdom He created, which Genesis tells us all about. Thank God that He hasn't given up on us and will create an even better paradise-kingdom when Jesus returns. Ask Him to let you be there!

THE BOTTOM LINE

God wants us to live with Him in perfection.

8 Would you Adam & Eve it?

Man's best friend.
A dog? A hamster? An iguana?
Nope. God has someone better in mind.

👁 Read Genesis 2 v 18–25

ENGAGE YOUR BRAIN

▶ What does the man need a helper for? (see Genesis 1 v 28)

TALK IT THROUGH

It might be a bit cheesy, but verses 21–23 have been summed up like this: *Woman was taken out of man — not out of his head, to rule over him; nor out of his feet, to be trampled on by him; but out of his side, to be equal to him — under his arm, that he might protect her, and near his heart that he might love her.*

▶ What do you think about that? Talk it through with friends.

ENGAGE YOUR BRAIN

▶ What are the three steps which make up marriage? (v24)

Miss any of them out and it's just not the way God designed it.

One man and one woman, leaving their parents, to be publicly, then physically, united (sex = God's invention for marriage!).

Notice verse 25. No clothes, no guilt, no fear. Life in God's garden was perfect (so far…).

GET ON WITH IT

"Marriage should be honoured by all" (Hebrews 13 v 4).

▶ Do your thoughts and behaviour honour God's design for marriage?

Sex outside of marriage and wrong thoughts of pre-marital sex don't please God.

▶ How might you tackle your wrong thoughts and desires?

THE BOTTOM LINE

Marriage should be honoured by all.

9 It's all gone belly up

And it was all going so well. But Genesis 3 marks a major turning point in human history; from now on things will be very different. Before you read verses 1–13, look back at Genesis 2 v 16–17. Remember what God says.

👁 Read Genesis 3 v 1–7

ENGAGE YOUR BRAIN

▷ *How does the snake encourage the woman to challenge what God has said? (v1, v4–5)*

When we doubt, distort or deny what God has said, things start going wrong. Think you wouldn't make the same mistake as Eve? Think again.

• "Does God really want what's best for me?"

• "Sex outside marriage was only wrong back in that particular culture."

• "God doesn't mind if I tell a white lie."

God's pattern for creation was Him in control with humans underneath Him, looking after His creation.

▷ *Can you see how that is changing in this chapter?*

This is more than just eating a piece of fruit; it's a full-scale rebellion against the way God planned His creation. Humans wanting to be in charge. To take God's place.

The Bible calls this *sin*.

👁 Read verses 8–13

God isn't asking these questions because He doesn't know the answers. He wants the man and woman to come clean about what they've done.

▷ *But what do they do in v12–13?*

The harmony we saw in Genesis 2 seems a long time ago.

PRAY ABOUT IT

Say sorry to God for specific times you've rebelled against Him. Ask Him to help you to change.

10 Free falling

Despite their excuses, the man and woman are guilty as charged. Now, in verses 14–19, God delivers His verdict.

👁 **Read Genesis 3 v 14–19**

ENGAGE YOUR BRAIN

▶ *Sum up the results of the rebellion on the following:*

1. Male/female relationships

2. Ruling over creation

3. Being fruitful and multiplying

What began in verse 6, with the woman telling her husband what to do, will continue. Verse 16 is not about sexual desire but the desire to be in charge of someone else. And no longer will the man care for his wife as his partner; he'll want to dominate or rule over her. The battle of the sexes started here.

Both of the jobs God gave mankind have suddenly become much harder.

Read verse 19 again. Despite the serpent's lies, God always keeps His promises (chapter 2 v 17).

SHARE IT

Our desire to rebel against God has huge consequences. It messes up relationships, as well as the world we live in. Maybe next time you're talking about relationships with friends or family, you can mention how people's failed relationship with God leads to so many problems.

PRAY ABOUT IT

If doing that sounds scary or impossible, ask God to help you.

THE BOTTOM LINE

The world is in a mess because of sin.

11 Die another day

It's not over yet. God's judgment ends with Adam and Eve being sent away from God's presence. It takes the rest of the Bible for mankind to come back.

👁 Read Genesis 3 v 20–24

ENGAGE YOUR BRAIN

▶ *What's the good news for Eve? (v20)*

▶ *What else does God do for them? (v21)*

Even in the middle of punishing Adam and Eve for their disobedience, God shows them great love and mercy! And it's totally undeserved.

All humans are descended from Eve — what an amazing privilege for her. And, even though God was banishing them from His presence, He made clothes for Adam and Eve, to cover their shame.

▶ *What were Adam and Eve no longer allowed to do? (v22)*

▶ *Why is that seriously bad news?*

▶ *What was even worse news? (v23)*

The man and woman could not eat from the tree of life any more — humans would no longer live for ever. They were condemned to death and they were thrown out of God's presence. From now on, they could no longer live with God — they were separated from Him.

Sin separates us from God. We're all doomed to die, far from God. But...

...the rest of the Bible tells us that God provided a way back to Him and eternal life — Jesus.

PRAY ABOUT IT

Thank God that He is fair in His judgment — rightly punishing sin. Praise Him for showing us incredible mercy and love by offering a way back to Him, through Jesus Christ.

12 Oh brother

Despite the disaster of chapter 3, things don't seem so bad. Adam and Eve are getting on with their jobs of being fruitful and multiplying (v1–2) and ruling over creation (v2). Nobody's dead yet. But hang on a minute...

👁 Read Genesis 4 v 1–7

ENGAGE YOUR BRAIN

🔟 *What is Cain's problem?*

🔟 *What is God's warning? (v7)*

Cain seems to have grabbed what was easiest and given it as a gift to God, rather than giving God the best, as Abel did.

Cain was furious and jealous of Abel. So God warned him that sin would take over his life if he wasn't careful and didn't control his anger.

👁 Read verses 8–16

🔟 *Like father, like son. Can you see any similarities between Cain's behaviour and Adam's?*

🔟 *How is God the same here as He was in the last chapter?*

Again we see God's judgment: He won't ignore evil or let it go unpunished (v9–12).

But we also see God's mercy: He protects Cain even though Cain doesn't deserve it (v13–15).

🔟 *Look again at verse 16. What is always the result of our sin?*

PRAY ABOUT IT

Thank God for the fact that He rightly judges evil but also shows mercy. Praise Him for the cross where Jesus took His Father's punishment on Himself so that we could be forgiven.

THE BOTTOM LINE

Our sin separates us from God.

13 | The good, the bad and the ugly

We're not given any details about where Cain manages to find a wife, but within a few generations, the population is growing nicely. Or should that be nastily?

👁 Read Genesis 4 v 17–24

ENGAGE YOUR BRAIN

▶ *What positive things are Cain's descendants involved in? (v20–22)*

▶ *What negative things do they get up to?*

▶ *Why is Lamech's attitude so bad? (v23–24)*

Despite some of the progress that seems to be going on, mankind is still messed up by sin: bigamy, murder and pride, just to pick three.

▶ *How is today's world similar?*

👁 Read verses 25–26

▶ *What signs of hope can you spot?*

God has mercy on Adam and Eve as individuals, giving them another child. But people in general also start calling "on the name of the LORD" (v26).

PRAY ABOUT IT

Thank God that however bad the world gets, there are still people who do turn to Him. Pray for people you know who are living without God, that they would learn to call on His name, and start living for Him.

THE BOTTOM LINE

The world without God is in a downward spiral.

LUKE

Jesus: the early years

Ever had a friend tell you that something unbelievable has happened? Maybe a huge celeb was shopping in the local mall. It's so outrageous that you don't believe a word of it until you see it in the local paper and a friend tells you they saw it with their own eyes.

CHECK THE EVIDENCE

There have been some outrageous claims about Jesus — His mother was a virgin; He could do miracles; He raised people back to life; He was God's Son. Without proof, we can easily ignore these claims. What we need is someone who was actually around at the time, and that's where Luke steps in.

DOCTOR DO-LOTS

Luke was a well-educated doctor, and one of Paul's mates. He did his own investigation into the claims about Jesus and even checked if all the stuff the Old Testament prophets claimed about the Christ came true in Jesus (it did).

He then compiled all his findings into "an orderly account" and sent it to his friend Theophilus, to convince him of the truth about Jesus.

PUBLIC INQUIRY

In the first few chapters of Luke's Gospel, we start with Jesus' early years and see how God was working in an incredible way right from the beginning.

Explore all the evidence and make up your own mind about Jesus.

14 Dumbstruck

It's a flying start from Luke. He explains why he's writing this essay and then jumps straight into the story. Although Jesus doesn't get a mention just yet.

👁 Read Luke 1 v 1–4

ENGAGE YOUR BRAIN

▶ Why did Luke do this investigation and write this account? (v4)

👁 Read verses 5–17

▶ Why was the angel's news so surprising? (v7, v13)

▶ What would John be like? (v14–15)

▶ And what would he do? (v16–17)

This couple were elderly and had given up on having kids, but God had other plans. Their son would become a great and godly man who would bring many Jews back to serving God. He would make them ready for King Jesus.

👁 Read verses 18–25

▶ Why was Zechariah struck dumb? (v20)

▶ How did Elizabeth react differently? (v25)

Unsurprisingly, Zechariah was surprised by the shock news and questioned Gabriel. So God's angel struck him dumb until birth-day.

This reminds us just how seriously we should take God's word. It's not to be taken lightly, but to be believed and treasured and allowed to change our lives.

GET ON WITH IT

▶ What can you do to make sure you take seriously what you read in the Bible?

▶ How can you treasure God's word as Elizabeth did?

PRAY ABOUT IT

Thank God that He works in people's lives in astonishing ways. Ask Him to change your attitude to His word.

15 | Pregnant pause

**It's time for part two of "Gabriel's Surprise Visits".
The scene is a house in the town of Nazareth. Get
ready to see another jaw drop and hit the floor in shock.**

👁 Read Luke 1 v 26–33

ENGAGE YOUR BRAIN

🔟 *What jaw-dropping promises did
Gabriel make about Jesus?*

He will be…

He'll be called…

The Lord will…

And He will…

His kingdom…

Out of the blue, God's messenger
told a young virgin that she would
become pregnant and that her
future baby would be called God's
Son and would rule the Jews for
ever. What a shock!

👁 Read verses 34–38

🔟 *How would Mary, a virgin,
become pregnant? (v35)*

🔟 *What great truth did Mary hear
about God? (v37)*

🔟 *What was Mary's response? (v38)*

We're not told exactly how this
virgin would get pregnant. All we
need to know is that "no word
from God will ever fail". Nothing is
impossible for God. Nothing at all.
Mary believed that God can do the
impossible and was prepared for
God to use her as His servant.

THINK IT OVER

🔟 *Do you truly believe that
nothing's impossible for God?*

🔟 *What do you find hard to believe
that God can do?*

🔟 *How can you serve Him more
willingly?*

PRAY ABOUT IT

Talk to God openly about this stuff.

16 Bump jump

Can you remember being really excited about something when you were young? What was it? How did you show your excitement? Elizabeth's baby got excited about stuff before he was even born!

👁 **Read Luke 1 v 39–45**

ENGAGE YOUR BRAIN

▷ *How did Elizabeth know about her relative's great news? (v41)*

Elizabeth was filled with the Holy Spirit, and her baby jumped for joy when pregnant Mary turned up on her doorstep. God clearly showed Elizabeth (and John inside her!) that Mary would give birth to the Christ — the promised Rescuer.

👁 **Read verses 46–56**

▷ *How had God treated Mary? (v46–49)*

▷ *How had He treated His people (Israel)? (v50–55)*

▷ *What about His enemies? (v51–53)*

Mary realised what a privilege it was that God had chosen to use her to serve Him in this unbelievable way. God often uses unlikely, humble people in amazing ways (v48, v52). He shows mercy to all those who fear Him and serve Him (v50). He proved this to the Israelites by doing many "mighty deeds" for them and defeating their wealthy, proud enemies (v51–53).

God's plan to save His people didn't start with these two babies — it had been His plan all along: "just as he promised our ancestors" (v55).

GET ON WITH IT

Try writing a poem or song or letter to God, like Mary's song (v46–56). Include things He's done specifically for you as well as for all Christians. Mention how it makes you feel. Don't hold back. Use it for your prayer time today.

17 Family fortunes

Mary (a virgin) is expecting a baby who will rule God's people for ever. Her elderly cousin Elizabeth is also pregnant with a special child and has a husband who's struck dumb for not believing an angel. Whatever next?

👁 Read Luke 1 v 57–66

ENGAGE YOUR BRAIN

▶ What did Elizabeth's neighbours recognise about what had happened? (v58)

▶ What effect did these events have on the local community? (v65–66)

When Zechariah showed he trusted God and gave his son the name John — as Gabriel had commanded — he got his voice back and immediately started praising God. Everyone was so flabbergasted by what had happened, the whole area was talking about it. They knew there was something special about John.

👁 Read verses 67–80

▶ What did Zechariah say about his son and what he'd do? (v76–79)

▶ What will God do for His people? (v69–75)

John would be God's messenger, a prophet. He'd prepare the way for Jesus — the "horn of salvation" — who would rescue God's people from their biggest enemy, sin. He would bring forgiveness and guide all believers in the path of peace.

SHARE IT

Read the verses again and think how they could help you to share with people what God has done for us by sending Jesus.

PRAY ABOUT IT

Zechariah's song reminds us what God was doing through Jesus — bringing a rescue. It reminds us of our deepest need — to have our sins forgiven. And it reminds us of the right response — living to please God.

THE BOTTOM LINE

Jesus is the great Rescuer.

18 Angel delight

You may have heard this story before. But try to see it with new eyes. As usual, Luke gives us the historical setting (v1–3) before he starts. Check out the excitement of the angels, the shepherds and the proud mum.

👁 Read Luke 2 v 1–12

ENGAGE YOUR BRAIN

▶ Who are the first to hear the great news? (v8–9)

▶ How does the angel describe the news? (v10)

▶ What two descriptions of Jesus does he give? (v11)

Not the first people you'd expect to hear the most impressive announcement ever. Regular shepherds out in the hills. But the angel gave them the most amazing *good news*, which would bring *great joy* to the world. It was news for *all people* — everyone needs to hear about Jesus.

Christ isn't Jesus' surname. It's a title. Like Messiah, it means "anointed one" — God's chosen King. Following Jesus means accepting Him as King and Lord of your whole life.

👁 Read verses 13–20

▶ How did the shepherds react to this news? (v15–18, v20)

▶ What about Mary? (v19)

The angels praised God for sending His Son to bring peace to people on earth. Peace for those who trust in Him. The shepherds believed, and showed it by rushing to the maternity room and then telling everyone about it. Look at the effect it had — verse 18.

And look at Mary, taking in exactly how huge and important this was and how privileged she was.

PRAY ABOUT IT

Thank God for sending His Son personally as our Saviour. Recognise His right to run your life as Lord.

THE BOTTOM LINE

Jesus is the Saviour of the world.

19 Simeon and Anna

Yesterday we saw how a bunch of ordinary shepherds were the first to hear the great news of Jesus' birth. Next to be let in on the news are two elderly temple workers.

👁 Read Luke 2 v 21–35

ENGAGE YOUR BRAIN

▶ *What had God promised Simeon? (v26)*

▶ *How did Simeon describe Jesus? (v30–35)*

▶ *Who would Jesus save? (v31–32)*

▶ *What other effect would Jesus have on people? (v34–35)*

Joseph and Mary took Jesus to the temple to offer sacrifices to God and vow that Jesus' life would be given to serving God. Simeon had been waiting his whole life to see the Christ — and here He was!

God showed Simeon who Jesus really was: the Saviour sent to rescue not just the Israelites, but Gentiles too (v31–32). But the message of Jesus isn't an easy one. He knows what's in our hearts (v35). Everyone who trusts Jesus' death to save them will "rise" to eternal life. But those who reject Him will "fall" to eternal death (v34).

👁 Read verses 36–40

▶ *What was Anna's reaction to seeing who Jesus really is? (v38)*

Anna spoke to people "looking forward to the redemption of Jerusalem" (v38) and Simeon was "waiting for the consolation of Israel" (v25). Israel, the people of God, needed to be comforted. But why?

It was about 400 years since the events at the end of the Old Testament. Israelites who trusted God were waiting for Him to bring His people back to Himself, as He'd promised. Simeon and Anna were shown by the Holy Spirit that *Jesus* was the one who would do it.

PRAY ABOUT IT

Using Simeon's words of praise (v29–32), make a list of things we can be thankful to God for. Add some things of your own too.

20 Missing Jesus

Today we look at the only event in Jesus' life between His birth and the age of 30 that's recorded in the Bible. Jesus' family were at the Passover feast in Jerusalem, celebrating God rescuing the Israelites from Egypt.

👁 Read Luke 2 v 41–52

ENGAGE YOUR BRAIN

▶ *Where had Jesus been for three days?*

▶ *What did His mother ask Him? (v48)*

▶ *How did Jesus describe where He'd been? (v49)*

▶ *What didn't they understand about His answer?*

▶ *What did Jesus do next? (v51–52)*

Understandably, Mary and Joseph were worried when their 12-year-old boy went missing. But Jesus was God's Son and spent the time in His Father's house (the temple), learning from Jewish teachers and asking them big questions. People were amazed at how much He understood.

At first, Jesus' answer to His mother sounds cheeky but later we're told that He obeyed His parents (v51) and that Jesus lived without sin (Hebrews 4 v 15). Yet even Joseph and Mary didn't fully grasp who Jesus was (Luke 2 v 50).

▶ *What does this Bible bit tell us about Jesus' identity?*

GET ON WITH IT

▶ *What specifically can you do to be more like Jesus?*

▶ *In what specific ways do you need to obey your parents more?*

PRAY ABOUT IT

Talk to God about these things.

21 Desert storm

Remember pregnant Elizabeth's bump jumping for joy when pregnant Mary came to visit? Well, the bumps have now both grown up and are about to make a huge impact on people's lives.

👁 Read Luke 3 v 1–6

ENGAGE YOUR BRAIN

▶ What was John teaching? (v3)

▶ What did the prophet Isaiah say John would do? (v4–5)

▶ What would be the result? (v6)

John baptised people who *repented* — who turned away from their sinful way of living, and turned back to God. John washed them in water as a sign of their repentance. It was a picture to show that their sin would be "washed away" and forgiven when Jesus died on the cross in their place. John was preparing people for Jesus, who would save mankind (v6).

👁 Read verses 7–14

▶ How does John shatter the Jews' false confidence? (v8–9)

▶ How should people who've turned back to God live? (v11–14)

Their sins wouldn't be forgiven just because they were descended from Abraham. They had to turn their backs on sin. Jesus was going to die so that people's sins could be forgiven. And He would also return as Judge. At that time, everyone who hasn't turned to Him for forgiveness will be punished in hell (v9).

But people who have repented should live God's way. John gives three examples in verses 11–14.

GET ON WITH IT

What three specific things do you need to start doing or stop doing so that you're living God's way?

1.

2.

3.

22 Burning question

John was making a big impact in the area. He preached that people needed to repent (turn back to God) and be baptised. But some people were confused about who John really was.

👁 Read Luke 3 v 15–20

ENGAGE YOUR BRAIN

▷ *Who did people think John might be? (v15)*

▷ *How did John answer them? (v16)*

▷ *How does John describe Jesus, the Christ? (v16–17)*

▷ *What do you think v17 means?*

Some people thought John might be the Messiah/Christ — the King who God had promised would rescue His people. But John spoke of "one who is more powerful" (Jesus), who would give people the Holy Spirit to help them live God's way.

The Messiah/Christ would also come with *fire*. Verse 17 uses the picture of harvest time — gathering good crops and burning the bad stuff. Jesus will judge people — gathering those who trust in Him, but punishing those who reject Him.

People often don't like this message. It sounds too harsh. They refuse to change their lives, or they just ignore this message, as Herod did (v19–20).

TALK IT OVER

Chat with Christian friends about the idea of Jesus coming with fire and "burning up the chaff".

▷ *How does this make you feel?*

▷ *Do you ever mention God's judgment when talking about your faith?*

▷ *How can you talk about both forgiveness and judgment when sharing the gospel?*

PRAY ABOUT IT

Pray about these issues and the thoughts rolling around your head.

THE BOTTOM LINE

Jesus will judge everyone.

23 | Father and Son

"Jesus is the Son of God." It's easy to say, but what does it mean? And what did it mean to all those Jews who were around when Jesus got baptised? Step into their sandals to understand what Luke's telling us.

👁 Read Luke 3 v 21–22

ENGAGE YOUR BRAIN

▷ *What four things are we told about Jesus in verse 22?*

1.

2.

3.

4.

When God said, "You are my Son", the Jews would have recognised those words from one of the psalms (Psalm 2 v 6-7), which says that God's King is His Son. So, God is saying that Jesus, the Son of God, is His appointed King.

When God said, "with you I am well pleased", He was quoting Isaiah, where God says His servant will rescue people from sin by suffering and dying. God is saying that Jesus is His Servant who will rescue people.

John spoke and people repented and were baptised to show they'd turned from sin. Is this why Jesus was baptised? No. The Bible says He had no sin. But in the queue by the Jordan, Jesus was standing in the place of sinners.

👁 Read verses 23–38

▷ *Why is David mentioned in the list? (Luke 1 v 32, 55, 69–70)*

Adam is also called the son of God (v38). But next, Luke will show us that Jesus is the true Son of God.

THINK IT OVER

▷ *What does it mean for us that Jesus is the Son of God?*

▷ *How does today's Bible bit show us that Jesus is unique?*

THE BOTTOM LINE

Jesus is God's Son.

Speak of the devil

Having the Holy Spirit doesn't stop Jesus from being tempted. In fact, the Spirit takes Jesus straight to a place where He can be tempted. Jesus will go three rounds with the devil. Luke is our ring-side commentator.

👁 Read Luke 4 v 1–4

ENGAGE YOUR BRAIN

▶ How did the devil try to tempt Jesus?

▶ What was he hoping to achieve?

👁 Read verses 5–8

▶ What's wrong with the devil's offer in verses 6–7?

The devil offered Jesus all the world's kingdoms. But Jesus is God's appointed King and He'll be given those anyway, as God promised in the Old Testament.

👁 Read verses 9–13

▶ How did Jesus beat each temptation? (v4, 8, 12)

▶ Why do you think He dealt with the devil's attack in this way?

If Jesus had given in to the devil, that would have been the end of God's rescue plan. Jesus kept trusting God, despite the devil's attacks. The Holy Spirit helped Him fight temptation, and He could rely on the truth of God's word from the Old Testament.

GET ON WITH IT

The more we know the Bible, the more armour we have against the devil's attacks. Flick through the book of Proverbs to find some practical advice about living for God. Pick a verse and learn it.

PRAY ABOUT IT

We must continually thank Jesus for fighting the devil's attacks and staying on His mission that led to the cross. If He hadn't, we'd have no Gospel of Luke, there'd be no Christians, and no salvation.

Also talk to God about specific temptations that don't seem to leave you alone.

25 Sweet and sour

Follow our simple recipe to create the fiery-flavoured dish "Sweet and Sour Synagogue". Its first taste is sweet but it soon turns so seriously sour, it's almost a killer.

👁 Read Luke 4 v 14–22

ENGAGE YOUR BRAIN

▶ *According to Isaiah, what five things had Jesus come to do? (v18–19)*

1.

2.

3.

4.

5.

▶ *What was the people's initial response to Jesus? (v22)*

It's a powerful scene. Jesus was in the synagogue in the town where He grew up. He read from the Old Testament and then told everyone it was about Him. Astonishing stuff.

Jesus announced His mission: preaching to the poor, bringing freedom to the oppressed, sight to the blind and to "proclaim the year of the Lord's favour" — God

rescuing His people. Jesus would release people from the devil's grasp by revealing the truth to them.

👁 Read verses 23–30

▶ *What point was Jesus making with His history lessons? (v24–27)*

▶ *How did the crowd's mood change? (v28)*

Already, people were turning against Jesus. What Simeon told Mary was proving to be true: "This child is destined … to be a sign that will be spoken against" (Luke 2 v 34). Jesus had come to save but not everyone wanted the sort of salvation He had come to bring. Especially if it included non-Jews.

PRAY ABOUT IT

People today just as readily reject Jesus. Many would get rid of Him permanently if they could. Pray for people you know who are like that.

26 Spirit splatter

So far, Luke wants his readers to know that Jesus is the Son of God and Saviour of the world, who will be accepted by some and rejected by others. It's all fulfilling what God promised in the Old Testament.

👁 Read Luke 4 v 31–34
ENGAGE YOUR BRAIN

▷ *How did people in Capernaum (v32) react differently to people in Nazareth? (v28–29)*

▷ *What did the evil spirit recognise about Jesus? (v34)*

The people of Nazareth had wanted to kill Jesus, but the Capernaum crowd were amazed at His teaching and authority. And so was the evil spirit, who recognised that Jesus was sent by God and could easily destroy evil spirits.

👁 Read verses 35–37

▷ *What did Jesus show authority over?*

▷ *What was the reaction of people in the area?*

Evil spirits could be terrifying and totally take over a person. But Jesus rules, and has power over everything. Evil spirits and murderous crowds (v30) are no match for Him. Tomorrow we'll see that illness is under His control too. Nothing is more powerful than Jesus.

THINK IT OVER

▷ *If nothing is more powerful than Jesus, how should that give us more confidence?*

▷ *What should we be afraid of?*

▷ *How can trusting Jesus' power help us as we talk to others about Him?*

PRAY ABOUT IT

Talk to God about your answers to those questions.

27 | Sickness and demons

Pack your bags and get on the tour bus. We're following Jesus on His preaching and healing tour of Judea. Yesterday we saw His authority over evil spirits. What next?

👁 Read Luke 4 v 38–39

ENGAGE YOUR BRAIN

▶ What else did Jesus have power over?

▶ How long before Simon's mother-in-law was completely healed?

Jesus healed her instantly. In a second, she was well and back to work. Jesus has authority over illness.

👁 Read verses 40–41

▶ What kinds of sickness could Jesus heal? (v40)

▶ Why do you think Jesus stopped the demons speaking? (v41)

Jesus had authority over every kind of illness, as well as demons and evil spirits. What power! But He wouldn't allow the demons to tell people that He was the Christ, the Son of God. It seems that Jesus wanted to show first by His words and actions what kind of Messiah He was, before He told people exactly who He was.

👁 Read verses 42–44

▶ What was Jesus' job, and who sent Him to do it? (v43)

The local people wanted Jesus to stick around — He'd become very popular — but His job was to spread the good news of God's kingdom to many different kinds of people. And it was a mission from God.

Today, Luke has given us a snapshot of Jesus' life. His miracles show us that Jesus has power over everything. And we've seen that His priority wasn't these miracles but to teach the good news of what God was doing through His Son — so that people would follow Him and become a part of God's kingdom.

PRAY ABOUT IT

Thank Jesus for who He is.

28 It's simple, Simon

Fishermen are tough lads. They have a very hard, physical job. And they smell a bit fishy too. Not really the kind of people you'd expect Jesus to hang out with.

👁 Read Luke 5 v 1–3

ENGAGE YOUR BRAIN

▷ *What was Jesus doing? (v1, 3)*

▷ *Remember from yesterday why He was doing this?*

Jesus was continuing His mission to teach God's word to people. But He wasn't just preaching from the boat…

👁 Read verses 4–11

▷ *What was impressive about Simon's words? (v5)*

▷ *And how did he feel when he saw what Jesus had done? (v8)*

▷ *What surprising new job did Jesus have for these fishermen? (v10)*

Jesus' command to fish some more was bizarre, as the best fishing in deep water was done at night. But there was something about Jesus that made Simon try it. When he saw the huge haul of fish, he fell to his knees and called Jesus "Lord". Simon also realised his own sinfulness compared to Jesus.

The nearer someone comes to God, the more they feel their own sinfulness and unworthiness to be near God. And Jesus outlined what He expects of His followers — to catch more people for Him (v10).

GET ON WITH IT

▷ *When you feel close to God, do you notice your sinfulness more?*

▷ *How close do you feel to God right now?*

▷ *Anything you can do about that?*

▷ *How can you fish more for Jesus?*

PRAY ABOUT IT

Talk over these things with God.

29 Skin deep

You've probably heard about Jesus healing people with the skin disease leprosy. Pretty impressive stuff, but not worth getting excited about, right? Wrong. Having leprosy didn't just harm your skin.

👁 Read Luke 5 v 12–14
ENGAGE YOUR BRAIN

▶ *What exactly did the man say Jesus could do? (v12)*

▶ *What did Jesus instruct him to do?*

Leprosy was more than a horrible disease. You were considered unclean and an outcast. You were kicked out of Jewish society, losing your family, friends, home and job. No one was allowed to come near you. It was a miserable existence.

But this man knew Jesus could make him "clean" again, if He was willing. Imagine how the man felt as his skin tingled and was healed. Not only was he healthy again, his broken relationships could now be healed too. He was no longer an outcast.

Jesus told the man to go to the temple priest so that his healing could be officially confirmed and he could rejoin society.

Jesus heals relationships. Especially our relationship with God. He came to ultimately die and make it possible for our broken relationship with God to be healed.

👁 Read verses 15–16

▶ *What did Jesus do regularly?*

Crowds of people hounded Him, wanted to hear Him and came to be healed by Him. But Jesus still found time to be on His own and pray.

PRAY ABOUT IT

We need to do the same. Do you have a time set aside each day to talk properly to God? Thank Him now for sending His Son to heal our broken relationships.

THE BOTTOM LINE

Jesus can make us clean.

30 Dropping in

Jesus had gained quite a reputation for life-changing words and astounding miracles. So much so that religious leaders flocked to see Him. And people would do anything to get their sick mates close to this healer.

👁 Read Luke 5 v 17–20

ENGAGE YOUR BRAIN

▷ *What do you think the men carrying their paralysed friend hoped Jesus would do?*

▷ *Yet what surprising thing did He say to them? (v20)*

These men were so desperate for Jesus to heal their friend that they ripped the tiles off the roof and lowered him into the house. They believed in Jesus. But the man needed to walk, so why was Jesus talking about sin?

Sin is doing what *we* want instead of what *God* wants. Sin separates us from God.

This man couldn't walk, but he had a far bigger problem — sin.

👁 Read verses 21–26

▷ *What were the Pharisees thinking? (v21)*

▷ *Why did Jesus heal the man? (v24)*

▷ *What was everyone's reaction?*

The Pharisees were half-right — only God can forgive sins. But this didn't mean that Jesus was blasphemous.

It meant He was God! It's much easier to say "Your sins are forgiven" because no one can see if it's happened or not. So Jesus healed the man in front of their eyes to prove it.

THINK IT OVER

▷ *Who do you think Jesus is?*

▷ *How would you back up your views when talking to others?*

PRAY ABOUT IT

Thank God for sending Jesus to deal with our greatest problem — the need to be forgiven.

31 Sin doctor

By His words and miraculous actions, Jesus had offended many of the religious big shots, especially the Pharisees. Imagine how they reacted to Him hanging out with "sinners" and undesirables.

👁 Read Luke 5 v 27–32

ENGAGE YOUR BRAIN

▶ How did Levi respond to Jesus' command to follow Him? (v28)

▶ What else did he do? (v29)

Levi was also known as Matthew — yep, the same one who wrote one of the Gospels. Tax collectors were usually dishonest and were hated.

But this tax collector's life was suddenly turned upside down by Jesus. There's no other way to follow Jesus than to give up everything and follow Him completely. And Levi held a huge banquet to let everyone know. Following Jesus requires devotion and means telling others.

▶ What did the Pharisees object to? (v30)

▶ What did Jesus say His priority was?

"The righteous" means people who think they're right with God — the Pharisees, for example. They couldn't understand why Jesus would spend time with "sinners".

But Jesus said that it was sinners — people who are aware of their sin and their need for forgiveness — who He came to help. Only people like that will turn to Him to be cured of their sin disease.

PRAY ABOUT IT

Pray that your non-Christian friends will realise their sinfulness and their need to turn to Jesus for the cure. Ask God to help you tell them about Jesus, the sin doctor.

Why not spend time learning verse 32 and thinking what it means for you and people you know?

THE BOTTOM LINE

Jesus came for sinners.

32 Fast and furious

Pharisees thought being right with God was all about keeping laws. So Jesus explains, in three pictures, that He is bringing a real cure for sin. But it will mean a radical change.

👁 Read Luke 5 v 33–35

ENGAGE YOUR BRAIN

▶ Who was the bridegroom?

▶ When would the disciples (wedding guests) be sad? (v35)

The Pharisees and many other Jews fasted (went without food) twice a week as a mark of their holiness. Fasting was also a sign of sadness.

But there was no reason why Jesus' disciples should fast. They were so happy to be with Jesus (the bridegroom). Why should they be sad and go without food?

Jesus knew that He would soon die. When that happened, His followers would be devastated, and then they'd fast. Yet their sorrow wouldn't last for long — God would raise Jesus back to life.

The message of Jesus was that He would die to rescue people from sin. But the Pharisees said you had to keep a set of rules to be right with God. The two messages don't mix.

👁 Read verses 36-39

▶ Why doesn't Jesus' new message mix with the Pharisees' old one? (v37)

Trying to fit the message of Jesus into a human set of rules won't work. The Pharisees said: "You must keep our rules to please God." Jesus said: "Repent (turn away from your sin) and believe the good news."

You can't become a Christian by keeping rules or being good. Only by trusting Jesus to forgive your sin.

PRAY ABOUT IT

Thank God that you don't need to keep a set of rules to be made right with Him. Thank Him for sending Jesus as our Saviour. Ask Him to help you share the message of Jesus.

COLOSSIANS

Life to the max

Col is a great guitarist. He's been practicing enthusiastically for hours every day for the last four years, and you can tell. But Sian's not so sure. She says to be a proper guitarist you need to have the right look, wear black all the time, know EVERY Jimi Hendrix riff and hang out with the right people. Following these simple rules, he can be a true guitarist. Col thought he already was one!

COME TO COLOSSAE

The year is 60 AD and the church in Colossae (in what is now Turkey) is packed with new Christians. They're full of enthusiasm for the message of Jesus, but people have been telling them that's not enough.

"Follow these rules and have these experiences if you want to be a true Christian."

"Believing in Jesus is one thing, but to know God deeply and please Him fully you need something more."

Heard anyone say stuff like that? The young Christians in Colossae had, and it sounded attractive. In his letter to the Colossian Christians, Paul says: *"HOLD ON GUYS! You don't need anything more to be a Christian; Christ is all you need."* A life based on faith in Jesus is the key for a full Christian life. That's the simple message of Colossians.

WHY READ THIS BOOK?

Paul's letter is a great read if you're a new-ish believer, as it's jammed with the truth of what it really means to be a Christian. And if you've been a believer a bit longer, Colossians is a great refresher course, spurring you on in the Christian life.

33 How to grow a Christian

How would you introduce yourself? How would you describe yourself in an email or letter to someone you've never actually met? Paul introduces himself as an apostle, someone sent by God to tell people about Jesus.

 Read Colossians 1 v 1–4

ENGAGE YOUR BRAIN

▶ *How does Paul describe the Christians in Colossae? (v2–4)*

They display the characteristics of growing Christians. They are...

• Holy (v2) — set apart for God.

• Faithful (v2) — serving God, letting their faith in Jesus shine through their lives (v4).

• Loving (v4) —they showed great love for other believers (if you're a Christian, you're a saint!).

 Read verses 5–8

▶ *Where did their faith and love spring from? (v5)*

They trusted God and loved other people because they were sure that their sins were forgiven through Jesus. They had a sure hope that they'd live with God for ever. This changed the way they looked at life — no longer grabbing the best for themselves, but living for God now, and serving Him, knowing that heaven was a sure thing.

▶ *How should the hope of eternal life affect the way you live?*

The gospel is the great news that Jesus died in the place of sinners, so that they could have their sins forgiven. This great news was "bearing fruit" all over the world (v6) — many people were becoming Christians. The gospel was spreading, just as it had in Colossae since Epaphras first told them about Jesus (v7).

PRAY ABOUT IT

Ask God to help you grow as a Christian and become more holy, faithful and loving.

Where do you want to see the gospel spreading and bearing fruit? Talk to God about it.

34 | The knowledge

Before an exam, we cram our heads full of knowledge. Why? So we can answer the questions in the exam and pass it. Well, that's the theory anyway.

👁 Read Colossians 1 v 9–11

ENGAGE YOUR BRAIN

▶ *What has Paul been praying for the Christians in Colossae? (v9)*

▶ *Why? (v10)*

▶ *So how does God want His people to live? (v10–11)*

What a great thing to pray — that these guys will know what God wants of them so they can live lives that please Him.

God wants us to bear fruit by serving Him in what we do; constantly learning from God; showing endurance and patience when we're given a hard time for living God's way. But it's not down to us — God gives us the strength to do it (v11).

👁 Read verses 12–14

▶ *What excites you most in these verses?*

Christians are God's children. They'll inherit eternal life with God. He's rescued them from sin (the dominion of darkness) so that they can live with Him for ever, totally forgiven for all their sins. Pretty amazing stuff, eh?

Read verses 12–14 again, changing "you" and "us" to "me". If we're Christians, Jesus has qualified us for eternal life and nothing can change that!

PRAY ABOUT IT

Pray verses 9–11 for your friends. And then for yourself. And thank God for the great inheritance Christians receive — forgiveness and eternal life with Him!

THE BOTTOM LINE

God rescues His children from darkness and helps them to live lives that please Him.

35 | Numero uno

Who is the number one athlete in the world? Number one fashion designer? Number one influence in your life? Paul wants to tell us who's really number one...

👁 Read Colossians 1 v 15–17

ENGAGE YOUR BRAIN

▶ *Paul is talking about Jesus. How does Paul describe Him in v15?*

▶ *Does anything surprise you in v16–17?*

In Bible times, the son who was born first got special rights and privileges. He was number one. Jesus is in charge of the whole of creation! He is the Creator of all things and everything was created for Him (v16). He's the one who holds the world together (v17)! Jesus is number one.

👁 Read verses 18–20

Jesus is number one in the church — head of all God's people, Christians (v18). Jesus became human but He was fully God (v19).

▶ *Despite being God, what was Jesus prepared to do? (v20)*

Jesus lived as a human so that He could die on the cross in our place and be raised back to life (v18). It was the only way to make it possible for us to be at peace with God.

People were telling the Colossian Christians they needed to do more than just believe in Jesus and be forgiven by Him. That's just not true! Jesus is enough, because He is Lord of everything. If you have Jesus, you've already got everything!

PRAY ABOUT IT

Read through the verses again, remembering who Jesus really is, thanking Him for all He's done.

THE BOTTOM LINE

Jesus is number one. Jesus makes it possible to be at peace with God.

36 | Before and after

Seen those before and after ads? BEFORE: someone chubby photographed in terrible light, from a bad angle, looking miserable. AFTER: they look half the weight (in great light, in great clothes and smiling!).

Yesterday, Paul told us that Jesus is number one. He is all we need to make peace with God. Now Paul shows us the Christian's BEFORE and AFTER pictures.

◉ Read Colossians 1 v 21–23
ENGAGE YOUR BRAIN

▶ Before people become Christians, what's their relationship with God like? (v21)

▶ After having their lives turned around by Jesus, how does God now see them? (v22)

Before someone becomes a Christian, they're an enemy of God. This is obvious from the way they disobey Him in their thoughts and actions (v21). But Jesus gave His body in death on the cross to take the punishment we deserve. If we trust in His death to put us right with God, then God sees us as holy and without guilt. Squeaky clean!

▶ So what should Christians do in response to what Jesus has done for them? (v23)

GET ON WITH IT

▶ What specific things in your life do you need to change in response to what Jesus has done for you?

▶ How can you make it more obvious that you are an AFTER, not a BEFORE?

THE BOTTOM LINE

Fill it in yourself today. In less than ten words, summarise what God has taught you today. Then pray about it.

37 | Solving the mystery

People were telling Christians in Colossae that they needed to understand secret and mysterious things to be true believers. But Paul says that's rubbish; you just need Jesus. So why is Paul now talking about a mystery???

👁 Read Colossians 1 v 24–27

Paul had suffered a lot for telling people about Jesus. In fact, he was writing this letter from prison. But he was happy to suffer for Jesus and for God's people (v24).

ENGAGE YOUR BRAIN

▶ *Paul describes the word of God as a mystery that had been hidden for ages. But did God keep it a mystery? (v26–27)*

Brilliantly, God chose to reveal the truth to people like these Christians in Colossae. Ordinary people like us!

Jesus Christ is the answer to this mystery (v27). For centuries, God had promised to rescue His people. He did it through Jesus! The mysterious treasure we all need is actually Jesus in our lives.

👁 Read verses 28–29

▶ *What did Paul work hard at, that we must work hard at too? (v28)*

See, it's no mystery at all! Everyone needs Jesus. God doesn't keep it a secret. He wants us to work hard at telling everyone about Jesus and what He has done. And Jesus gives us the energy to do it! (v29)

PRAY ABOUT IT

Thank God for revealing the truth to you.

Ask Him to give you the strength and opportunities to tell others the amazing truth about Jesus.

THE BOTTOM LINE

God has revealed the mystery to us — that Jesus is the only way to have our sins forgiven.

38 | What's the secret?

What's the secret to a successful relationship? What's the secret to passing exams? What's the secret ingredient that makes chocolate so yummy? What's the secret to knowing God?

👁 Read Colossians 2 v 1–5

ENGAGE YOUR BRAIN

▶ What does Paul want for the Christians in Colossae? (v2)

▶ Do you ever pray these things for Christians you know?

Paul says his purpose is for them to be encouraged, united, showing love for each other — and he wants them to know Jesus. Paul was prepared to work hard and go through all kinds of struggles for this. Do you want the same things for yourself and for your friends that Paul wanted for these Christians?

▶ So what's the secret to knowing God? (v2–3)

Sorry, trick question! There is no secret! You don't need any secret knowledge or need to do anything weird or have special abilities. You just need Jesus. All the treasures of God are found in Jesus!

👁 Read verses 6–7

Paul says: You've started well following Jesus — now stick at it!

▶ How are Christians encouraged to live?

As Christians grow, they need to continue living Jesus' way, building their lives on Him, becoming strong in their faith. Jesus gives Christians everything they need. He saved them from their sins. He's given them the Bible to teach them, and the Holy Spirit to help them live for Him! So they should be bursting with thankfulness (v7)!

PRAY ABOUT IT

Thank Jesus that He's all you need. Take some extra time now to thank Him for what He's done in your life.

39 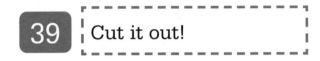 Cut it out!

Some food packaging is designed to look as if there's more food in it than there really is. Like a nice big bag of nachos that actually contains about three of them. Annoying, eh?

Paul warns us about people whose ideas about life promise a lot, but are really just hollow and empty.

👁 Read Colossians 2 v 8–10

ENGAGE YOUR BRAIN

▶ *Paul says watch out for teaching that relies on what rather than what? (v8)*

We're bombarded with attractive ideas all the time. A lot of them have great principles involved (save the planet, end poverty, be a better person) but if they're based on human traditions and not on Jesus, then they're not the real deal. First and foremost, Christians live for Jesus. He's the basis of our lives, not man-made traditions and ideals.

👁 Read verses 11–12

Uh-oh, Paul mentions circumcision. Don't worry guys, he's not saying we have to cut off bits of our wotnots!

▶ *What does Paul say Christians cut off (or "put off") from their lives? (v11)*

In Old Testament times, circumcision was a sign of belonging to God. For Christians, cutting off our old sinful ways is a sign of belonging to God.

Paul says that when people become Christians, they're both buried with Jesus and raised with Him. Christians have buried their old sinful way of living and are raised to a new life with Jesus!

GET ON WITH IT

▶ *What sins do you need to cut out from your life?*

Talk to the Lord about it.

THE BOTTOM LINE

Cut out sins from your life.

40 Nailing the truth

Paul now reminds Christians exactly what God has done for them through His Son, Jesus.
Listen up, because this applies to YOU.

👁 Read Colossians 2 v 13–15

ENGAGE YOUR BRAIN

▶ *How does Paul describe Christians before they're rescued by Jesus (v13)?*

Before turning to Jesus, people are as good as dead — separated from God by their sins against Him. But when God forgives their sins, He makes them alive again, bringing them back to Him, giving them new life.

▶ *What does Paul say was cancelled when Jesus died on the cross? (v14)*

▶ *What else has God done for His people, Christians? (v15)*

The "written code" (or "charges" or "legal indebtedness") means the debt we owe God. It's like a bill showing the huge debt we owe God for our sins against Him. We've treated God so badly that it's a debt we could never pay. But by His death in our place, Jesus has nailed our debts to the cross, paying them for us.

By trusting in Jesus' death on our behalf, all our sins are forgiven (v13). Wiped out for ever! God has rescued His people from the powers of evil. When Jesus died and was raised back to life, God publicly defeated death, sin and evil powers (Satan). God's people are rescued from the sin that had control of their lives.

PRAY ABOUT IT

Read today's verses again and tell God how they make you feel.

THE BOTTOM LINE

Through Jesus' death on the cross, God has forgiven Christians' sins and rescued them from the grip of evil.

41 Chasing shadows

Laura has a photo of her boyfriend, Tom, in her purse, which she looks at all the time. But when Tom's with her, she doesn't look at the photo at all. Why waste your time with a picture when you have the real thing?

Read Colossians 2 v 16–17

ENGAGE YOUR BRAIN

▶ *What were the Christians in Colossae being judged about?*

People were telling them that they had to follow loads of rules to be right with God. But these Old Testament laws pointed to Jesus coming to save His people. Now that Jesus is here, He's the only way to be forgiven. Keeping these rules just isn't enough. Don't settle for the shadow when you've got the real thing in Jesus (v17)!

Read verses 18–23

▶ *What's the biggest mistake made by people who say you need to obey certain rules to be a Christian? (v19)*

▶ *Who is the head of God's people ("the body")?*

If anyone says you need to follow certain rules or have certain experiences for a full Christian life, they've missed the point. Jesus is enough. Yes, we want to obey God's commands, but it's only Jesus' death that brings us forgiveness.

TALK IT THROUGH

What do people sometimes say we need as well as Jesus? What rules and traditions can get in the way of living for Jesus? Why not talk about these things with Christian friends.

THE BOTTOM LINE

Trying to keep rules won't put you right with God. Only trusting Jesus to forgive you leads to a full Christian life.

PRAY ABOUT IT

You're on your own today. There must be loads of things to talk to God about.

PSALMS

Psongs from the heart

JUST FOR STARTERS

In these *Engage* Bible readings, we want to throw ourselves into God's word, discover what He wants to say to us and grow closer to Him, living for Him more and more. And there's no better place to do that than Psalms.

HEART ON THEIR SLEEVES

Psalms is the longest book in the Bible, but it's also the most personal. Each psalm is a very honest song to God. David and the other psalm writers are incredibly honest about how they feel, expressing their feelings to God — anger, despair, rejection, love, sorrow, joy, frustration, thanks, fear, loneliness, persecution, trust, happiness… the lot.

Psalms has the whole range of emotions that you and I go through.

TALK TIME

The psalms remind us that we can talk to God in ANY situation. They encourage us to be open and honest with God. And they teach us loads about His character. They make us turn to God to remember what He's like and hear what He's got to say. And they point us to Jesus too.

KING SONG

David, King of Israel, wrote loads of the psalms (you can read his story in 1 and 2 Samuel). We get to see into his heart and explore his feelings; celebrate his highs and sob with his lows. But most of all, we get to see his awesome, powerful, protective, loving God.

Please turn to number one on your psong psheet…

42 Two ways to live

There are loads of ways of dividing people into two groups. Male and female. Dog lovers and cat lovers. Those who can wiggle their ears and those who can't. Psalm 1 shows us another way.

 Read Psalm 1 v 1–2

ENGAGE YOUR BRAIN

▶ *Who are the two groups of people mentioned in Psalm 1?*

▶ *What does the "blessed" person do? And what don't they do?*

Blessed means favoured by God; happy. People blessed by God want to live His way, not hang out with the wicked, copying what they do (v1). Instead, God's people fill their minds and hearts with God's law, the Bible.

Meditate means to fill your mind, not empty it. Using all your spare moments to get God's word into your mind and heart. We want to explore God's word fully and let it impact our lives in incredible ways.

👁 **Read verses 3–6**

▶ *What's the result for the person who walks God's way? (v3)*

▶ *What about the person who doesn't? (v4-6)*

People who walk God's way are successful! That doesn't mean they'll be millionaires. Much better than that — they'll become more like Jesus.

As we read the Bible, we're being taught directly by God, learning about Jesus and His great promise of rescue. We'll learn how to become more and more like Jesus. What could be better than that?!

Unfortunately, the future's not so bright for those who reject God (v6).

PRAY ABOUT IT

▶ *Which group do you belong to?*

Talk to God about your answer, and what you want to do about it. And ask Him to help you meditate on His word as you use *Engage*.

43 | Who's the boss?

Think of the people around you every day. What's their opinion of Jesus? What do they say about Him? Good stuff? Offensive stuff? Nothing at all? Does it even matter how people respond to Jesus?

👁 Read Psalm 2 v 1–6

ENGAGE YOUR BRAIN

▷ *What's the world's attitude towards God? (v1–3)*

▷ *What does God think about this? (v4–6)*

People refuse to let God be in charge of their lives. They want to shut Him out, get rid of Him. The Anointed One (v2) is the person God chose to rule His people, as king. When this psalm was written, King David was top dog, but now Jesus is King of God's people. Yet most people reject Jesus as King of their lives. Big mistake.

👁 Read verses 7–12

▷ *How powerful is King Jesus? (v8–9)*

▷ *So what's the wise response to all-powerful King Jesus? (v10–12)*

God won't turn a blind eye to the evil in the world. He has given His Son Jesus immense power, and one day, Jesus will return as the perfect Judge. He will rightly destroy all those who reject Him (v12).

The message is clear: serve the Lord, and "kiss the Son" — give Jesus the love and respect He deserves as our all-powerful King.

PRAY ABOUT IT

▷ *What is your attitude towards Jesus?*

▷ *Do you let Him rule your life?*

Tell Him how you feel. If you mean it, ask Him to rule your life as King.

THE BOTTOM LINE

Jesus is King!

44 | Prayer changes things

So far, the Psalms have shown us how important it is to engage with the Bible, live God's way and meet King Jesus. Next up — the power of prayer.

David was king of Israel. His son, Absalom, wanted to murder him and take over. So David was on the run, fearing for his life.

 Read Psalm 3

ENGAGE YOUR BRAIN

▶ *What was David's problem? (v1)*

▶ *What did God do for David? (v5)*

▶ *How does David now feel about his enemies? (v6)*

Prayer changes things. David was in a tight spot, his enemies all around him, hungry for his blood. So David cried out to God, pouring out his fears and asking God to protect him. Then he went to bed.

Amazingly, God gave him a good night's sleep (v5). David woke up encouraged that God was in control, would protect him, and would smash his enemies' teeth in! (v7)

God hears our prayers and answers them. Prayer is vitally important. Because of Jesus' death in their place, Christians get to know God personally. They can talk with Him; share their lives and worries with Him; ask for His help; and give Him the praise He deserves.

GET ON WITH IT

Don't go to sleep, or go into the day, with worries on your mind. Try this...

1. Tell God about your worries.

2. Remind yourself how powerful and in control God is. Maybe by reading a psalm or two.

3. Ask God to deal with the situation that's on your mind.

4. Get some sleep.

5. Wake up, praise God, and keep asking Him to help you.

What are you waiting for? Bring your worries to God now!

45 Genesis – In the beginning

Have you ever watched those TV shows where they start with a recap by Voiceover Man and his big booming voice: "Previously on..." Well, verses 1–3 of chapter 5 remind us of the story so far in Genesis.

Read Genesis 5 v 1–3

ENGAGE YOUR BRAIN

- *Verses 1–2 sound great but what is the problem with Seth? (v3)*

- *Whose likeness was Adam made in (v1)?*

- *What is the problem with being like Adam rather than like God?*

Have a read through the whole section, verses 1–32.

- *Which phrase is repeated again and again?*

- *Are there any exceptions to this?*

- *What's different about this person? (v21–24)*

"And then he died." Despite the amazing lifespans — check out Methuselah — God's judgment on Adam and his family still holds. They all die eventually. We're still looking for the descendant who will crush the serpent's head (Genesis 3 v 15).

SHARE IT

Death. They call it the ultimate statistic: 1 in 1 will die. But not Enoch, and there are a couple of other exceptions in the Bible too. Why not chat about it to a friend today? Are they frightened of death? What would happen if everyone lived for ever? Do they believe in life after death? Why / why not?

PRAY ABOUT IT

We know from the rest of the Bible that this life is not all there is. All humans die once and face God's judgment. Pray for people you know who are not trusting in Christ. Pray that they would turn to Him before it's too late.

THE BOTTOM LINE

Death is not the end.
Good news for some...

46 | Grieving God

Andrew means "brave", Sophie means "wisdom", Kevin means "beautiful at birth". Look back at Genesis 5 v 28–29. Was Noah's dad just being optimistic when he named him? Will he bring comfort from the curse? Let's find out...

👁 Read Genesis 6 v 1–4

So the population is increasing, but they're still sinning and God's judgment (as we saw yesterday) is still in place. Some Bible experts think the 120-year limit refers to the amount of time they have left before the flood. Others think God was reducing people's lifespan.

And don't worry too much about the identity of the *"sons of God"*. They might be angels, might not. What is clear is that they were disobeying God.

👁 Read verses 5–8

ENGAGE YOUR BRAIN

▶ *How bad have things got?*

▶ *What reaction(s) does God have?*

▶ *Is there any glimmer of hope? (v8)*

Have you ever made something that took a lot of care and hours of work? A painting, sculpture, design project or model? How wrong would it have to go before you destroyed it or threw it away?

The world had become very different from God's very good creation (Genesis chapter 1). Though nothing had happened outside of His control, God was still grieved and troubled by the evil and ruin He saw.

PRAY ABOUT IT

Have you ever thought that your sin grieves God? Spend some time saying sorry to Him.

THE BOTTOM LINE

Our sin pains and offends God.

47 | Ark and ride

Have you ever seen one of those enormous cruise ships? They look like five floating football stadiums in one. Well, the ark was pretty big — but it wasn't a cruise ship. It was a lifeboat.

👁 Read Genesis 6 v 8–10

ENGAGE YOUR BRAIN

▶ *What is special about Noah?*

▶ *OK, that was a trick question! Who decides Noah will be special? (v8)*

👁 Read verses 11–22

▶ *What is the problem with the earth? (v11–12)*

▶ *How exactly is God going to deal with it? (v13)*

We sometimes think God's judgment is unfair — an overreaction maybe — but take another look at verse 5 and verses 11–12.

TALK IT THROUGH

Chat to another Christian about God's judgment. Do you find it difficult to understand? Does it seem fair? Why does it matter that God can't ignore evil? How does the cross show how seriously He takes sin?

Noah didn't deserve to be saved by God, but God chose him to be rescued.

▶ *What was God's wild rescue plan for Noah? (v13–21)*

▶ *List some of the ways in which God shows His mercy in this passage. Jot them down on the lines on the right.*

PRAY ABOUT IT

None of us deserves to be saved by God. We're just as wicked as the next person, but God has always been the God of rescue. Can you think of any other examples of God rescuing His people? Thank God for them.

48 Flood warning

If you've ever seen a flood on TV, you'll know how destructive loads of water can be. But the flood in Genesis was seriously devastating — every living thing on the face of the earth was destroyed.

Read Genesis 7 v 1–24

ENGAGE YOUR BRAIN

▷ Jot down the basic order of events (on the lines on the left).

▷ Why do Noah and family escape?

▷ Why do you think Noah has to take more of some animals than others? Think about it!

▷ Who shuts the door of the ark? (v16) What does that show us?

▷ Remember the pattern of sin, judgment and mercy we've been seeing since Genesis 3? Fill in the table for chapters 6 and 7:

Sin?	
God's judgment?	
God's mercy?	

GET ON WITH IT

"And Noah did all that the LORD commanded him" (v5). If you've ever seen footage of a rescue team at work up a mountain or at sea, you'll know that the people being rescued have to do exactly what they're told. If someone threw you a rope when you were drowning and told you to take hold of it, you'd be pretty stupid to argue.

Jesus is our lifeboat — have you accepted that? The alternative is just as terrifying as verses 21–23.

THE BOTTOM LINE

Will you get into the lifeboat before it's too late?

49 Home and dry

Look back at the end of chapter 7 for a minute. "Only Noah was left, and those with him in the ark." Pretty scary, being the only living creatures left.

Chapter 8 starts with the words "But God…" — probably one of the best phrases in the Bible!

👁 Read Genesis 8 v 1–14

ENGAGE YOUR BRAIN

▶ *What happens to halt God's terrifying judgment?*

▶ *What does this tell us about God?*

▶ *What did God make happen to stop the flood? (v1–2)*

▶ *What does this tell us about Him? Any ideas?*

People remember the whole 40 days and 40 nights of rainfall but it took nearly a whole year before the earth was dry enough to stand on again.

▶ *What was Noah's nifty way of checking whether it was safe to disembark from the ark?*

Noah sent a dove to see if there was dry land or not. God had flooded the earth to wash away all the sin and evil. *"But God remembered Noah"* (v1).

God remembered that Noah had obeyed Him, and He rescued Noah and blessed him loads (more on that in the next few days).

God is in total control of the world, and He cares for everyone and everything that lives in His world.

PRAY ABOUT IT

Thank God that He cares about you. Thank Him that He is powerful enough to help you, and to rescue you from sin. Those are two very good reasons to pray.

THE BOTTOM LINE

But God remembered Noah.

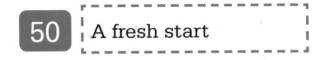

50 A fresh start

**So all the wicked have been swept away by the flood.
The earth is clean.
Time for a fresh start?**

👁 Read Genesis 8 v 15–22

ENGAGE YOUR BRAIN

▶ *Who makes the decision to disembark? (v15–16)*

▶ *How do you think Noah felt to be on dry land again?*

▶ *What is Noah's first act on dry land? (v20)*

▶ *What does this show?*

▶ *How does God react? (v21–22)*

Another command to be fruitful and multiply (v17) and no further curse on the ground (v21). Perhaps things are looking up. So has anything changed? Are human beings any better? Well, no. Their hearts are still inclined to do evil right from the start (v21).

Yes, that means your heart too.

But no more world-destroying floods, not like the last one, even though we deserve to be punished.

Do *you* believe that your heart is naturally inclined to do evil? Or do you think you're basically a good person? If you're a Christian, you know the answer is the first one.

We all do wrong stuff. But God sent Jesus so that we can be forgiven.

SHARE IT

Do your friends recognise the fact that we are ALL capable of evil, not just a few criminals? That we all do wrong? It's a truth everyone needs to understand — that we're all sinful and need God's forgiveness.

THE BOTTOM LINE

God loves us despite the way we live, not because of it.

51 Lifeblood

"God bless ya!" People often say that simple phrase without really knowing what it means. Noah knew — he received God's blessing. God was doing business with him and his family. Let's look at the deal.

👁 Read Genesis 9 v 1–7

ENGAGE YOUR BRAIN

▶ *In the journalling space on the right, list the ways God blesses Noah and his family.*

▶ *What is Noah warned against doing? (v4)*

▶ *Why is that?*

▶ *Who will be held to account for the spilling of human blood? (v5–6) Any surprises?*

In the Bible, blood = life. Here God is reinforcing just how valuable human life is. Whether another human or even an animal killed someone, then their life would be taken in return.

▶ *What reason does God give for placing such a high value on human life? (v6)*

TALK IT THROUGH

Christians have different views about what the punishment for murder should be. How do you think verse 6 applies today, if at all? Does the New Testament change anything?

We may not think that verses 5–6 apply to us. We're not murderers, surely? But Jesus says that being angry with another person is just as bad (Matthew 5 v 21–22). God will hold us all responsible for our actions. But we're not the ones to dish out the punishment — Jesus will do that when He returns.

PRAY ABOUT IT

Thank God that He's given us the world to look after and enjoy. Ask Him to help you treat other people better, as they're made in His image.

THE BOTTOM LINE

Human life is valuable.

52 Promises promises

What do a wedding ring, an IOU and a rainbow all have in common? Any ideas? Well, they're all things that represent a promise.

👁 Read Genesis 9 v 8–17

ENGAGE YOUR BRAIN

▷ *What does God promise?*

▷ *Who is God's covenant agreement with? (v8–10, 17)*

▷ *How long will it last? (v12, 16)*

▷ *What sign does God give to show He will remember His promise?*

The flood was a huge event. Just in case people were frightened it might happen again, God chose a sign which occurs naturally at the same time as wet weather, to reassure the world of His promise.

Can you think of any other examples of God keeping His promises in the Bible? Jot down as many as you can think of.

PRAY ABOUT IT

Thank God for His covenant, because it's a promise for you too. Thank God that He cares about all that He has made. Pick one of God's great promises and spend time thanking Him for it.

THE BOTTOM LINE

God keeps His promises.

53 Drunk and disorderly

Things are looking good for Noah. Time for a celebratory drink? Or ten? Bottoms up!
Don't take that too literally, Noah...

👁 Read Genesis 9 v 18–23

ENGAGE YOUR BRAIN

▶ Try to sum up Noah's behaviour in verse 21 in one word.

▶ What's so bad about Ham's behaviour?

▶ What is good about Shem and Japheth's response?

Not only does Noah have a few too many and make a fool of himself, but Ham decides to have a laugh at his dad's expense and broadcast his drunkenness. Neither of them acts in a way that honours God.

GET ON WITH IT

God says we should honour our parents and treat them with respect (Exodus 20 v 12).

▶ Do you?

▶ How can you show that today or tomorrow?

👁 Read verses 24–29

ENGAGE YOUR BRAIN

▶ What is Noah's hung-over reaction?

▶ Have we found our serpent-crusher yet? (v29)

An ugly tale and a sad end. So Noah is definitely not the promised serpent-crusher. However, he announces God's blessing on two of his sons (v26–27) and God's punishment on the other (v25). Then he dies. The story of God and His people goes on.

THE BOTTOM LINE

Does your behaviour honour God?

History-shaper

So Ham, Shem, Japheth — the world's your oyster... sorry, you've probably had enough of sea creatures for a while... So, H, S, and J — where are you gonna go?

Read Genesis 10 v 1–32

Some of Shem's descendants eventually became God's people Israel, and their relationships with the nations around them (Ham and Japheth's descendants) were influenced by the judgment and blessings Noah handed out to his sons in Genesis 9 v 25–27 (Ham's descendants would be slaves to the descendants of Shem and Japheth).

ENGAGE YOUR BRAIN

▶ *Check out Ham's descendants (v6–20). Can you spot any future enemies of Israel?*

We get a little taste of some of the events to come in the rest of the Old Testament here — Egypt, Nineveh, Babylon and the evil cities of Sodom and Gomorrah. All places and people who would have an impact on God's people over the years.

None of this happened by accident. God knows exactly what's going on. All of this shows us how, from the very beginning, God is in control of history. Amazing.

PRAY ABOUT IT

God is in control of the whole world. Pray about countries and places that really need prayer today. Here are a few suggestions for you to research on the internet: Somalia, Sudan and Syria.

THE BOTTOM LINE

God is in control of history.

55 | Babel babble

If you could build anything at all (given endless time and resources), what would you build? I bet your project isn't as ambitious as this one...

👁 Read Genesis 11 v 1–9

ENGAGE YOUR BRAIN

▶ What is the motivation behind this project? (v4)

▶ Where have we seen this attitude before?

What's your greatest ambition — to win a reality TV show? To get signed as a professional footballer? To get straight "A"s in all your exams? If so, maybe you're interested in making a name for yourself. What do you spend time thinking and dreaming about? Does it make God look good? Or just yourself?

▶ What is God's response to Project Babel?

▶ Why do you think God stops them achieving their ambition? Is He just trying to spoil their fun?

Think for a minute about what might happen if human beings could do whatever they wanted with no restrictions (v6). What would the world look like (bearing in mind that people are naturally sinful and greedy)? You want something? Just take it. If someone's in your way, step on them. You don't like someone? Shoot them.

PRAY ABOUT IT

Thank God that He has given us a conscience plus laws and governments which, most of the time, keep us from the chaos of everyone going their own way (Romans 13 v 1–4).

GET ON WITH IT

The Lord's Prayer says: "Hallowed (honoured) be your name". How can you honour God's name, rather than your own, today? Think of something practical you can do!

56 Man hunt

Uh-oh. It's another one of those lists of names, or "genealogies" if you're being clever. So is this bit of the Bible about as interesting as reading the credits at the end of a movie, or is there more to it?

👁 Read Genesis 11 v 10–32

ENGAGE YOUR BRAIN

▶ *Any signs that the serpent-crusher might be on his way?*

God's death sentence on mankind is still going. We've seen that despite the hopeful signs, Noah wasn't the serpent-crusher. But what about this next guy, Abram?

▶ *What facts do we learn about Abram?*

•

•

•

•

Keep those in mind — they'll be significant later. We're standing on the edge of Abram's adventures with God — it's going to be awesome. But for now, look back at all you've learned in Genesis so far…

▶ *What have you learned about God?*

▶ *What have you learned about human beings?*

▶ *What have you learned about yourself?*

PRAY ABOUT IT

You know what to do.

THE BOTTOM LINE

God has a perfect plan.

LUKE

Jesus on tour

Quick. Grab a bag and stuff some clothes into it. You won't need many possessions because you're going on tour with Jesus, and people will provide you with all you need as you go from town to town, seeing history being made.

THE LOWDOWN

Luke wrote his book to tell the true story of Jesus. He wanted believers to know the facts about their Saviour, to strengthen their faith and to answer accusations and attacks on Christianity by unbelievers.

LIFE ON THE ROAD

In chapters 6 to 11 of Luke, we go on a tour with Jesus as He travels around Galilee and Judea. We'll see many mind-boggling things — miracles, life-changing teaching and plenty of controversy. And we'll get to see how the disciples reacted and how they began to see who Jesus really was.

CONTROVERSY

Jesus did and said many controversial things — He upset the Jewish leaders repeatedly, He spent time with not-so-respectable people, He went against Jewish tradition, He fought hypocrisy and said seemingly ridiculous things about His own death and about loving your enemies.

GET READY

Prepare to be blown away as Jesus defeats demons, heals diseases, controls storms, brings the dead back to life and does even weirder stuff (Luke 9 v 28–36). And His teaching could even change your life. If you act on it.

As you go on this road trip with Jesus, notice how the disciples' attitude changes as it starts to dawn on them who this incredible man really is. OK, let's get going…

57 Against the grain

The Jewish bigwigs were hoping to catch Jesus breaking the law. But there was a big difference between God's law in the Old Testament and all the extra laws made up by Jewish leaders that made life harder for people.

👁 Read Luke 6 v 1–5

ENGAGE YOUR BRAIN

▷ *What were the Pharisees upset about?*

▷ *How did Jesus answer them? (v3–4)*

▷ *What did He claim in verse 5?*

The Pharisees said that no work was allowed on the Sabbath rest day — not even picking corn to eat. Does that sound like work to you? Jesus pointed out that their hero, David, had done something far more shocking, but he did it to feed his starving companions. It was much more important to save life than keep specific rules.

Even more shocking than that, Jesus claimed to be "Lord of the Sabbath" (v5). Jesus is God, so the Sabbath was His day — He created it. And more than that, He's in charge of the biggest rest day of all — eternal life.

👁 Read verses 6–11

▷ *What point did Jesus make? (v9)*

▷ *How did the religious leaders react? (v11)*

According to these guys, even healing someone on the Sabbath counted as work and was breaking God's law. But they'd totally missed the point. How can it be wrong to heal someone, to show compassion?

This story isn't really about the day of rest or even about rules. It's about Jesus. He is God, so He was in charge of God's holy day. Jesus came to complete what was written in the Old Testament. So serving God no longer meant just obeying the law, it now meant following Jesus.

PRAY ABOUT IT

Thank God for sending His Son Jesus. Ask Him to help you follow Jesus with your whole life, rather than just trying to keep the rules.

58 | Team talk

Jesus had harsh words for those who rejected Him. But now He turns to those who follow Him, to give them a team talk. If you're on Jesus' team, then you'd better listen up.

👁 Read Luke 6 v 12–19

ENGAGE YOUR BRAIN

▷ What other name/role was given to the 12 special disciples? (v13)

▷ Why did the crowd want to be near Jesus? (v18–19)

Before Jesus made the big decision of choosing His twelve closest followers, He spent the night in prayer. That's a pointer for us when we have big decisions to make — take it to God first. He called these guys "apostles", which means they were "sent out by God". And notice the huge effect Jesus had on people — they saw His power and were desperate to get near to Him.

👁 Read verses 20–26

▷ What bad things can Jesus' followers expect? (v20–22)

▷ But what will they be given? (v20–23)

▷ What about those who live for themselves? (v24–26)

Jesus calls His followers poor and hungry because they realised how pathetic they were compared to God and were hungry for God to rescue them from sin. Christians can be given a tough time for following Jesus (v22), but they can leap for joy because they'll be rewarded with life in God's kingdom (v20, 23). There's no greater prize.

Those "who are rich" means people who are happy with the rewards of this life and think they're OK with God. But people who live for themselves, not God, will end up weeping and mourning.

PRAY ABOUT IT

▷ What will you thank God for?

▷ Which "rich" people do you need to pray for?

59 Behind enemy lines

You've had enough of Shannon. She bad-mouths you in front of your friends, "borrows" stuff without returning it and even slapped you once. Hard. The question is, what will you do about it?

👁 Read Luke 6 v 27–31

ENGAGE YOUR BRAIN

- ▶ *How does Jesus say we should treat people? (v31)*

- ▶ *What about when friends treat you badly? (v27–29)*

- ▶ *What does Jesus say about lending and giving? (v30)*

This is radical stuff. It's so easy to get annoyed when people use you or treat you like dirt. Jesus not only says, *Expect it*, He also says, *Be prepared to take more of it*. Give without expecting to get things back; take the abuse you get for being a Christian; pray for people who hate you.

👁 Read verses 32–36

- ▶ *Why should Christians love their enemies and give to them?*

Believers need to be different from everyone else — more generous, less hate-filled, not seeking revenge.

When it all seems too hard, go back to verses 35–36. Disciples of Jesus need to live like this because of what God's done — forgiving us and giving us a place in His kingdom. So we'll put up with hardships along the way because we're looking forward to eternal life.

GET ON WITH IT

- ▶ *Who do you need to treat differently?*

- ▶ *How can you be more generous with your possessions?*

- ▶ *How can you show God's love to an "enemy"?*

PRAY ABOUT IT

Spend some time talking to God about your answers.

THE BOTTOM LINE

Love your enemies.

60 Get the picture

"A picture is worth a thousand words" according to some people. Mostly artists. Jesus often spoke in picture language to put across His radical message. Luke now shows us three of Jesus' pictures.

👁 Read Luke 6 v 37–38

ENGAGE YOUR BRAIN

▶ *What does Jesus command?*

▶ *From what we've already learned, when will Christians receive their reward?*

Jesus' first picture carries on from where we finished yesterday. We should show generosity and forgiveness to people, not for the reward ("measure"), but because God has been merciful to us.

👁 Read verses 39–40

▶ *Who should and who shouldn't we learn from?*

We behave like the people we learn from. So if we have short-sighted teachers (like the Pharisees) who don't teach God's word properly, we're less likely to live God's way. If you follow a blind guide, you'll fall down a big hole. Choose your Bible teachers and role models carefully.

👁 Read verses 41–42

▶ *When we see faults in others, where else should we look?*

Don't be a plank-eyed fool, picking faults with people but not bothering to deal with your own. First, take a long hard look at yourself and list the things you need to change to serve God better. Only then are you able to help out friends with their issues.

GET ON WITH IT

▶ *List three things you need to sort out after reading Luke today.*

1.

2.

3.

Now talk to God, confessing your sinfulness and pleading for His help with what you've written down.

61 | Words in action

Thorn bushes, figs, grapes, builders, rock and sand. It may sound like a list of random objects, but Jesus uses them to make some big points about our lives.

👁 **Read Luke 6 v 43–45**

ENGAGE YOUR BRAIN

▶ *What reveals what we're really like on the inside?*

Jesus shares one way you can tell whether someone belongs to God or not — by what they say. A prickly bush won't produce tasty pineapples, and it's the same for us. People can't produce good fruit — living God's way — if their evil heart is unchanged. Only people rescued by Jesus will really live for God. And the evidence is in what we do and say.

👁 **Read verses 46–49**

▶ *What mistake were some of Jesus' "followers" making? (v46)*

▶ *What's true for people who put His words into practice? (v48)*

▶ *And those who don't? (v49)*

Some people called Jesus "Lord" and yet refused to obey Him and do what He said. Right now there are people who call themselves Christians and yet live only for themselves and ignore Jesus' commands. When Jesus returns as Judge, such people will be washed away. Only those whose lives are built on firm foundations — obeying Jesus — will stand firm through the Day of Judgment.

THINK IT OVER

▶ *What do the things you say reveal about your heart?*

▶ *Do you put Jesus' words into practice?*

▶ *Which of His commands do you need to seriously work on?*

PRAY ABOUT IT

Talk to God about the issues raised today and commit your whole life to serving Him.

62 Faith from afar

Next, Jesus takes His tour to Capernaum. So far, it's been mostly Jews who've been amazed and impressed by Him. But even the Romans are starting to hear of Jesus.

👁 Read Luke 7 v 1–6

ENGAGE YOUR BRAIN

▶ What do we learn about the man who sent for Jesus' help? (v1–5)

▶ What did he understand about himself? (v6)

This guy was an important soldier in the Roman army, in charge of many men. Yet he cared greatly for his dying servant. The Romans were generally hated by the Jews, and yet this centurion had built a synagogue for the Jews and clearly got on well with them. More importantly, he realised that Jesus was someone special and far greater than he was.

▶ What's your attitude towards Jesus?

▶ How much respect do you give Him?

👁 Read verses 7–10

▶ What amazed Jesus?

▶ What had the centurion realised about Jesus? (v7)

▶ What was the outcome?

Surprising stuff. This Roman showed more faith in Jesus than any Jews had. He believed Jesus could heal his servant — even from a distance. Jesus demonstrated His power and authority by making it happen. Great faith from the Roman. Greater power from Jesus, the ultimate Healer.

THINK IT OVER

In the space on the right, write a definition of faith from these verses:

▶ How do you measure up to that?

PRAY ABOUT IT

Thank Jesus for His authority over sickness. Ask Him to strengthen your faith and trust in Him.

63 | Coffin buster

The Jesus tour rolls on — to the little-known town of Nain. Yesterday we saw Jesus heal a dying man without even going to see him. Today He tops that...

👁 Read Luke 7 v 11–13

ENGAGE YOUR BRAIN

▶ *What was Jesus' first reaction to this sad scene? (v13)*

In a society where only men could go out and earn money, the loss was doubly devastating for this woman. Jesus was filled with compassion for her. He has great love for people, especially those in unfortunate situations. Jesus reaches out to those who need Him most.

👁 Read verses 14–17

▶ *What does this miracle teach us about Jesus' attitude to death?*

▶ *What did the people say about Jesus? (v16)*

▶ *Were they right, wrong or both? Why?*

Coffins were open so you could actually see the dead body. Jesus touched the coffin which, according to Jewish law, made Him "unclean".

But for Jesus, death wasn't the end. He came into the world to bring life — eternal life. And by His resurrection He would defeat death for ever. In raising this boy back to life, Jesus not only showed His love and care for the bereaved woman, He also revealed His power over death itself.

Onlookers were amazed and called Jesus a prophet. Many people know things about Jesus that are right: good teacher, perfect man, prophet etc. But that's not enough. They need to see who Jesus really is — the Son of God, Saviour of the world, risen from death, Judge, King — and submit to His rule.

PRAY ABOUT IT

Pray for friends / relatives who don't yet realise who Jesus really is.

64 | Who's who?

John the Baptist's message to Jesus: "Some of my guys are confused. I've been preaching that you're the Ruler sent by God to be Saviour and Judge of the world. But some of my friends aren't sure. Tell em!"

👁 Read Luke 7 v 18–23

ENGAGE YOUR BRAIN

▷ *How does Jesus answer any doubters? (v22)*

Jesus' miracles and extraordinary teaching proved that He was the Christ — God's promised Ruler. They also fulfilled what, 700 years earlier, the prophet Isaiah said would happen (Isaiah 35 v 5–6; 61 v 1). Jesus wasn't the conquering warrior many were expecting. In fact, most people didn't understand who Jesus was at all.

👁 Read verses 24–30

▷ *What was John's role? (v27)*

▷ *What surprising thing does Jesus say about other believers? (v28)*

How can Christians, like us, be better than John the Baptist??? Well, John was greatest at that time — he understood who Jesus was better than anyone else. Now, because we have the Bible, every Christian knows who Jesus is and exactly why He came. So we're greater. Greatness is understanding who Jesus is.

👁 Read verses 31–35

▷ *What did people think of John? (v33)*

▷ *And what about Jesus? (v34)*

Jesus was saying: *Most of you misunderstood John and you don't understand who I am. But my way — mixing with sinful people — is right. Some will grasp it and follow me.*

PRAY ABOUT IT

Some people followed Jesus; others failed to understand who He was. Pray you'll never tire of learning about Jesus, discovering who He really is and enjoying living for Him.

65 Transformer

It's time to play spot the difference. Two very different people met Jesus at a party. Some of their differences are blatantly obvious, others are more surprising. See Jesus transforming people — there's more than meets the eye.

👁 Read Luke 7 v 36–39

ENGAGE YOUR BRAIN

ⓘ *How did the woman treat Jesus?*

ⓘ *What did the Pharisee think about all this? (v39)*

The man was a Pharisee — religious, respectable. Attended all synagogue events. Talked about God and studied Old Testament law. A bit snobbish.

The woman was a woman (so in that society had no rights and was owned like property). She was "sinful" (v37), probably a prostitute. Feel the Pharisee's disgust (v39) — just touching a woman like that would make you "unclean".

Her action: disgraceful. Jewish women had to have their hair tied up in public. She interrupted the dinner party by kissing Jesus' feet (strange, but a sign of deep respect).

His action: respectable. See his first move (v36). But Jesus saw the truth about these two people.

👁 Read verses 40–50

ⓘ *What point does Jesus make with His story? (v41–43)*

ⓘ *What did the woman need and what did she receive? (v47–50)*

The story shows us that love for Jesus follows being forgiven by Him. The woman knew she needed to be forgiven and came to show her love for Him, believing He could forgive sins. The Pharisee rated Jesus as a prophet (v39) but thought he himself was OK with God. He wasn't. Only the sinful prostitute was forgiven.

THINK IT OVER

Think of your sinful actions, attitudes, words. Then think of how much Jesus did so that you could be put right with God. If you're thankful, tell God.

66 Sow far, sow good

Luke is painting a picture of Jesus for us. So far, he's shown that Jesus is the Son of God, who's calling sinners to repent. The Jews are rejecting Him, but a few people (including non-Jews and "sinners") have faith in Him.

👁 Read Luke 8 v 1–3

ENGAGE YOUR BRAIN

▷ What was Jesus doing on His tour? (v1)

Notice how Jesus and His disciples were supported by wealthy women. But if He was preaching such good news, why was He getting such a mixed reaction? Jesus tells us why in a parable.

👁 Read verses 4–10

▷ Why did Jesus speak in parables? (v9–10)

Does God hide truth from some people? Well, yes! He's in charge. He chooses what He wants to do. Those serious about following Jesus, like the disciples, were given an explanation of the parable. Those who weren't, who refused to take in what He said, were left in the dark.

👁 Read verses 11–15

▷ What are the four possible responses to Jesus? (list them on the right)

GET ON WITH IT

▷ How will you hear God's word?

▷ How will you retain/keep it?

▷ How will you stick at living God's way?

▷ How will you spread the good news?

Now talk these things over with God, asking His help.

THE BOTTOM LINE

He who has ears, let him hear.

67 Do the light thing

"Remembering these five rules could save your life one day." Do you listen up and act on what you learn, or does it slip from your mind immediately? Jesus is teaching us how to listen and respond to His words.

👁 Read Luke 8 v 16–18

ENGAGE YOUR BRAIN

▷ *What should you do with a bright light in a dark room?*

▷ *So what should we do with the truth about Jesus while living in a dark and sinful world?*

▷ *What's true for whose who do and those who don't accept Jesus' teaching? (v18)*

Imagine a power-cut plunging your house into total darkness. It would be dumb to hide your torch/flashlight, leaving everyone to stumble around blindly. We have something far more powerful — the good news of Jesus. The world is a dark place full of sin with people in need of Jesus' light to guide them. So don't hide it — the truth needs to get out there (v17). People who accept Jesus' words will understand more and more. But those who refuse to listen will lose the little they already know (v18).

👁 Read verses 19–21

▷ *What incredible thing does Jesus say about hearing God's word?*

This is awesome stuff. Jesus wasn't rejecting His mother and brothers, He was making a much much bigger point about responding to His teaching. People who receive it obediently are on the same level as Jesus' family! Accepting Jesus, repenting of your sin and being forgiven by Him brings you into His family. Christians are close to Jesus. Very close.

SHARE IT

▷ *Are you excited? What will you say to God?*

▷ *And what will you say to your friends who are in the dark?*

THE BOTTOM LINE

Don't hide your light!

68 Storming performance

If someone asked you: "Who is Jesus?" what would you say? If you're not entirely sure how to answer, don't worry. Even the disciples weren't sure! Through a series of stories, Luke is building a picture of who Jesus is.

Read Luke 8 v 22–25

ENGAGE YOUR BRAIN

- How did the disciples react to the terrifying storm? (v24)
- How about Jesus? (v24)
- Why did Jesus criticise the disciples? (v25)
- What did they learn about Jesus? (end of v25)

It's understandable to panic when the boat you're in could be destroyed by a wild storm. At least the disciples turned to Jesus for help (and so should we when we're afraid). But they hadn't yet fully grasped who Jesus really was.

They panicked, thinking no one in the boat could save them. They were wrong. If they'd fully understood that Jesus was God's Son, they would have known He could control winds and waves and weather. So Jesus demonstrated His immense power to them, and the storm calmed. "Where is your faith in me?" He wanted to know. Yet they still didn't understand who Jesus was (v25).

THINK ABOUT IT

- How does your faith stand up in times of difficulty?
- How do you react when something bad happens?
- What do you need to remember about Jesus?

PRAY ABOUT IT

Talk to God about any worries or fears you have at the moment.

Thank Him that He's more powerful than anything you face. Turn to Him for help and trust in Him.

THE BOTTOM LINE

Jesus is God's Son — He's in control.

69 Pigging out

Luke now hits us with another of Jesus' miracles as he continues to build his picture of Jesus. Notice...
a) what it tells us about Jesus;
b) how people responded to Him.

👁 Read Luke 8 v 26–33

ENGAGE YOUR BRAIN

▶ *What effect did these demons have on the man? (v27, v29)*

▶ *What does the miracle show Jesus has authority over?*

The demons were tearing this guy apart. They gave him great anger and strength, yet they knew who Jesus was and greatly feared Him. They knew He could destroy them and begged Him not to (v31). This bunch of demons were terrifyingly evil, yet Jesus had power over them, giving them permission to go into a herd of pigs. Jesus rules.

👁 Read verses 34–39

▶ *How had the man been changed by Jesus? (v35)*

▶ *How did the locals react?*

▶ *What did Jesus tell the man to do? (v39)*

This man's life was completely turned around by Jesus. Yet people who saw this incredible change didn't celebrate it — it scared them. They refused to accept Jesus and asked Him to leave!

▶ *Have you seen people react to Jesus or Christianity like that?*

But the ex-demonic man was truly changed. He even wanted to go with Jesus (v38). But when Jesus told him to stay and tell everyone about God, he obeyed. Even though it would be tough living with people who'd rejected Jesus.

PRAY ABOUT IT

Pray for God's help to obey what you know already and to keep trusting Jesus even when faith seems difficult.

70 A crush on Jesus

Next, Jesus returns to the other side of the lake to a hero's welcome. Huge crowds swarm around Him, but Jesus is more interested in two individuals — a sick outcast and a grieving dad.

Read Luke 8 v 40–48

ENGAGE YOUR BRAIN

▶ *What was surprising about Jairus' actions? (v41)*

▶ *What did Jesus say to this trembling, embarrassed, "unclean" woman? (v48)*

First, a respected religious leader fell at Jesus' feet, begging Him to heal his dying daughter. Then a woman that doctors couldn't heal, who was considered "unclean" because of her bleeding, showed great faith in Jesus. She knew that only He could heal her; all it would take was a touch. Now that's how to respond to Jesus — total faith, trusting Him to turn your life around completely.

Read verses 49–56

▶ *What does the miracle show about Jesus' authority?*

▶ *How does it show His care?*

Even death wasn't a barrier to Jesus. After news that the girl was dead, He still asked her father to believe. And he did! Notice that no one else did (v53). Jesus had great compassion for this family and brought the girl back to life. Jesus didn't raise her back to life to impress anyone; in fact, He told her parents to keep it quiet. Jesus wanted people to follow Him because they understood who He was, not because they enjoyed His miracles. Jesus wants faith and obedience.

PRAY ABOUT IT

Read through today's verses again. What most amazes you about Jesus? Thank Him for these things. And what have you learned about your own faith today? Tell Jesus and ask Him to help you trust Him more.

THE BOTTOM LINE

Jesus demands faith and obedience.

71 | Colossians – Back to the future

In Colossians 1 and 2, Paul has been explaining the truth about Christianity: it's all about Jesus.
That's the theory; now he moves on to the practice — how to live as a Christian.

👁 Read Colossians 3 v 1–4

Paul tells us what's happened to Christians in the *past*, what's true for them in the *present*, and what will happen in the *future*.

THE PAST

Christians have died to their old way of life and have been raised with Jesus to live for Him and with Him.

THE PRESENT

▶ *What's true for Christians now? (v3)*

If you're a Christian, Jesus died for YOU. You're one of His people now, and your life is kept safe ("hidden") with Him in heaven. Your future with God is safe!

THE FUTURE

When Jesus returns, Christians will be revealed to be God's children. They'll be like Jesus!

▶ *So what should Christians be doing now? (v2)*

We shouldn't get bogged down with our everyday lives, as if that's all there is. We must live our lives for Jesus, remembering that we'll live with Him for ever, becoming more like Him.

▶ *How can you "set your heart on things above"?*

▶ *How can you focus your thoughts on better things?*

PRAY ABOUT IT

Thank God for the past, present and future Christian life. Thank Him that your future is safe with Jesus!

THE BOTTOM LINE

If you're a Christian, your past, present and future are safe with Christ. Our eyes should be fixed on a glorious future with Jesus.

72 Get it sorted

Oi! Sort your life out! That's what Paul said to the Colossians (well, sort of) and it's what God is saying to us...

👁 Read Colossians 3 v 5–11

ENGAGE YOUR BRAIN

▶ What kinds of things do we need to throw out of our lives? (v5, v8–9)

▶ What is God's reaction to sin? (v6)

▶ Why should we be fighting the sin in our lives? (v9–10)

God hates sin; He won't stand for it and will punish those who sin against Him (v6). But Christians have had all their sins forgiven by God, so they want to please Him by throwing out sin from their lives.

It's a real struggle, but God helps us do it, helping us become more and more like Him (v10). This is true for all Christians, no matter who they are or where they're from (v11)!

GET ON WITH IT

Look again at verses 5, 8 and 9.

On the right-hand side of this page, make a list of specific sins you need to kick out of your life. Be brutally honest with yourself.

PRAY ABOUT IT

Spend time bringing these things to God in prayer.

TALK IT THROUGH

We all have sin issues we need to deal with. It's often easier if we have someone we're accountable to. Pluck up the courage to talk to an older Christian about the stuff you really struggle with. They can pray with you and encourage you.

THE BOTTOM LINE

Don't delay. Tackle that sin.

73 | Holy wardrobe

Is there a common "Christian look"?
Is the equation SOCK + SANDALS = CHRISTIAN true?
Does it matter what Christians wear?
Paul says that it does...

👁 Read Colossians 3 v 12-14

ENGAGE YOUR BRAIN

Christians are God's own people. They are holy, set apart to serve Him. And God loves them massively! OK, so Paul doesn't tell us where to go shopping, but he does tell us the characteristics Christians should clothe themselves in.

▶ *Below, list the 7 qualities we should wear (v12–13).*

1.

2.

3.

4.

5.

6.

7.

▶ *Which ones do you struggle with?*

▶ *What's the motive for us to forgive other people? (v13)*

▶ *What's the key ingredient to all of these good qualities? (v14)*

For Christians, God has forgiven all their disobedience and sins against Him, so they should show the same forgiveness when people wrong them (v13). Just as our love for others (even those people who get on our nerves) should be motivated by God's endless love for us (v12).

GET ON WITH IT

On the left, list two people you get on with and two you don't. Make them a mix of ages. Next to each one, write down how you can actively show one of the 7 qualities to them.

PRAY ABOUT IT

Thank God that He loves you so ridiculously much! Ask Him to help you do the stuff you scribbled down.

74 Body language

Christians are perfect. They're always loving, helpful and encouraging. Christians always get along brilliantly together and never argue, right? You don't look convinced!

OK, maybe we struggle sometimes. Here are Paul's tips for getting along with other Christians…

TIP 1 – Read Colossians 3 v 15

▶ *How are Christians described?*

▶ *So how should we act towards other Christians?*

All Christians are part of the same "body", with Jesus as our head. He's forgiven our sins and made us at peace with God. So He expects us to act in peace and kindness towards other believers. That makes sense!

TIP 2 – Read verse 16

The word of Christ — the awesome message of what Jesus has done for us — should be at the centre of our lives. We need to study the Bible together, teaching each other from God's word, and singing praise songs to God together, thanking Him for all He's done.

TIP 3 – Read verse 17

▶ *What command is repeated in each of verses 15, 16 and 17?*

Are you grateful to God for what He's done in your life? Christians show their gratitude to God by living their whole lives for Him. Everything we do and say should be done and said for Jesus. What a challenge!

GET ON WITH IT

▶ *How can you get on more peacefully with "difficult" Christians you know?*

▶ *Are you reading the Bible together with other Christians?*

▶ *Who could you start reading God's word with?*

PRAY ABOUT IT

Pray about your response to the *Get on with it* section.

75 | Family fortunes

Someone once said: "Life would be easy if it wasn't for other people." Actually, I said it. But it's true, our relationships can be a cause of real difficulty sometimes. They're HARD WORK!

Yesterday we read: "Whatever you do … do it all in the name of the Lord Jesus." Paul says we must serve God in our relationships. Today we'll look at two of those relationships…

👁 Read Colossians 3 v 18–19

ENGAGE YOUR BRAIN

- ▶ *What do you think verse 18 means?*

- ▶ *And what responsibility do husbands have? (v19)*

This is a really tricky subject that people can get upset about. So if you're starting to fume, check out Galatians 3 v 28, which reminds us that men and women are equal in Christ, even though they have different roles from each other.

But since most of us aren't married yet, let's look at a relationship a little closer to home…

👁 Read verses 20–21

- ▶ *How much should we obey our parents? Why?*

- ▶ *And what's the news for fathers?*

Did you get that? We must obey our parents in everything!

OK, obviously not if they're going against God's commands, but in everything else we must obey them because it pleases the Lord. Yes, it's really hard sometimes, but what better reason to honour our parents? We do it out of love for God.

GET ON WITH IT

- ▶ *How can you obey your parents more? What do you need to work really hard on?*

PRAY ABOUT IT

Talk to God about any issues raised today. Ask Him to give you clear guidance, and to help you serve Him in your relationships.

76 Working class

What's your attitude towards work (school work, a job you have, chores around the house)? Do you plod along grudgingly or throw yourself into it wholeheartedly?

👁 Read Colossians 3 v 22 – 4 v 1

Back when Paul was writing, rich people had slaves working in their homes. But Paul's advice is relevant for any kind of work we do.

ENGAGE YOUR BRAIN

▷ What should a Christian's attitude be towards their boss or teachers? (v22)

▷ Do you work harder only when someone's watching?

▷ Why should Christians work hard? What's their motivation? (v23–24)

Paul says: Go for it! Obey your boss, even if they annoy you. Don't work hard just to keep them happy but give your all as if you're working for God (v23). You are!

It's not about the money you earn or the grades you get here on earth. It's about serving Jesus with your whole being, giving everything for Him. He has already promised Christians their reward — eternal life with Him (v24).

Working your socks off is a way of showing your gratitude for everything Jesus has done for you and everything you'll receive in eternity.

GET ON WITH IT

▷ How will you change the way you work this week?

PRAY ABOUT IT

Ask God to help you work harder for Him. Ask Him to keep reminding you that it's Him you're serving.

THE BOTTOM LINE

Work hard; you're doing it for God.

77 Talking to God

How are you finding prayer right now? How often do you talk to God? What do you say? Paul has been giving us some great advice on how to live as Christians. Now he turns to prayer...

👁 **Read Colossians 4 v 2–4**

ENGAGE YOUR BRAIN

▶ *What does it mean to be devoted to something?*

▶ *How can you be more devoted to talking to God?*

Yet again Paul says: Go for it! This is God, the Creator of the universe. And YOU get to talk to Him! As often as you want! So what are you waiting for???

Devote yourself to talking to your heavenly Father. You've got so much to thank Him for, so do it (v2).

▶ *What did Paul ask the Colossians to pray for? (v3–4)*

Paul was in prison for telling people about Jesus, and he wanted these Christians to pray for him. To pray that he would have the opportunity to tell more people about the gospel, and that he'd be able to do it clearly (v4).

We need to pray hard for Christians we know who spread the gospel. Anyone spring to mind?

PRAY ABOUT IT

Take longer today to talk to God. Make a list of things to thank Him for. Use verses 3–4 to help you pray for Christians you know who tell others about Jesus. Ask God to give you opportunities to spread the gospel too.

THE BOTTOM LINE

Be devoted to prayer. Pray for gospel-spreaders.

78 Talking about God

Are you a good talker? What do you enjoy chatting about? How good are you at talking about God? Bet that last one silenced you!

As Paul continues to train the Colossian Christians in living for God, he gives them some top talking tips.

👁 Read Colossians 4 v 5–6

ENGAGE YOUR BRAIN

▷ *How should Christians behave towards outsiders — people who don't know Jesus? (v5)*

▷ *What does it mean to be wise in our behaviour towards outsiders?*

Paul says be wise — watch how you act. Are you drawing people in to know more about Jesus or pushing them away with the way you behave? Do you take up opportunities to talk about your faith or do you listen to the whooshing sound as the chances fly by? Paul encourages us to grab opportunities with both hands.

▷ *What might conversation that's full of grace and seasoned with salt sound like? (v6)*

Full of grace means full of Jesus — talking about Him and how He's turned your life around.

Full of salt means interesting. Don't bore people to death when you talk about church. Don't make Christianity sound like a list of rules. Not enough salt makes your food too bland; too much is overpowering. Get the balance right. Try to be lively and interesting in conversation when you're talking about Christian stuff.

SHARE IT

Time to go for it! How will you mention God more in your daily conversations? Are you ready to answer people's questions? If not, what can you do about that?

PRAY ABOUT IT

Ask God to help you grab those opportunities!

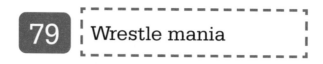

79 Wrestle mania

We've reached the end of Paul's letter to the Colossian Christians. He's warned them about people who say you need more than Jesus to be a Christian. And he's given them loads of practical advice on living for Christ.

Now, some of Paul's friends say "Hi" to the Colossians...

👁 Read Colossians 4 v 7–18

ENGAGE YOUR BRAIN

▷ *How is Tychicus described? (v7–8)*

▷ *Why did Paul send him to Colossae (v8)?*

Like Tychicus, all Christians are fellow-servants, working for Jesus. Tychicus' job was to encourage these Christians by telling them what Paul and his friends had been going through to spread the message of Jesus. All Christians need encouragement. Which means we all need to be encouragers too.

▷ *How does Paul describe Epaphras? (v12)*

It was Epaphras who first told these guys about Jesus (Colossians 1 v 7–8), and he was still praying for them. And not just a quick prayer every now and then. He was "wrestling in prayer" for them. Prayer can be a struggle and hard work sometimes. It shouldn't be hit-and-run. We should throw ourselves into it, praying intensely for other Christians, as Epaphras did — that they will stick at it, grow in their faith, and be certain of their eternal future with Jesus.

GET ON WITH IT

▷ *Which Christian friends can you encourage this week?*

Try to pick at least one to encourage in person, one to phone, and one to text or email.

PRAY ABOUT IT

Now think of three other Christians you know. Pray Epaphras' prayer for them from verse 12.

80 Psalms – Night night

If you want to get in the mood for Psalm 4, put your pyjamas on. David is talking to God just before going to bed. And he gives us some brilliant advice on living for God in a messed-up world.

👁 Read Psalm 4

ENGAGE YOUR BRAIN

▶ *How confident is David that God will answer his prayers? (v1, 3, 8)*

▶ *How were other people treating God? (v2)*

David gives us loads of top tips for right living. First, he asks God to hear his prayer (v1); then he grumbles about people worshipping fake gods instead of the one true God (v2); he warns against sinning (v4); then he sings God's praises before settling down to sleep (v6–8).

▶ *Which verse jumps out and speaks to you personally?*

▶ *What word of advice on sin does David offer? (v4)*

GET ON WITH IT

What can you do to control yourself when you're angry? Why not make an *anger plan* to help you next time your temper rises. Base it on verse 4:

• Count to 10 and calm yourself

• Keep your mouth shut

• Search your heart and get to the root of the problem

• Ask yourself if you're reacting in a good and right way

• Talk to God and ask for His help

God filled David's heart with joy, much more than any wine could (v7). We often look for happiness everywhere except in God, who brings us real joy. We sometimes think alcohol or good times are what we need, when only God can truly satisfy us.

PRAY ABOUT IT

Read the psalm again.

▶ *What can you change in your life, so you're living for God more?*

Now ask the Lord's help…

81 Rise and shine

How do you like to start the day? Up at dawn for a two-mile run and a bowl of muesli? Or a long lie-in before crawling into the shower?

👁 Read Psalm 5 v 1–3

David is having trouble with enemies again. So he starts his day by talking to God and asking for His help (v3). And expecting an answer!

▶ *How would starting your day off with God benefit your life?*

David says there are two kinds of people — those hated by God and those accepted by God...

👁 Read verses 4–6 and 9–10

ENGAGE YOUR BRAIN

▶ *From these verses, describe God's enemies in one sentence.*

▶ *How does God treat those who rebel against Him? (v4–6)*

David's enemies are God's enemies. It's not wrong to pray against people who do evil. That doesn't mean praying against people who get on your nerves, but those who are fighting against God and His people.

👁 Read verses 7–8 and 11–12

Brilliant news! God's people are allowed into His presence (v7);

God leads them in the right way to live (v8); they are protected by Him (v11); He shows them great favour (v12). There's every reason to celebrate! Being one of God's people is a fantastic privilege!

PRAY ABOUT IT

▶ *Will you set your alarm a little earlier this week, so you start your day by talking to God?*

Make a list of many of the great privileges of being a Christian, and thank God for them every morning before you launch into your day.

GENESIS

Promises promises

Lies, deception, war, daring rescues, surprising babies, angels in disguise, circumcision (ouch!), child sacrifice (almost!), incest, a woman turned into a salt stack, and evil cities destroyed by burning sulphur — it's all in Genesis 12–25.

NEW BEGINNINGS

There are some incredible stories here in Genesis, but at the heart of it all, we meet an awesome God in control. If Genesis 1–11 was about the beginning of the human race, then chapters 12–25 are about the beginning of the people of God. We meet Abraham — a man faithful to God — and his, er, *interesting* family. And we see how they fit into God's plans for a nation ruled by Him.

PROMISES PROMISES

In Genesis 12–25, God makes amazing promises to Abraham and his family (who would become God's chosen people, the Israelites). The promises God makes here in Genesis are kept throughout the whole of the Bible. And they ultimately come true through Jesus. Even at the beginning of the Bible, we're pointed to Jesus Christ!

REVEALING STUFF

In the Bible, God reveals Himself to His people in stages, gradually showing them more about Himself, building on what He's already taught them. Through His promises to Abraham, we begin to see more of what God's like and His incredible plans for His people.

If you want great stories, you've come to the right place. But delve a little deeper, and you'll also see the incredible, powerful, loving God behind it all.

OK, take it away, Abraham. Or should that be Abram…

82 Get up and go

Some stories are slow to start, gradually building an atmosphere. Not so with Abram. We're thrown straight into the middle of things, with God giving Abram mind-boggling orders and promises right away...

👁 Read Genesis 12 v 1–5

ENGAGE YOUR BRAIN

▶ *What did God command Abram to do?*

▶ *Why was it hard for Abram? (v1)*

▶ *But what amazing promises did God make?*

God suddenly told Abram to leave his home and his people and step into the unknown. Abram trusted God to guide him and took his family on this mysterious adventure (v4–5). And the Lord made some history-shaping promises to Abram...

Promise 1 — Children
Abram's family would grow into a great nation (v2). But look back at Genesis 11 v 29–30: Abram was 75 and his wife Sarai couldn't have kids. God's first promise looked unlikely.

Promise 2 — Blessing
Through Abram, God would bless everyone on the planet (v3). Again, it seems improbable. But the rest of the Bible shows us that *Jesus* was a descendant of Abram. It was Jesus who would be a blessing to the whole world.

👁 Read verses 6–9

▶ *What new promise did God make? (v7)*

Promise 3 — Land
The Lord promised to give the whole land of Canaan to Abram's descendants. Another unlikely promise, but Abram believed God.

Christians have the Bible and know Jesus. Abram had neither and yet was prepared to trust God and step into an unknown future.

▶ *How is he an example to you?*

PRAY ABOUT IT

Thank God for His awesome promises. Pray that, like Abram, you'll trust and obey God.

83 Who do you trust?

You're in a tight spot. You fear for the worst and you don't know what to do. Do you trust your own instincts? Phone a friend? Or maybe even turn to God for help?

👁 Read Genesis 12 v 10–16

ENGAGE YOUR BRAIN

▶ *What did Abram do when famine hit the land? (v10)*

▶ *What did he do when he feared for his safety? (v11-13)*

▶ *How many times is God mentioned in verses 10-16?*

Abram was living in Canaan, the place God led him to. But when famine struck, Abram didn't seek God's help — he ran off to Egypt. And when he feared the Egyptians might kill him and take Sarai, Abram told a half-truth (Sarai was his half-sister) to save his skin.

God isn't mentioned in these verses because Abram didn't turn to the Lord for help. He tried to sort his problems out by himself. It's always a big mistake to tackle a problem without asking God's help.

👁 Read verses 17–20

Because of Abram's lies, Sarai became Pharaoh's wife, God gave Pharaoh serious diseases, and Abram and Sarai were thrown out of the country. Yet God was still with them!

It's so easy to take matters into our own hands. We sometimes trust ourselves more than we trust God. But because of Jesus, we can turn to God for help in living His way.

PRAY ABOUT IT

Tell God about difficult situations you're facing at the moment. Ask Him to help and guide you.

THE BOTTOM LINE

Trust God, not yourself.

84 Time to split

Abram had made a mess of things in Egypt by not turning to God for guidance. But, amazingly, God was still with him and his family. So, would Abram learn from his mistakes?

👁 Read Genesis 13 v 1–4

ENGAGE YOUR BRAIN

▷ *What did Abram do this time? (v4)*

That's a good pattern to follow: when you've done wrong, go quickly back to God. Talk to Him, ask Him to guide you.

Abram's back trusting God, but how will he react when he's tested again?

👁 Read verses 5–13

▷ *What was the problem? (v7)*

▷ *How did Abram deal with it? (v8–9)*

▷ *How wise was Lot's choice? (v12–13)*

Abram and his nephew Lot had become so rich that the land wasn't big enough for both of them and their families and animals. Abram had the right to choose who farmed where because he was top man in the family. But he showed great generosity by letting Lot choose.

Lot chose perfect farming land, near the river Jordan. But it was near the sin-infested city of Sodom. Later on, we'll see what a bad move this was.

GET ON WITH IT

How can you be more generous to people around you? List three specific things you can do:

1.

2.

3.

PRAY ABOUT IT

Ask the Lord to remind you to do those things. And bring any problems or decisions you have to God, asking Him to guide you.

85 Showing promise

In the best thrillers, the plot is revealed slowly. Bit by bit, we're given new facts, until we can start to piece together what's happening. Things gradually start to make sense.

God made three great promises to Abram (Genesis 12 v 1–7). Gradually, the Lord reveals more and more about these incredible promises. And He also reveals more about Himself.

Read Genesis 13 v 14–18

ENGAGE YOUR BRAIN

- What does God reveal about His promise of land? (v14–15)

- And what about the promise of children? (v16)

- How does the Lord get Abram to appreciate His promises? (v17)

God is so good to His people and treats them far better than they could imagine! God revealed to Abram just how amazing His promises were — Abram's family would become a huge nation (v16), and they would have this great land, as far as the eye could see (v15).

Throughout the Bible, we gradually begin to see how awesome, loving,

forgiving and powerful our God is. He gives us far more than we could ever deserve or imagine. Sending His Son to die for us was the ultimate example of this.

GET ON WITH IT

Abram walked around the country, taking in all that God had promised to give him.

- What can you do to make sure you appreciate the great things God has given you?

PRAY ABOUT IT

Thank God for some of the specific things He's given you. Ask Him to reveal more and more of Himself to you as you read your Bible.

THE BOTTOM LINE

God is so good to His people!

86 | Lot of trouble

Remember how Abram let his nephew Lot have first choice of where to live? Lot chose great farming land, but it was near Sodom, where people sinned against God in disgusting ways.

Keep that at the back of your brain. But first, a big battle between loads of kings with crazy names…

👁 Read Genesis 14 v 1–12

ENGAGE YOUR BRAIN

▶ *Where was Lot living before? (Genesis 13 v 12)*

▶ *Where's he living now? (Genesis 14 v 12)*

Four powerful kings attacked five cities (including Sodom) on the plain of Jordan. By now, Lot had moved into the evil city. What a bad move!

GET ON WITH IT

▶ *Is there anywhere you go or people you hang out with that tempt you away from living God's way?*

▶ *What will you do about it?*

Lot was kidnapped along with all his possessions. Time for Abram to come to the rescue…

👁 Read verses 13–16

▶ *How was Abram able to rescue Lot so successfully? (see v20)*

With the help of his allies and some cunning night-time tactics, Abram made a successful attack and rescued Lot. Nice work. But it was God who was behind Abram's victory.

PRAY ABOUT IT

Thank God that He's in control. Spend time thanking God for specific things He's enabled you to do.

THE BOTTOM LINE

God's behind the good stuff.

87 Two for one offer

Know anyone who's got two jobs? Waiter and actor. Teacher and mother. Taxi driver and ballet dancer. Today, Abram meets a man who has two seriously important jobs...

👁 Read Genesis 14 v 17–20

ENGAGE YOUR BRAIN

▷ *What two impressive roles did Melchizedek have? (v18)*

▷ *What did he recognise about Abram's victory? (v20)*

Not only did Melkich... Meldizzy... Milkyway... this king/priest have two great jobs and say some great things to Abram, he also reminds us of someone.

▷ *Any ideas who?*

The book of Hebrews tells us that Melchizedek reminds us of *Jesus*. Jesus is king and priest. He's the *King over everything* and He was the *ultimate priest* because, when He died and rose again, He took away the sins of God's people. Stunning.

👁 Read verses 21–24

▷ *How did the king of Sodom want to divide the people and things Abram had captured?*

▷ *What's Abram's surprising answer?*

Usually, the reward for winning a battle was to keep everything (and everyone) you captured. But Abram refused to keep anything the king of Sodom gave him. He wanted people to know that everything he had came from God. And he gave a tenth of his possessions back to God too (v20).

GET ON WITH IT

▷ *Everything you have comes from God. What can you give back to Him? Time? Money? Possessions?*

▷ *How exactly will you do that?*

PRAY ABOUT IT

You must have loads to thank God for today — and a few things to ask Him.

88 | Game of two halves

What promises had God made to Abram? Flick back through the last few pages if your brain has frozen. Today, we'll see God confirm those promises in a spectacular way.

👁 Read Genesis 15 v 1–6

ENGAGE YOUR BRAIN

▶ *What was Abram worried about? (v2–3)*

▶ *How did God answer Abram and encourage him? (v5, v1)*

▶ *What was Abram's response? (v6)*

The Lord said He would protect Abram. In fact, having God with him was Abram's greatest reward (v1). Yet Abram still doubted God's promise to give him a huge family. So God said: *Go count the stars — that's the number of offspring you'll have!*

Abram believed and trusted God (v6). It's one of the brilliant moments in the Bible. For us, too — as we trust God to forgive us by what Jesus has done, He counts us right with God.

▶ *How does your life show that you trust God?*

👁 Read verses 7–21

▶ *What would you say is happening here? Any ideas?*

Abram wanted to be sure that God would keep His promises. So the Lord reminded Abram of how He'd been faithful in the past (v7) and would be in the future (v14–16).

God made a *covenant* (agreement) with Abram. When making a covenant, two people would sacrifice animals and walk between the bodies. If you broke the agreement, you'd be cut to pieces too. Ouch. The fire pot and torch were a sign that God was there, making this promise.

PRAY ABOUT IT

God has promised to forgive His people and keep them safe for ever. He always keeps His promises. Spend a while praising and thanking God.

89 | You've got Ishmael

How good are you at waiting? Are you really patient, or do you tear your hair out when you're waiting for stuff? It had been ten years since God promised Abram and Sarai a son...

👁 Read Genesis 16 v 1–6

ENGAGE YOUR BRAIN

▶ *How would you describe Sarai's feelings?*

▶ *What happened because of Sarai's and Abram's impatience and failure to trust God?*

Abram and Sarai gave up on God giving them the son He'd promised. They tried to fix the problem themselves, but the result was a pregnant slave girl (v4), hate (v4), blame (v5), and a runaway mum-to-be (v6).

Sometimes it seems to defy logic to trust God's word, so we try to fix things ourselves. But God wants us to trust Him so that our faith gets stronger.

👁 Read verses 7–16

▶ *God cared for this pregnant Egyptian slave girl. What does that tell you about God?*

▶ *What did Hagar recognise about God?*

Hagar felt unloved and alone. Yet God saw her misery and cared for her. But Ishmael wasn't the son God had promised Abram. He and Sarai would have to wait a little longer.

TALK IT THROUGH

Grab a Christian friend or two and talk about...

• times you're tempted to not trust God and do things your way instead;

• the consequences of doing things your way instead of God's;

• how you can encourage each other to trust God and hold on to His promises.

PRAY ABOUT IT

Talk to God about what's on your mind today.

90 Lifetime guarantee

What do you think you'll be doing in 13 years time? Will you still be walking God's way? From yesterday's story, we now jump forward 13 years with Abram. But is God still with Abe?

👁 Read Genesis 17 v 1–8

ENGAGE YOUR BRAIN

▷ *What did God promise…*

- *for Abram? (v4–5)*

- *for Abram's family? (v6, 8)*

- *for ever? (v7)*

▷ *What did God demand of Abram? (v1)*

God was definitely still with Abram. He confirmed His brilliant covenant promises again and gave Abram a few more details. He would now be called Abraham which means "father of many".

God promised Abraham he'd have loads of descendants, including kings. God promised to give Abraham's family the land of Canaan (they were still aliens/foreigners there at this point). The Lord promised to be their God and He would keep His promises for ever!

God told Abraham to keep obeying Him and living for Him. Oh, and to do something else too…

👁 Read verses 9–14

▷ *What did Abraham's family have to do?*

▷ *Why? (v11)*

Sounds weird and painful (hands up if your eyes are watering). But it was a sign of God's covenant. Like wearing a badge saying: *Hey, I'm part of God's people and He's looking after me!* But it wasn't a ticket to heaven; you still had to trust and obey God (v1).

PRAY ABOUT IT

Read verse 1 again.

Are you ready to live like that? What needs changing? Talk to God about it and ask His help.

91 Promise keeper

Yesterday we read about the awesome promises God made to Abraham. And God's not finished yet... But how do we know God keeps His promises?

👁 Read Genesis 17 v 15–22

ENGAGE YOUR BRAIN

Four more promises here. Find them and sum them up in your own words.

▶ *Promise 1 (v16):*

This promise came true. Whole nations were descended from Abraham and Sarah. Some of them were kings like David and Solomon.

▶ *Promise 2 (v19):*

A baby for this doddery couple? Surely not! If you want to find out what happened, flick ahead to Genesis 21 v 1–7.

▶ *Promise 3 (v20):*

It happened in Genesis 25 v 12–18.

▶ *Promise 4 (v21):*

God would have a covenant with Isaac too. His many descendants would live in Canaan, and the whole world would be blessed through a member of his family — Jesus.

All of these promises came true, giving us even more evidence that God keeps His promises.

👁 Read verses 23–27

Don't worry, we don't have to get circumcised these days (phew!) The Bible later talks about a circumcision of the heart — it's our attitude He's most concerned about. God wants people to trust and obey Him. In everything.

THE BOTTOM LINE

God ALWAYS keeps His promises.

92 | Luke – On the road again

We're back in Luke, and Jesus' disciples are receiving training in how to spread the news about God's kingdom. And Jesus is also training them to understand who He really is.

👁 Read Luke 9 v 1–6

ENGAGE YOUR BRAIN

▶ *What task were they given?*

▶ *What attitudes must they adopt to follow Jesus' instructions? (v3–5)*

Jesus was training the twelve disciples to do His job. They may not have realised it, but Jesus was preparing them to carry on His work after He was gone. He was also teaching them to have His attitude: relying on God (and other believers) to give them everything they needed.

GET ON WITH IT

▶ *In what areas don't you trust God to provide for you?*

▶ *What can you do to rely more on God and less on yourself?*

👁 Read verses 7–9

▶ *Who did the people think Jesus was?*

▶ *Why does it matter that they thought this?*

Herod (and the people around him) hadn't worked out who Jesus was. And neither had the disciples. Over the next few days we'll see them start to get the idea.

It's not obvious why Luke mentions Herod's reaction and his beheading of John the Baptist. Maybe it's there to remind us that being a disciple of Jesus means facing hard times along the way. Possibly even death.

PRAY ABOUT IT

Ask God to help you to understand who Jesus really is and to be prepared to serve Him, whatever it takes.

93 Feeding time

Today we read Luke's version of a very famous miracle. It must be important, because it's in all four Gospels. Try to read it with new eyes — taking your time and looking out for new things.

👁 Read Luke 9 v 10–11

ENGAGE YOUR BRAIN

▷ How did Jesus react when people interrupted His disciple training?

▷ How do you react when people "bother" you?

▷ How ready are you to talk to people about God's kingdom?

👁 Read verses 12–17

▷ What does this miracle reveal about Jesus and His power?

▷ If you were one of the disciples, what would you learn here?

Jesus feeding thousands of people would have reminded them of God feeding His people in the desert with manna and quail (Exodus 16). God provides for His people. He looks after their physical needs.

The miracle also showed Jesus creating something out of nothing — only God can do that. It was another pointer to *who* Jesus really is. Tomorrow we'll see the disciples finally start to get it!

SHARE IT

▷ How can you be more welcoming to people?

▷ How can you point people to Jesus and who He really is?

PRAY ABOUT IT

Thank Jesus that He meets both our spiritual and physical needs. Talk to Him about the needs of yourself, your friends and your family.

94 Who is Jesus?

There's a riddle to solve. The disciples have lots of clues — His teaching, miracles, priorities, people He's met... but there's no solution so far. WHO IS JESUS???

👁 Read Luke 9 v 18–20

ENGAGE YOUR BRAIN

▶ What had Peter realised about Jesus?

▶ Why is this so important?

▶ How does it differ completely from the other views? (v19)

Peter realised that Jesus was the Christ, the Messiah — the ruler sent by God to rescue His people, as promised by Old Testament prophets. "Christ" is a Greek word. "Messiah" is Hebrew. They both mean the same thing: "the anointed one" (ie: God's chosen King).

Peter solved the riddle. And solving riddles leads to hidden treasure. In fact, Jesus was about to give them a gold nugget of information...

👁 Read verses 21–22

▶ What did Jesus say must happen to Him?

▶ Why do you think the disciples were not allowed to tell anyone what they'd realised?

The Jews were expecting the Messiah to beat the Romans; they didn't think the Christ would suffer and die. At the hands of the most religious Jews too. Imagine the disciples' reaction to this shocking news. No wonder Jesus told them to keep quiet. This was shocking news that people were not ready for yet. And the disciples still had much to learn about exactly what kind of Messiah Jesus was and what He expected of His followers.

PRAY ABOUT IT

Read slowly through verse 22, thanking Jesus for each of the painful things He went through to rescue undeserving sinners like us.

THE BOTTOM LINE

Jesus is God's promised Messiah.

95 Dying for life

If someone asked you: "What does living as a Christian involve?" how would you answer? Write your answer in the space on the right, being honest. Then read what Jesus demands of His followers.

👁 Read Luke 9 v 23–25

ENGAGE YOUR BRAIN

▶ How should Jesus' disciples live? (v23–24)

▶ Why should they live this way? (v24–25)

▶ What does it mean to "lose our lives"?

Being a Christian is no easy ride. Jesus demands that His followers "deny themselves" — stop living for themselves and give their whole lives to serving Jesus. That's not easy. Neither is "carrying your cross". People carried their own cross on their way to be crucified. Jesus says His disciples must be prepared to sacrifice their lives for Him in this world, knowing He has saved them for real life in eternity.

👁 Read verses 26–27

▶ What does Jesus warn us against? (v26)

Jesus is coming back in glory. When He does, those He has saved will live with Him eternally, but those who were ashamed of Him will themselves be rejected by Jesus. Tough but fair.

TALK IT OVER

Verse 27 is confusing and different people have different theories of what it's referring to. I'll not tell you mine. Instead, grab a Christian friend and look into it together. Read what comes before it and after it in Luke. Read the other versions of it (Matthew 16 v 28, Mark 9 v 1), and what Bible teachers have written about it.

GET ON WITH IT

▶ What changes will you make to be the sort of disciple Jesus wants?

▶ Jesus' followers deny themselves and take up their cross. Do you?

96 Transfigure it out

Peter has realised that Jesus is the Messiah/Christ — the ruler who would rescue His people. God Himself now confirms who Jesus is in a dramatic display for three of the disciples.

👁 Read Luke 9 v 28–32

ENGAGE YOUR BRAIN

▶ *What happened to Jesus?*

▶ *What did Moses and Elijah speak about with Jesus?*

Peter, James and John saw an incredible display of Jesus' glory. And they saw two Jewish heroes with their Master. Moses had given God's law to the Israelites and Elijah was a prophet — God's messenger to His people. They both pointed forward to someone even more important — Jesus. And the most important event in history would be the "departure" — Jesus' death.

👁 Read verses 33–36

▶ *What does Luke think of Peter's suggestion? (v33)*

▶ *What's the big news from God? (v35)*

Peter had realised that Jesus was the Messiah/Christ (v20), but he and the other disciples still hadn't fully understood who Jesus was and why He came. Even when they saw His glory. They hadn't grasped that Jesus was far greater than Moses or Elijah. The voice of God spelled it out to them: "This is my Son … listen to Him." Listen to Jesus first, above anyone or anything else.

GET ON WITH IT

Listening to Jesus means taking the Bible seriously. Grab a notebook or create a file on your PC or phone. Divide it up into sections called "Bible passage", "What it teaches about Jesus", "What I've learned" and "What I'm going to do about it". Every time you read about Jesus in the Bible, fill it in.

THE BOTTOM LINE

Jesus is God's Son — listen to Him.

97 Faith failure

Amazing scenes on the mountain with Jesus' glory and identity revealed. But when He gets back to civilisation, He finds chaos, with His disciples and a demon in the middle of it.

👁 Read Luke 9 v 37–41
ENGAGE YOUR BRAIN

▷ *What was the problem? (v38–40)*

▷ *Why does Jesus criticise His disciples? (v41)*

Jesus came back to a disturbing situation — a demon had control of a boy, was throwing him around and the disciples could do nothing about it. Jesus called everyone there "unbelieving and perverse". The disciples hadn't trusted God to heal the boy and the rest of the people still didn't believe that Jesus was God's Son, the Christ.

👁 Read verses 42–45

▷ *What did this miracle show about Jesus? (v42–43)*

▷ *But what about the bigger news? (v44)*

▷ *Why did the disciples need to understand this?*

Jesus was making it clear to His disciples that He would have to die. But they simply didn't understand, and were even afraid to ask Him about it. It is absolutely vital that we understand who Jesus is, why He came and why He had to die.

PRAY ABOUT IT

Ask God to help you really understand who Jesus is and why His Father sent Him to die. Ask God to help you believe and trust in Jesus. Then spend time praising God for how great and powerful and loving He is.

THE BOTTOM LINE

God sent His Son Jesus to die. Believe in Him.

98   How to be the best

Ever try to prove you're better or "more Christian" than some of your friends? Ever look down on Christians from different backgrounds and churches to yours? If so, Jesus is about to give you a slap...

👁 Read Luke 9 v 46–48

ENGAGE YOUR BRAIN

▷ *How have the disciples gone wrong again?*

▷ *What is true greatness, according to Jesus? (v48, also v23–26)*

Back then, kids were considered unimportant with no rights. Jesus came back to what He was saying earlier: *If you want to follow me, you've got to stop putting yourself first. Serve me by serving each other and looking after people who are looked down upon and treated badly — like kids. That's how you live for me. That's true greatness.*

👁 Read verses 49–50

▷ *What did John not understand?*

You've probably noticed that Christians come in all shapes and sizes, and, let's face it, some of them seem pretty weird. We won't always agree on every issue, but the bottom line is this: if someone trusts in Jesus' death to rescue them, they're your Christian brother or sister. You're in the same family.

GET ON WITH IT

▷ *What has Jesus challenged you about today?*

▷ *What practical steps will you take to follow Jesus' teaching?*

▷ *Who do you need to pray about?*

PRAY ABOUT IT

Only you know what you need to talk about with God today.

99 Follow the leader

**Jesus calls people to come and follow Him.
But some just walk away. So Jesus has to warn them in
crystal clear terms. Like this...**

👁 Read Luke 9 v 51–56

ENGAGE YOUR BRAIN

▶ *How would you describe Jesus' attitude? (v51)*

▶ *Why was He like this?*

Jesus' death and resurrection were still over a year (and 10 chapters!) away, but Luke says that's where Jesus was heading. And what about James and John's angry outburst? Samaritans and Jews hated each other, but J & J's question is classic: *Shall we zap them now, Jesus?* As if they could! Jesus' reply shows it was not yet time for His enemies to be destroyed.

👁 Read verses 57–62

▶ *In the space on the right, jot down what it would mean for each of these characters to follow Jesus: Man 1 (v57–58), Man 2 (v59–60), Man 3 (v61–62).*

Jesus isn't saying that families and homes aren't important. But He is saying that serving God is *more* important — throw yourself into it. Once we've seen how much Jesus has done for us, there's no other way to follow Him — whatever that might mean you have to give up or miss out on. Go all out to obey Him first.

THINK IT OVER

Think what these verses might mean when there's a choice between comfort or following Christ.

▶ *Can you think of some situations coming up when you may have to face a choice like this?*

PRAY ABOUT IT

Following Jesus is seriously hard. Ask God to help you stick at it, putting Jesus first in your life.

100 Kingdom come

Jesus has told people to come and follow Him — because He's more important than anything else. Now He tells those followers to go... and tell others about Him. Urgently. Watch now as 72 disciples join in.

👁 Read Luke 10 v 1–11

ENGAGE YOUR BRAIN

▶ *What could these guys expect? (v3, v10)*

▶ *What message were they to preach about? (v9–11)*

This was important work — these men were preparing the way for Jesus, healing the sick and telling people about Jesus and God's kingdom coming. They were to trust God to provide them with food and places to stay, and they must expect a tough time. Like lambs surrounded by wolves.

👁 Read verses 12–16

▶ *What will happen to those who reject the message of Jesus?*

▶ *When will this happen? (v12, v14)*

This is what "the kingdom of God has come near" means — the time is closer when Jesus will come to judge all people. It's an urgent message. Sodom (v12), Tyre and Sidon (v13–15) were places in the Old Testament that were full of sin and were enemies of God and His people. Jesus says: *If you think they were bad, look at places like Chorazin, Bethsaida and Capernaum* — places that had actually seen Jesus but still not turned to follow Him.

▶ *What will be their fate when God judges?*

SHARE IT

▶ *Do you ever mention to friends that Jesus is coming back?*

▶ *Are you urgent enough in sharing the gospel?*

PRAY ABOUT IT

Ask God to give you an urgency to talk to people who are rejecting Him and heading towards destruction.

101 Better than demon-bashing!

Jesus sent out 72 of His followers to heal the sick and preach about God's kingdom coming. Now they're back, full of exciting news.

👁 Read Luke 10 v 17–20

ENGAGE YOUR BRAIN

▶ *What were they excited about? (v17)*

▶ *What does Jesus say they should be more thrilled about? (v20)*

Look at Jesus' view of what was happening (v18–19). He was in charge and was defeating His (and our) greatest enemy, the devil. Even Satan can't really harm Christ's followers: Jesus protects them. In fact, He has already defeated Satan.

But Jesus said there was something to be even more excited about than defeating demons. Knowing you're saved by God and will live with Him in eternity is the best news ever.

👁 Read verses 21–24

▶ *What did Jesus get extra excited about? (v21)*

▶ *What was He referring to?*

Jesus had seen His followers grasp the good news and go out, spreading it around. His disciples were not high-powered super brains. They were ordinary men. That's why Jesus referred to them as "little children". Yet God revealed His truth about His Son to these regular guys. God often uses the least likely people to do incredible things.

SHARE IT

We're not on our own. Yes it's nerve-wracking to talk about Jesus. But it's not down to us — Jesus Himself makes it possible to do far more than we could on our own.

PRAY ABOUT IT

Ask Jesus to give you the courage and the words you need to spread the message.

Then thank God as you "rejoice that your names are written in heaven."

102 | Big questions

How does the Good Samaritan story go? Do you know it pretty well? Try to look at it with new eyes today, and look for answers to this question: *how do we get eternal life?*

👁 Read Luke 10 v 25–28
ENGAGE YOUR BRAIN

▶ *So how does someone inherit eternal life?*

▶ *Is it possible for anyone to keep these commands fully?*

Many people believe it's what you do that earns you a spot in heaven. Jesus says: *Sure — if you always love God with every part of you and put others first.* The problem is — we just can't do it.

👁 Read verses 29–37

▶ *How difficult would this Jewish law expert have found it to treat Samaritans (his worst enemies) better than himself... ALL the time?*

▶ *So what was Jesus teaching him?*

Remember this man's opening question? He wanted to know how you get eternal life. Jesus' story isn't just saying *"love your enemies"*, although that is important, and one way we serve God.

Jesus was teaching Him that we need to live *perfect* lives to be good enough for God and earn eternal life. And that's simply impossible. We never love God or other people perfectly. Never. We need someone to get us to heaven. To rescue us.

PRAY ABOUT IT

Jot down your response to Jesus' teaching. Then talk it over, line by line, with God.

THE BOTTOM LINE

We can't earn our way to eternal life.

103 Lord vs Supper

Life is full of choices. "What shall I wear?" "What shall I do next year?" "Burger or curry?"
Here's a big choice we all have to face: what's the most important thing in your life?

👁 Read Luke 10 v 38–42

ENGAGE YOUR BRAIN

▷ *What was Martha most bothered about?*

▷ *What did Mary realise about Jesus?*

It's easy to picture Martha rushing around nervously at her house party, making sure everything is OK and everyone has enough food. It's understandable that she got annoyed with Mary; I'd probably do the same. But Martha totally missed the point.

She got distracted by what was most important to her — being a good hostess. It's great that she wanted to please other people but there was something far more important right under her nose. Jesus, God's Son, was in her house! Forget the food, Martha — this man can show you eternal life! But Mary got the message. She saw how incredible and important Jesus was.

THINK IT OVER

▷ *What distracts you from Jesus?*

▷ *What do you give more time to than learning from Him?*

▷ *What will you do to give Jesus more of your time?*

PRAY ABOUT IT

If you dare, ask God to shake up your thinking, so that you drop some of the things that take over your life. Ask God to help you choose Jesus first.

THE BOTTOM LINE

Nothing is more important than Jesus.

104 Pray as you learn

It has been said you can tell how someone's getting on as a Christian by how much they enjoy praying. In the next bit of Luke, Jesus is teaching about how to pray and what to expect from God. Sign on for the refresher course...

▶ On the left-hand side, write down how you're getting on with God and what you normally talk about with Him.

Read Luke 11 v 1–4

ENGAGE YOUR BRAIN

▶ How are the disciples told to address God? (v2)

▶ What are they to pray for first? (v2) Why?

"Hallowed" means honoured or respected. Praying "Your kingdom come" means a) praying that we and others would let Jesus rule our lives, and b) looking forward to His great return as King.

▶ What's the reminder in v3?

▶ What else is it vital to pray about? (v4)

It's very easy to focus on ourselves and our own wants and needs. But praying is all about putting God first.

Praying for His kingdom; praying for others to become Christians; remembering He gives us everything we need; recognising our sinfulness and need for God's forgiveness; and His help in forgiving others and fighting temptation.

GET ON WITH IT

▶ What are the important things to pray for and about?

▶ Look at what you wrote earlier. How will you now change the way you pray?

PRAY ABOUT IT

Now's your chance!

105 Powerful prayer promises

Jesus is teaching us about prayer. This is God's Son telling us how to talk to His Father, so listen up. Re-read Luke 11 v 1–4 so you know where we've got to so far.

👁 Read Luke 11 v 5–10

ENGAGE YOUR BRAIN

▷ *What point do you think Jesus is making with His bedtime story?*

▷ *Sum up verse 9 in one word, and verse 10 in two.*

The man waking up his friend was persistent, and no doubt annoying. In those days, if you didn't answer someone asking for help, you'd be branded a pretty lousy neighbour. As we keep asking God, His honour is at stake. So He will answer — in His time and way.

THINK IT OVER

Have you been asking God for something important, like a friend or relative becoming a Christian? It's easy to give up if you don't get an immediate answer. Jesus says ask, ask and keep asking. Never give up. God promises to answers our prayers.

👁 Read verses 11–13

▷ *What fantastic promise are Christians given here?*

God gives His children the ultimate gift — the Holy Spirit. So what? Well, the Spirit helps us do the stuff we've been told to pray in verses 2–4. Through His Spirit working in us, God will help us to honour Him more, help us know we're forgiven, help us forgive others, protect us from sin and care for our needs. And more!

PRAY ABOUT IT

▷ *Same question as yesterday: how will you change the way you pray?*

Talk to God right now.

106 | Speak of the devil

Some Jews are starting to accuse Jesus, testing Him, turning people against Him. Luke now shows Jesus answering them. He pulls no punches. His first reply gives a glimpse into His battle against the devil.

👁 Read Luke 11 v 14–22

ENGAGE YOUR BRAIN

- ▶ *What did some people accuse Jesus of? (v15)*

- ▶ *How did Jesus shoot down their claims? (v17–19)*

- ▶ *And what did He claim about Himself? (v20–22)*

Rather than believe in Jesus, the Son of God, some people accused Him of being from the devil (Beelzebub, which means "Lord of the flies"). That's madness, says Jesus. If He was from the devil, He wouldn't be driving out the devil's evil spirits. Plus it would mean that Jews who were doing the same were from Satan too.

Jesus smashed their silly claims and then told them what was really going on. He was proving that He was far stronger than the devil ("the strong man"). This miracle showed people that Jesus was God's chosen King (v20).

👁 Read verses 23–28

- ▶ *Is it OK to have no opinion about Jesus? (v23) Why/why not?*

- ▶ *What's a better way to live? (v28)*

Verses 24–26 are tricky, but the focus again is: *who is Jesus?* Do you think He's from the devil, from God, or just a good man? We can't avoid the issue — if we're not actively with Him, then we're against Him (v23). There's no sitting on the fence when it comes to Jesus.

SHARE IT

- ▶ *How does this change your attitude towards fence-sitters?*

- ▶ *How can you challenge friends who are neutral about Jesus?*

PRAY ABOUT IT

Pray specifically for people you know who are indifferent about Jesus. Ask God to reveal the real Jesus to them.

107 | See and believe

Look back at 11 v 16: "Come on Jesus, do another miracle. Show us some magic!" These people had already seen and heard so much and still didn't believe. Jesus has tough words for those who refuse to see.

Read Luke 11 v 29–32
ENGAGE YOUR BRAIN

▶ Why was it wrong to keep wanting more proof from Jesus?

▶ How should Jesus' listeners respond to Him? (v31–32)

God sent Jonah to tell the sinful people of Nineveh that the Lord would punish them. The "sign of Jonah" (v29) is when total outsiders (like God's enemies in Nineveh and this powerful queen, v31–32) turn to trust God. For Jesus' Jewish listeners, the sign would be the same — non-Jews coming to follow Jesus and know God. Read about it in Acts.

▶ What will happen to those who ignore Jesus' message? (v31–32)

Read verses 33–36

▶ What point is Jesus making? (v34)

Jesus had publicly shone the light of the gospel clearly and yet people still asked for more spectacular signs. Jesus says we all need to see clearly (v34). We all need to recognise who Jesus is and why He came. If you can't read the signs (evidence) about Jesus, there's no hope for you. We have all the information we need — there's no excuse not to believe.

PRAY ABOUT IT

Read today's verses again.

▶ What do you need to pray for yourself?

▶ What about your unbelieving friends?

THE BOTTOM LINE

There's no excuse for spiritual blindness.

108 Sin side out

The Pharisees believed getting eternal life was all about keeping the rules. And they were more worried about what others thought of them than God. It's time for Jesus to shock these comfortably confident religious types.

👁 Read Luke 11 v 37–44

ENGAGE YOUR BRAIN

▶ *What surprised this Pharisee about Jesus? (v38)*

▶ *What had the Pharisees got wrong? (v39–41)*

▶ *How else had they missed the point? (v42–43)*

Pharisees believed they could please God with their huge amount of rules about life. Jesus said they were trying to impress others by appearing holy, but not dealing with the sin inside (v39). They kept the rules, but it was empty religion — they were neglecting justice and the poor.

Jews painted graves white so no one would accidentally touch them and become unacceptable to God. Hanging out with these sinful Pharisees made you even more unclean than touching a grave! (v44)

👁 Read verses 45–54

▶ *Instead of apologising for insulting the Jewish leaders, what did Jesus say about them? (v46)*

▶ *Why is rejecting God's prophets and apostles so serious? (v47–51)*

▶ *What is the dreadful result of their teaching? (v52)*

"Woe to you" is a warning that they'll be punished…

a) for making life unbearably difficult for their followers (v46);

b) for rejecting, persecuting (and even killing) God's messengers (v49);

c) for leading people away from God instead of to Jesus (v52).

PRAY ABOUT IT

Thank Jesus that He's passionate about people getting eternal life, and avoiding God's punishment, by trusting in Him.

ACTS

What Jesus did next

BOOK 1: LUKE'S GOSPEL

His first book, *The Gospel*, was a huge bestseller. In his biography of Jesus of Nazareth, Luke had given the world his carefully researched history of Jesus' miracles, teachings, death and resurrection. It was action-packed, edge-of-the-seat stuff, with a fantastic twist at the end — and all of it was true!

BOOK 2: ACTS

Here's Luke's second book, his follow-up. It's called *Acts*, it probably hit the shelves around AD65, and it's the history of what Jesus did next. Not physically — He spends almost all of it in heaven. This time, Jesus will work through His people. And there's just as much drama, suspense, triumph and tragedy as Luke crammed into his first chart-topper.

In The Gospel, Jesus only visited an area the size of Wales; in Acts, the message about Him will reach some of the greatest cities of the world.

In The Gospel, Jesus only ever had a handful of real followers; in Acts, those who worship Him will come to number tens of thousands.

In The Gospel, Jesus had never been able to rely on His friends, who had failed him repeatedly; in Acts, He'll give them the strength to stand up and be counted.

OVER TO YOU

In Acts, you'll see normal Christians, no more special than you or me, do extraordinary things in the power of Jesus their Lord. And hopefully, as you see them loving Jesus, living for Jesus, and speaking about Jesus, it'll inspire you to do in your day what they did in theirs; to stand up and be counted.

109 Mission impossible?

At the start of each episode in a TV series, you get a recap of what's already happened. That's what Luke gives us at the beginning of part two of his story.

👁 Read Acts 1 v 1–8

ENGAGE YOUR BRAIN

▷ What was Luke's "former book" (called "Luke") about? (v1–3)

▷ What did Jesus tell His followers to wait for? (v4–5)

▷ What would God's gift enable them to do? (v8)

Acts 1 v 8 is a useful summary of what the whole book is about — Jesus' followers spreading the good news of their Saviour. The Holy Spirit isn't a force like electricity, He's a person. He's God. On their own the disciples were pretty ordinary, few in number and muddled (v6). But with God's help, they'd be equipped to tell others about Jesus.

👁 Read verses 9–11

▷ A cloud often signifies God's presence — so what's happening here then?

▷ Is that the last the world will see of Jesus? Why, or why not? (v11)

SHARE IT

▷ What do we need to tell people about what Jesus has done?

▷ What should we tell them about the future?

PRAY ABOUT IT

Write the names of three people you're going to try to witness to about Jesus this week.

1.

2.

3.

Now ask God to help you do it.

110 Decisions, decisions

Eleven players on a soccer team; two people in a marriage; four members of the Beatles; twelve disciples of Jesus... but hang on a minute, He's only got eleven!

👁 **Read Acts 1 v 12–26**

ENGAGE YOUR BRAIN

▶ *Who's Peter talking about? (v16)*

▶ *What had he done? (v16)*

▶ *Who had he been before that? (v17)*

Now Judas wasn't around — not only had he betrayed Jesus to death, but he himself had died (v18–19). He couldn't be brought back into their number (v20).

▶ *What needed to happen? (end of v20)*

▶ *What experience did potential apostles need, and why? (v21–22)*

The twelve apostles were to be the leaders of the mission team taking the good news about Jesus to the world. But, before they could start the task, the gap left by Judas had to be filled. These verses give us a great model for how to make decisions as Christians.

Step One: Start by reading God's word (v20)

Step Two: Continue by thinking hard about what's best (v21–23)

Step Three: Pray about it (v24–25)

Step Four: Trust God to help you make the final decision (v24–26)

This doesn't have to be by drawing lots. Once we've been guided by the Bible, thought hard, and prayed hard, we can take a decision, trusting God to help us make it the right one.

THE BOTTOM LINE

Christians can trust the apostles' writings about Jesus, and follow their example when making decisions.

111 Public spirit

Often Christians are a bit confused about who the Holy Spirit is and what He does. So let's see what the history-changing events of Acts 2 tell us about the Spirit and His relationship with believers.

👁 Read Acts 2 v 1–4

ENGAGE YOUR BRAIN

▶ What could they hear? (v2)

▶ Where did it come from? (v2)

▶ What could they see? (v3)

God often signifies His presence on earth as a fire — a blazing, pure, powerful fire (for instance in Exodus 19 v 16–19).

▶ What did they see the "tongues of fire" do? (v3)

▶ What did they find they could do? (v4)

▶ The wind and the fire were a sign that something had happened. What? (v4)

What we learn about the Holy Spirit in these verses:

• He is powerful (v2)

• He is from heaven (v2)

• He is God (v3 — think about what fire signifies)

• He lives in all believers (v4)

• He changes people drastically (v4)

• He enables people to do amazing things for God (v4)

👁 Read verses 5–13

▶ What did people notice? (v7–8)

▶ What two responses did people have to the Holy Spirit's work?

v12:

v13:

PRAY ABOUT IT

Every Christian has this Holy Spirit dwelling in them. Amazing! Spend some time thanking Jesus for sending His Spirit into you.

112 | Spread the message

Confronted with men who'd been changed by the Holy Spirit, the people in Jerusalem asked: "What does this mean?" "Oh, they're just drunk!" laughed some onlookers. Not so, replied Peter...

👁 Read Acts 2 v 13–28

ENGAGE YOUR BRAIN

▷ How does Peter react to people laughing at him?

▷ Who is Peter's message in these verses all about?

▷ On the right, scribble down what Peter says about him in...

v22:

v23:

v24:

▷ What does Peter say has now happened because of all this man did? (v17)

▷ What is now on offer? (v21)

And all this had been predicted by God hundreds of years before. Notice that Peter uses the Bible to back up what he's saying. He quotes from Joel, a prophet from 700 years before, and David, a king from 1000 years earlier. Jesus is the one God had been pointing to for centuries — and we can know Him and tell people about Him!

THINK ABOUT IT

▷ How should we respond to people who laugh at us for living Spirit-driven lives? (v13–14)

▷ When people ask us what Christianity means, what should be the content of our reply? (v22–24)

PRAY ABOUT IT

Thank Jesus for saving you through all He did; ask Jesus to change you through His Spirit; ask Jesus to give you chances to tell others about Him.

THE BOTTOM LINE

Jesus was chosen by God, crucified, raised, and offers salvation and the Spirit — that's the message Jesus' people bring to others.

113 | Fact, response, effect

Firm fact: **More work and sleep means better exam results.** *Right response:* **Study and rest.** *Immense effect:* **great grades! But there's a firm fact, right response and immense effect far more important than any exams...**

👁 Read Acts 2 v 25–36

ENGAGE YOUR BRAIN

▶ *What's God done for and through Jesus? (v32–33)*

▶ *What's God made Jesus? (v36)*

"Lord" means God Himself. "Christ/ Messiah" means God's eternal, all-powerful King.

That's the **firm fact** about who Jesus is: so it's eternally important to respond in the right way.

👁 Read verse 37–41

Right response one:
▶ *How do the people feel? (v37)*

They knew they hadn't always treated Jesus as they should (they'd helped kill Him), and that they were in trouble with the Messiah/Christ. They desperately asked: "What shall we do?" Thing is, we haven't always treated Jesus as He deserves either; so "What shall *we* do?"

Right response two:
In verse 38, Peter tells the people to repent and be baptised. "Repent" means to turn away from sin and turn to Jesus as your King. Baptism is a public way of saying: "Jesus is now my King".

Immense effect:
▶ *What will anyone who responds rightly be given? (v38)*

▶ *How many people responded rightly? (v41)*

THINK ABOUT IT

Have you ever actually turned from your sinful ways to have Jesus as your King? Have you stated publicly that He's now your ruler? If not, now would be a good time to respond in the right way.

THE BOTTOM LINE

Jesus is Lord and Christ — how will you respond to Him?

114 How church should be

**How would you describe "church"?
Where would you start — the building, the music,
the uncomfy seats?**

Read Acts 2 v 42–47

ENGAGE YOUR BRAIN

▶ *Which word in verse 42
describes these new Christians'
commitment to church?*

▶ *What does that word mean?*

▶ *What four things did they commit
themselves to? (v42)*

▶ *What was Jesus doing through
this devoted church? (v47)*

This is what church can be like! A
Holy Spirit-filled, loving, learning,
praying and sharing community,
being used by Jesus to bring more
people to faith in Him. What a
wonderful church to be part of!

THINK IT THROUGH

These Christians were totally, 100%
committed. Does that describe
your attitude to your church? Are
you devoted to the Bible teaching,
to the other members, to taking

Communion/the Lord's Supper,
and praying together? That means
actually being there on Sunday, and
meeting up in the week too (v46).
And it means giving 100% while
you're there. It means not waiting
for others to make your church more
like this one, but getting on with it
yourself!

GET ON WITH IT

What two specific things can you
start doing / do more of to make
verse 42 describe your commitment
to church?

1.

2.

PRAY ABOUT IT

Ask God to make you devoted to
your church, in attitude and action.

115 | Even better than gold

What's the most valuable thing you can do for someone this week?

👁 **Read Acts 3 v 1–12**

ENGAGE YOUR BRAIN

▶ How would you sum up these verses in one sentence?

▶ And how would you sum up what this is telling us about how to live as Jesus' people today?

▶ What did the crippled man expect from Peter and John? (v5)

▶ What did he get? (v6–7)

▶ Where did the power to heal come from, and where did it not come from? (end of v6, end of v12)

▶ How did the man react to what had happened? (v8)

Here's the end result of Jesus' amazing intervention in this man's life. He hadn't expected to have one of his greatest needs met: but when it was, he praised the one who'd helped him — God.

THINK IT THROUGH

▶ You probably know people with great needs — physical, emotional, material, and most of all the spiritual need of forgiveness. Can Jesus help them?

▶ How will really believing this change the way you pray?

▶ What should you be praying will be the end result of Jesus' work in their lives? (think back to v8–9)

PRAY ABOUT IT

Why not spend time now praying in this way for people you know?

Look back to your summary sentences, and think about if you want to change them at all. Then write them down as today's…

THE BOTTOM LINE

116 Good news, bad news

Last time Jesus' apostles told people about Him, 3000 of them turned back to Him as their Lord. Now the apostles have another chance to talk about Jesus. What'll happen this time?

👁 Read Acts 3 v 11–26

Good news

The message Peter had for those people that day is the message we're to share today. In answer to each question, write a sentence you could say to a friend who's not a Christian.

- ▷ Who is Jesus? (v15)

- ▷ How have people treated Jesus? (v13–14)

- ▷ So what do people need to do? (v19, first word)

- ▷ What will happen if they do? (v19)

And that's not all… one day God will send Jesus Christ (v20) to "restore everything" to perfection (v21) — and anyone who's turned back to Him will be part of that. Wow!

GET ON WITH IT

- ▷ Who can you share this message with this week?

👁 Read Acts 4 v 1–4

- ▷ How did some people react to the message about Jesus? (v4)

Bad news

- ▷ How did some other people react? (v1–2)

- ▷ What happened to Peter and John? (v3)

So was it worth it? Yes! 2000 more people had become Christians. But Peter and John are still in loads of trouble, arrested by the people who'd killed Jesus only months before. Will this be the end of the church?

THE BOTTOM LINE

Anyone who turns back to Jesus as Lord has their sins wiped out; anyone who talks about Jesus being Lord will face very different reactions.

117 Message: Unstoppable

Serious trouble for Peter and John — imprisoned, on trial, facing death for talking about Jesus. What will they do? What would you do?

👁 Read Acts 4 v 5–12

Peter and John are questioned by the men who'd murdered Jesus. Two fishermen face the most powerful men in the country. Their options: keep quiet about Jesus or stand up for Jesus.

ENGAGE YOUR BRAIN

▶ *What do they do? (v10)*

▶ *Why's verse 10 seriously brave?*

▶ *What does verse 12 tell us about why they want to witness about Jesus?*

PRAY ABOUT IT

All over the world today, what happened to Peter and John is happening to Christians who witness publicly about Jesus.

Take a minute to pray for them now, asking the Holy Spirit to help them as He helped Peter (v8).

👁 Read verses 13–22

The leaders have a problem; they want to get rid of Peter and John, but because of the man who'd been healed, they can't (v14–16).

▶ *What do they do instead? (v18)*

▶ *How do Peter and John respond, and why? (v19-20)*

What looked like *Mission: Impossible* for the church is actually *Message: Unstoppable!* Peter and John's words encourage us to keep talking about Jesus, because He's the only way to be saved (v12). They also challenge us: no matter who tells us to shut up, no matter what the cost is, Christians should obey God by talking about Jesus at every opportunity.

THE BOTTOM LINE

"There is no other name under heaven … by which we must be saved."

118 Praying proper prayers

You've just had a really tough day — you talked about Jesus and got laughed at and treated badly. Who do you turn to? What do you do?

👁 Read Acts 4 v 23–31

ENGAGE YOUR BRAIN

- *What are verses 23–24 teaching us about who to turn to and what to do when we get persecuted for talking about Jesus?*

- *What are they doing at the start of their prayer? (v24)*

- *Where does the next part of their prayer come from? (v25–26)*

- *What do they ask God to help them do? (v29)*

- *What do they ask God to do? (v30)*

This is pretty amazing! You'd expect, after the day they've had, that Peter and John would ask for protection from persecution. But instead they ask for power to preach, to live how God has called them to live (back in Acts 1 v 8). They know they'll face even more trouble for talking about Jesus — so they ask God to help them do it. Amazing praying!

- *What's the result of these Christians' prayers? (end of v31)*

THINK IT THROUGH

Our first instinct when we face trouble as Christians should be to get support from other believers. Even more importantly, we should get talking to God, praying in a way that's shaped by who we know God is, what we know God has said, and how we know God wants us to live.

PRAY ABOUT IT

Write your own prayer, shaped by Acts 4 v 24–30...

THE BOTTOM LINE

Write your own today:

119 Walk the walk

Some people talk a good game ("I'll be there at 10am, can't wait!"), but don't deliver ("Errmm... sorry, I forgot"). Sometimes, doing that can have deadly consequences.

👁 Read Acts 4 v 32–37

ENGAGE YOUR BRAIN

🄳 *What did Barnabas do? (v36–37)*

This is sacrificial giving — going without so you can give financially to others. Check out 2 Corinthians 8 v 1–7, where Paul talks about a church which gave "beyond their ability" (v3), and encourages all Christians to "excel in this grace of giving" (v7).

👁 Read Acts 5 v 1–11

🄳 *What was the difference between Barnabas, and Ananias and Sapphira? (v1–2)*

🄳 *What did they tell people they were giving? (v7–8)*

🄳 *Why's what they did so serious? (v3–4)*

The problem wasn't keeping some of the money, but pretending they'd given it all. They were talking the talk, wanting to look good to everyone... but not walking the walk, not doing what they'd said. That's hypocrisy.

🄳 *What's the serious result? (v5, v10–11)*

The lesson is this — God hates and punishes hypocrisy. He doesn't like it when church-goers try to convince people they're sacrificially serving others, when in fact they're not. We might be able to get away with lying to Christians; but we can't get away with lying to God.

GET ON WITH IT

Have a look through your life. Are there any areas where you're pretending to live as a Christian, talking the talk, but actually not bothering to walk the walk? Deal with them now!

God hates hypocrisy. So live like Barnabas, not like Ananias and Sapphira.

120 Psalms – Pain relief

Guess what! King David is having a hard time again. In pain, ill, hounded by his enemies. Let's listen in on his painful groans…

👁 Read Psalm 6 v 1–7

ENGAGE YOUR BRAIN

▶ *David was worried that God might be against him. How did this make him feel? (v2–3, 6–7)*

▶ *Why would the Lord rescue David? (v4)*

When you've let God down, how do you feel? David was incredibly upset at the thought that he'd offended God. He wouldn't rest until he knew the Lord's forgiveness and healing.

We can sometimes be arrogant and think we deserve God's help. David knew this wasn't the case. If God rescued him, it was because of His unbeatable love (v4), nothing else.

👁 Read verses 8–10

▶ *After talking to God, what was David confident of?*

v9:

v10:

PRAY ABOUT IT

David knew he didn't deserve to be rescued by God. And *we* don't deserve rescue from sin. It's only because of God's great love that He sent Jesus to die for us, so that we can be rescued from the punishment we deserve.

Talk to God now and tell Him exactly how that makes you feel.

TALK IT THROUGH

What's getting you down? What sin are you feeling bad about? Grab some Christian friends you trust, and bring these things before God in prayer, confident that He will answer your cries.

121 Fair enough

"Life's not fair!" "Why do bad people seem to get away with evil and do well in life?" Well, David says they don't get away with it at all...

👁 Read Psalm 7 v 1–10

ENGAGE YOUR BRAIN

▶ *What did David do when his enemies were after his blood? (v1)*

▶ *What did David want God to do? (v6–7)*

As God's chosen king, David's enemies were God's enemies. They were out to kill David and were rejecting God. David asked God to rescue him (v1) and knew the Lord would keep him safe (v10).

David didn't seek revenge on his bloodthirsty enemies. He left it to God to deal with them.

👁 Read verses 11–17

▶ *Will evil people get away with it?*

▶ *What will happen to them? (v16)*

God is completely fair. It's not for us to get revenge on people who wrong us. In the end, God treats everyone fairly. People who choose to live without God will ultimately end up frustrated (v14), trapped (v15) and causing their own downfall (v16). Justice will be done!

GET ON WITH IT

Who treats you badly? How can you make sure you act in a godly way towards them, not seeking revenge? Will you hand the situation over to God and ask Him to deal with it?

PRAY ABOUT IT

God is completely fair. He is perfect. So we should thank Him and praise His name (v17). Right NOW.

THE BOTTOM LINE

Justice will be done. By our perfect, completely fair God.

122 Stars in your eyes

Have you ever seen a breathtaking starry sky or huge, awe-inspiring mountains? Something which made you realise how huge and magnificent God must be to have created all that?

👁 **Read Psalm 8**

ENGAGE YOUR BRAIN

▶ *How would you define majestic?*

▶ *What evidence does David have that God is awesome and powerful?*

▶ *On the right-hand side of this page, list the ways God shows He cares for people (v5–8):*

David has grasped two huge truths about God in this psalm and they are repeated in verses 1 and 9.

God is majestic — He is the Creator, the Ruler, the King.

But He is also *our* God — He cares for us and we have a personal relationship with Him. Doesn't that make you want to praise Him?

SHARE IT

The heavens are the work of God's fingers. The world around us shows God's amazing power. Do your non-Christian friends agree or do they think this world is a random accident? Why not chat to them about it?

▶ *The book of Hebrews tells us this psalm is also about Jesus. How does that come across in verses 4–8?*

Jesus, God's Son, became the perfect man. He ruled over God's creation and is now crowned with glory and honour. Jesus is our great King.

PRAY ABOUT IT

Use Psalm 8 to praise God for how awesome He is, to thank Him for caring for you and for sending His Son Jesus as the perfect King.

THE BOTTOM LINE

Our God is the King of all the earth.

123 Compare and contrast

Ever noticed you look taller when standing next to someone short? Or that your grubby t-shirt looks much cleaner compared to your cruddy pair of jeans? Today, David compares God's people with God's enemies.

Read Psalm 9 v 1–12
ENGAGE YOUR BRAIN

▶ How many phrases can you find that show that God is King and in control?

▶ What sort of King is He?

▶ Find a verse that shows how long God will be around for. Then find another one that shows how long his enemies last.

David knew that God was the everlasting King, and he'd seen God's power and justice in defeating David's enemies. So what did he do? He gave thanks and told everyone by writing this song.

SHARE IT

Can you praise God by telling someone this week about some of the wonderful things He's done? The death and resurrection of Jesus is a pretty good place to start…

Read verses 13–20

▶ What is David asking God to do?

▶ What are the two outcomes? Look at:
a) those who trust in God
b) those who forget Him.

God is known for His justice. He is the perfect and fair Judge. He will punish the wicked who reject Him, and He won't forget His people who are struggling and in need.

PRAY ABOUT IT

Pray for people you know who are not currently putting their trust in God. And pray for people you know who are in need, that God would show them His love and care.

124 Genesis – Promises promises

You're watching TV when the doorbell rings. You reluctantly get up to answer it — and gasp. It's God. Nowadays we meet God as we read the Bible. But Abraham actually met God at his front door.

👁 Read Genesis 18 v 1–8

ENGAGE YOUR BRAIN

▷ How did Abraham react to getting surprise visitors? (v2)

▷ What did Abraham do for his guests?

Abraham must have realised he had three pretty special visitors — God (v13) and two of His angels (more on the two angels in a couple of days). Abraham gave the Lord great respect (v2) and begged Him to stick around before preparing a slap-up dinner.

▷ Do you go out of your way to show people friendship?

▷ What about God? How do you treat Him?

▷ How can you give Him the respect He deserves?

👁 Read verses 9–15

▷ What surprise did God have up His sleeve? (v10)

▷ Why do you think Sarah reacted the way she did? (v11-12)

▷ What should Sarah have remembered? (v14)

Remember God's great promises to Abraham (Genesis 12 v 1–3)? Sarah thought she was far too old and wrinkly to have kids! But nothing is impossible for God. If He promised it, then it would happen — no matter how unlikely it seemed. Sarah also learned that we can't hide anything from God (v15).

PRAY ABOUT IT

Nothing's too hard for God, so stop putting limits on your prayers. Bring some BIG things before God right now, knowing that nothing is impossible for Him.

125 | God in conversation

Ever begged for anything? Maybe pleaded with your parents for something you desperately wanted? Or begged your brother to stop bugging you? Abraham pleaded with God for people's lives.

👁 Read Genesis 18 v 16–19

The Lord and His two angels were about to leave Abraham. But Abraham was God's friend and his descendants would be God's chosen people. So God wanted to share with Abe what He was about to do.

It wasn't good news...

👁 Read verses 20–33

ENGAGE YOUR BRAIN

▷ *What was God going to do?*

▷ *Remember who's living in Sodom? (Genesis 14 v 12)*

▷ *As he pleads for any godly people in Sodom, what did Abraham remember about God? (v25)*

▷ *And about himself? (v27)*

God was going to see if Sodom and Gomorrah were as disgustingly sinful as was claimed. If so, they'd be destroyed. Fair enough.

There's just one problem — Abraham's nephew Lot and his family were living there.

Abraham pleaded with God to save Sodom, so that the godly people there (like Lot) wouldn't be destroyed too. You can sense how desperate he was becoming to save Lot, as the numbers he asked for got smaller and smaller. He knew that God is completely fair — brilliantly, God agreed to Abraham's requests.

PRAY ABOUT IT

Thank God that He's the *"Judge of all"* and is totally fair.

Think of people you desperately want God to save. Will you plead with God for them? Will you keep pleading, every day?

THE BOTTOM LINE

God's the Judge, yet He listens to our cries.

126 | Lot in a hot spot

God was going to destroy the evil city of Sodom. But Abraham pleaded with God to save his nephew Lot. So God sent two angels to check out the sinful city.

👁 Read Genesis 19 v 1–11

ENGAGE YOUR BRAIN

▷ How would you describe the people of Sodom?

▷ What did Lot do right? (v1-3, 6-7)

▷ What did he get wrong? (v8)

▷ How did God rescue Lot? (v10-11)

Sodom's inhabitants were evil and depraved. No wonder God was offended by their actions. They deserved destruction. Lot was right (and brave) to stand up to the mob.

When people around us are going against God, it's good (though really hard) to try and talk them out of it. Even when we know they'll probably ignore us, it's good to make a stand.

But Lot stuffed up by offering his own daughters to this sex-crazed gang. How could he? Lot had made a bad choice by moving into this evil city. It had clearly corrupted him,

and now look at the mess he was in. Having the wrong circle of friends can affect us more than we think.

GET ON WITH IT

▷ How are you affected by the people around you?

▷ Any bad habits you've got into?

▷ What do you need to make a stand about?

PRAY ABOUT IT

Spend time thinking about this issue, bringing these things to God in prayer.

THE BOTTOM LINE

Check your surroundings.

127 Word of warning

You wake up in the middle of the night to hear someone screaming "THE HOUSE IS ON FIRE! QUICK, GET OUT!" You're sooooo comfy in your bed, but it would be madness to ignore the alarm bells.

👁 Read Genesis 19 v 12–16

ENGAGE YOUR BRAIN

▶ What was God's verdict on the city of Sodom? (v13)

▶ What big mistake did Lot's in-laws make?

▶ Lot hesitated too, but how did God show him mercy? (v16)

Lot's sons-in-law ignored his warnings, the idiots. And today, people ignore God's warnings to turn away from sin and avoid His punishment. God shows His great mercy to us, sending His Son to rescue us. But if we keep ignoring His warnings, we'll face destruction too.

👁 Read verses 17–29

▶ How did God again show His mercy to Lot? (v21)

▶ What big mistake did Lot's wife make? (v17, 26)?

Maybe Lot's wife couldn't bear to leave Sodom. Or maybe she doubted God. Whatever the reason, she disobeyed God, and paid the price.

God hates sin. That's why He punished Lot's wife and why He destroyed evil Sodom and Gomorrah. And yet God showed great love and mercy too. He remembered His promise to Abraham and He rescued Lot.

TALK IT THROUGH

▶ What does this story tell us about
• what God is like?
• the way people treat Him?
• what our response to God should be?

PRAY ABOUT IT

Praise and thank God that He deals fairly with sin. Thank Him for warning us and giving us many more chances to escape than we deserve.

128 What a mess

Why is it that just after we've experienced God's grace in an amazing way, we go and mess things up? God rescued Lot and his daughters from Sodom's destruction. But then...

👁 Read Genesis 19 v 30–38

ENGAGE YOUR BRAIN

▶ *Why did Lot's daughters do what they did? (v31–32)*

▶ *Was Lot innocent in all this?*

▶ *Do you think good or bad came out of it? (v37–38 give us a clue)*

Continuing the family line was a big big thing in those days. It was shameful if you had no children. So it's understandable how Lot's girls talked themselves into doing it. But that doesn't make it right. The Bible is clear that sex belongs only within marriage.

▶ *What things do you persuade yourself it's OK to do, but know deep down dishonour God?*

Lot wasn't innocent either. His daughters got him drunk, but it was his responsibility to look after his body. Too much alcohol can cloud our judgement or leave us vulnerable and open to sin.

👁 Read 1 Samuel 14 v 47

The descendants of Lot and his daughters became enemies of Israel, and enemies of God (Numbers 25 v 1–3 is another nasty example).

Straight after a spiritual high, we can let our guard down and let God down. When that happens, there's no point wallowing in it. We need to say sorry to God, thank Him for His forgiveness, and get back to living His way.

PRAY ABOUT IT

The issues raised today must have left you with loads to say to God...

129 Old habits die hard

Do you learn from your mistakes? Or is there something you just keep getting wrong? How do you feel when you know you've done that same stupid thing yet again?

👁 Read Genesis 20 v 1–2

ENGAGE YOUR BRAIN

▷ *What was Abraham's mistake?*

▷ *Why do you think he lied?*

Abraham was worried that Abimelek would kill him and take Sarah for himself, so he lied. But he'd made this mistake once before (Genesis 12 v 11–13).

👁 Read verses 3–18

▷ *What problems did Abraham's lies cause Abimelek?*

▷ *Yet what did God call Abraham? (v7)*

▷ *Who had Abraham trusted in this situation — God or himself?*

Abraham had deceived Abimelek out of fear and because he hadn't trusted God to protect him. It's easy to rely on our wits rather than turning to God for help.

Yet God's in control of everything — who better could we turn to?!

Despite Abraham messing up again, God called him a prophet! He's the first person in the Bible to be given that honour — God's messenger. God doesn't turn His back on His people when they let Him down. He's with them… for ever. (Check out John 5 v 24.)

PRAY ABOUT IT

▷ *What sin do you keep falling into?*

Talk honestly with God about it. Ask Him to help you fight it, and to trust in Him and not your own abilities. Thank Him that, despite repeatedly messing up, He's still there for you.

THE BOTTOM LINE

Rely on God, not your own abilities.

130 Abe's babe

"Expect the unexpected". That's an oxymoron — a statement that seems to contradict itself (like "genuine imitation", "pretty ugly" and "Fun Run"). But it's a good phrase for Abraham and Sarah.

👁 Read Genesis 21 v 1–2

ENGAGE YOUR BRAIN

▷ *What does this tell us about...*

- *God's character*
- *God's promises?*
- *God's timing?*

Sarah had laughed at the idea of having a baby in her 90s. But God was gracious. As always. He kept His seemingly impossible promise. As always. And His timing was perfect. As always.

👁 Read verses 3–7

▷ *How did Abraham respond to God's incredible gift to them?*

▷ *What about Sarah?*

God kept His promise; now it was Abraham's turn. He gave his son the name Isaac (it means "he laughs") as God had told him to (Genesis 17 v 19). And he kept his promise to circumcise Isaac, to show that his whole family belonged to God.

Sarah had laughed mockingly at the notion of having a son. But now she laughed with joy at what God had done for her. God is so gracious to His people, especially when they least deserve it.

▷ *When God answers your prayers, how do you react?*

GET ON WITH IT

List some of the things God has done for you in your life.

PRAY ABOUT IT

Spend time going through your list, thanking God that He gives you far more than you could ever deserve.

THE BOTTOM LINE

God is full of grace, and always keeps His promises.

131 Outcast outcry

God kept His promise. Sarah had a baby when she was nearly 100 years old! Everyone was over the moon when Isaac was born. Well, nearly everyone...

👁 **Read Genesis 21 v 8–16**

ENGAGE YOUR BRAIN

▶ *What was the problem?*

▶ *What was God's solution? (v12)*

▶ *Yet what did God promise Hagar and Ishmael? (v13)*

Isaac was the son God had promised Abraham. It was through Isaac and his descendants (the Israelites) that God would bless the whole world.

Abraham hadn't trusted God to give him a son with Sarah, so he took matters into his own hands and slept with Hagar. Ishmael was the result. But he wasn't the son God had promised. So Abraham sent Hagar and Ishmael away. Yet God promised to make Ishmael's family into a big nation (v13). So why is He letting them die in the desert??? (v14–16)

👁 **Read verses 17–21**

▶ *What amazing things happened? (v17-19)*

▶ *What was the most amazing part for Ishmael the outcast? (v20)*

God kept His promise to Hagar and Ishmael. Even though Ishmael wasn't the son God had promised Abraham, God still cared for him.

SHARE IT

God cares for everyone, no matter what their background.

▶ *Who do you know who's a bit of an outcast?*

▶ *How could you talk to them about God's love for them?*

PRAY ABOUT IT

Thank God that He sent Jesus to the whole world. Pray for people you know who are outsiders. If you dare, ask God to give you opportunities to get to know them better.

132 Oh well

What do you find hardest about being a Christian surrounded by people who aren't interested in God? Abraham lived in a land where God wasn't worshipped. But he still had to live with those people...

👁 Read Genesis 21 v 22–24

ENGAGE YOUR BRAIN

▷ *Remember where you've seen Abimelek before? (Genesis 20)*

▷ *What did he notice about Abraham? (v22)*

Abraham had brought trouble upon Abimelek when he pretended that Sarah was his sister. But Abimelek had shown great kindness to him. And now Abimelek wants Abraham to promise that he'd do the same and treat Abimelek's family fairly. (v23).

👁 Read verses 25-34

▷ *What might have caused a fight between the two? (v25)*

▷ *How did Abraham make peace? (v27–30)*

Where Abraham lived, water was rare and often the cause of conflicts. Abraham had been wronged when Abimelek's servants seized his well.

But to avoid a fight, he struck a peace deal and even gave Abimelek gifts!

In life, we're often faced with conflicts or people treating us unfairly. As God's people, Christians must act in a way that brings Him honour. Sometimes that means compromise or even showing kindness when we've been wronged.

GET ON WITH IT

▷ *What conflicts do you need to sort out peacefully?*

▷ *What will you do to show kindness and sort things out?*

PRAY ABOUT IT

You know what you need to do...

THE BOTTOM LINE

God's people need to live God's way in a godless world.

133 The toughest test

What's the hardest choice you've made this week? Which socks to wear? What to get your sister for her birthday? Maybe even a choice that affects your future? Abraham was about to face the toughest choice of his long life...

👁 Read Genesis 22 v 1–2

ENGAGE YOUR BRAIN

▶ *What did God command?*

▶ *Why? (v1)*

▶ *How do you think Abraham felt?*

Abraham was used to making sacrifices. He would kill an animal or bird, cook it and offer it to God. It was the way God's people said sorry or thank you to the Lord.

Abraham had waited so long to have a son and now he was being asked to sacrifice him! Shocking. God was testing Abraham. Did he really trust God? Did he love the Lord more than his own son?

👁 Read verses 3-10

▶ *How did Abraham show his trust in God? (v5, 8)*

▶ *Was he really prepared to sacrifice his own son for God? (v10)*

Incredible stuff. God had asked the unthinkable of Abraham. Imagine Abraham's thoughts on the three-day trip. Yet Abraham picked up the knife to kill Isaac. He showed that he loved and trusted God more than anything. He clearly loved Isaac, but God came first.

God tests *our* trust, too, to make it genuine and strong. To make us more like Jesus, who trusted and obeyed God fully. How does He test us? By calling us, as we read the Bible, to obey Him whatever the cost. When it goes against logic and our feelings. And He'll be there to see us through.

PRAY ABOUT IT

Ask the Lord to strengthen your faith in Him and to help you last the course even when it's tough.

THE BOTTOM LINE

Our faith is revealed in our actions.

134 In the nick of time

Yesterday we ended with a cliffhanger. Abraham had a knife poised, ready to kill his son Isaac. Would God really make him go through with it?

👁 Read Genesis 22 v 9–14

ENGAGE YOUR BRAIN

▶ *What did God find out about Abraham? (v12)*

▶ *What did Abraham find out about God? (v14)*

The Lord stopped Abraham from killing Isaac. God saw that Abraham really did love Him and trust Him above anything else. He wouldn't hold anything back from God, not even his own son.

But the sacrifice still had to be made. So God provided a sheep to take Isaac's place. Later on in the Bible, John the Baptist said that the "Lamb of God … takes away the sin of the world" (John 1 v 29). The Lamb of God is Jesus.

God gave Abraham a ram to take Isaac's place. And He gives us Jesus to take our place. We deserve to be punished for our sins. But God sent Jesus to die in our place.

👁 Read verses 15–19

▶ *How did God encourage Abraham?*

God mentioned His three great promises again:

1. Abraham would have loads of descendants (v17).

2. God would give them a land to live in (v17).

3. The whole world would be blessed through Abraham's descendants (v18). This last promise was fulfilled when God sent His only Son, Jesus, into the world as a blessing for the whole world. He died so that we can be forgiven.

PRAY ABOUT IT

Anything you want to thank and praise God for?

THE BOTTOM LINE

God provides. God provided His own Son to be sacrificed in our place.

135 Tomb with a view

Are you a trusting person?
Have you got trust issues?
Can you be trusted?
How much do you trust in God?

👁 Read Genesis 23 v 1–15

ENGAGE YOUR BRAIN

▶ *What did Abraham want? (v8–9)*

▶ *What's Ephron's generous-sounding offer? (v11)*

▶ *But how much did he really want for the field? (v15)*

Devastating news for Abraham: Sarah died at the grand old age of 127. He wanted to buy some land so he could bury her. At first it seemed that Ephron was being hugely generous, but it was all a show. When pressed to name a price, he claimed it was worth 400 shekels (4.5kg) of silver. What a rip-off.

▶ *Are you ever crafty like that?*

▶ *Ever help people out only so you can get something out of it?*

▶ *Or maybe you're not entirely honest with your friends?*

👁 Read verses 16–20

▶ *Why did Abraham want Sarah to be buried in Canaan rather than where they both came from?*

Remember God's three big promises to Abraham? (See yesterday's page.) One was that God would give Abraham's family the whole land of Canaan. Well, he's just bought his first plot of land there.

It was a small start, but Abraham buried Sarah in Canaan, trusting that one day God would give his descendants the whole land. That's full-on faith.

PRAY ABOUT IT

Ask God to help you trust Him and His promises much more. Tell Him about times you've been less than honest with people. Ask God to help you be more generous and genuine.

136 Thigh will be done

If someone said to you, "Put your hand under my thigh," how would you react? Give them a funny look? Slap them hard? Let's see what Abraham's servant did...

👁 Read Genesis 24 v 1–9

ENGAGE YOUR BRAIN

▸ *What did Abraham get his servant to promise?*

▸ *Why didn't he want Isaac to marry a girl from Canaan?*

▸ *How did Abraham again show his trust in God? (v7)*

Abraham didn't want Isaac to marry anyone outside of his family — God's chosen people. He also didn't want Isaac to leave Canaan, the land God had promised to give Abraham's descendants. This meant so much to Abraham, he made his servant swear an oath. Putting his hand in a very, er, personal place showed how serious a promise it was.

Yet again, Abraham showed how much he trusted the Lord. He knew God would lead his servant to find the perfect wife for Isaac (v7).

👁 Read verses 10–16

▸ *What did the servant ask God?*

▸ *How soon did God answer?*

Now that's prayer in action! God answered before this guy had even finished talking! Sometimes God answers lightning fast, and other times we have to wait and keep praying. Notice how the servant didn't go wandering around for days, looking for the right girl. He asked God to help and show kindness to Abraham. And God did just that.

PRAY ABOUT IT

▸ *How do you need God's help?*

▸ *Who would you love God to show kindness to?*

▸ *So what are you waiting for?*

THE BOTTOM LINE

Bring your requests to God. He's listening.

137 | She's the one

What prayers have you seen answered recently? Have you got a long and exciting list? Or do you forget to check whether or not God's answered your prayers? Time to catch up with Abraham's servant...

👁 Read Genesis 24 v 15–27

ENGAGE YOUR BRAIN

▶ *Did God answer the servant's prayer?*

▶ *How did he react? (v26–27)*

Abraham sent his servant to find a wife for Isaac. The servant had asked God to lead him to the right family and the right girl. And God did!

Nice one — nose rings and bracelets all round (v22). The servant realised God was behind it all and so thanked and praised the Lord for this brilliant answer to prayer.

If you've got time, read verses 28–49. If not, here's what happens:

• Rebekah's brother, Laban, welcomed Abraham's servant into their house.

• The servant told them all about Abraham and how good God had been to him.

• And all about the mission Abraham had sent him on and how God answered his prayer.

👁 Read verses 50–54

▶ *How did Rebekah's brother and father respond to the servant?*

▶ *What did they recognise? (v50)*

God was in complete control. He showed great kindness to Abraham yet again, and answered the servant's prayer. God was looking after His people. Laban and Bethuel saw that God was behind this chain of events, so they let Rebekah leave home.

PRAY ABOUT IT

Make a list of things you've prayed for and how God's answered them. Thank Him for these things. Ask Him to help you notice when He answers your prayers.

138 Showing promise

God led Abraham's servant to Rebekah and her family. Rebekah is the one God wants Isaac to marry. Time for a tearful farewell...

👁 Read Genesis 24 v 54–60

ENGAGE YOUR BRAIN

▶ What was the great blessing that Rebekah's family gave her? (v60)

▶ How does that fit in with God's plans and promises? (See Genesis 22 v 15–18.)

Rebekah's family wanted her to stay a little longer, but she decided it was time to go and meet the man she would marry. Fair enough.

Rebekah's family hoped she'd have a huge family. Well, she was about to marry Isaac, Abraham's son. God had promised Abraham that His family would be uncountably massive! God was keeping His promise. Abraham and Isaac would have loads of descendants, and they would become God's nation.

👁 Read verses 61–67

▶ What's the happy ending to this, the longest chapter in Genesis?

Rebekah and Isaac finally met. They got married and Isaac loved his new wife. Perfect. God had promised to give Isaac a wife, and here she was. God always keeps His promises.

SHARE IT

We've seen throughout Abraham's life how God keeps His promises and kept giving Abraham far more than he deserved.

▶ Which of God's promises can you share with your friends?

▶ What experiences of God giving you more than you deserve can you share with them?

PRAY ABOUT IT

It's down to you today...

THE BOTTOM LINE

God keeps ALL His promises.

139 End of the road

What would you like to achieve before the end of your life? Abraham had done some great stuff and seen God do incredible things in his long life. But now his time on earth was at an end.

👁 Read Genesis 25 v 1–6

ENGAGE YOUR BRAIN

▶ *Why did Isaac get much more than Abraham's other children?*

Isaac was the son God had promised to give Abraham. And it was through Isaac's family that God would keep His most staggering promise.

Find it in Genesis 12 v 3.

Isaac got the best inheritance of all. Jesus would be one of his descendants. God would bless people from every nation through Jesus.

👁 Read verses 7–11

▶ *What was the final promise to Abraham that God kept? (See Genesis 15 v 15.)*

Abraham lived until he was 175. God had been so good to His servant Abraham. And even though

Abraham was now dead, God would continue to bless his family. And God's plan to bless the whole world would continue…

GET ON WITH IT

▶ *What have you learned about God from Abraham's story?*

▶ *What have you learned about Jesus?*

▶ *What have you learned about yourself?*

▶ *What are you going to do about it? What do you need to change?*

PRAY ABOUT IT

Take your time, talking to God about each of your answers.

LUKE

Walking with Jesus

Who would you most like to meet? If you could go for a walk with them one afternoon, what would you ask them? What tips would you want from them about how to approach life?

BACK TO LUKE

In Luke 12–18, God's Son, Jesus, has got more than an afternoon with His friends and the crowds who followed Him — but He is still on limited time. Jesus is walking to Jerusalem, and He knows that when He gets there He won't be placed on a throne; He'll die on a cross in agony.

So in this section of Luke's historical account of His life, Jesus is telling those around Him why it's worth following Him, and what it'll be like to live that way. He does this in a variety of ways: meeting people, answering questions, telling stories, reacting to events.

But all the time He's answering these two questions:

Why is it worth following Jesus?

What does it mean to follow Jesus?

JOIN THE CROWD

You're 2,000 years too late to walk with Jesus to Jerusalem; but thanks to Luke you can still be part of each scene, and listen to Jesus speak to you about your life.

Maybe you're still working out for yourself who Jesus is. The crowd around Him were trying to do that too — so over the next few weeks you'll have the chance each day to see for yourself.

And if you're already a friend of Jesus, dive in and find out how the Lord of life tells you to approach your own life.

140 Don't don't don't

It's annoying when people say: "Don't do that!" without giving a good reason. Here, Jesus has three "don'ts" — but gives us three massive reasons why.

👁 Read Luke 12 v 1–3

ENGAGE YOUR BRAIN

▶ *Jesus and the Pharisees often disagreed. What's their problem according to Jesus? (v1)*

It's easy to be a hypocritical Christian — to say we follow Jesus but then not bother when it gets hard.

▶ *Why can't we get away with that? (v2–3)*

Jesus is describing the day He returns, when everything, even what's hidden in our hearts, will be "made known".

👁 Read verses 4–7

▶ *What's the next don't? (v4)*

If we care what other people think, we'll be afraid of standing up for Jesus. But the worst a man can do is kill you (v4). But Jesus has the power to send people to hell. We should be more concerned about what Jesus thinks of us than what people do!

👁 Read verses 8–12

▶ *What's true if we stand up for Jesus? (v8)*

SHARE IT

▶ *How can you speak out more for Jesus?*

▶ *What's the great news when you do make a stand? (v11–12)*

PRAY ABOUT IT

What's on your mind after today's study? Talk to God about it.

THE BOTTOM LINE

When He returns, Jesus will reveal everything, send people to hell, and welcome those who stood up for Him. So don't be hypocritical, don't be afraid of people and don't disown Jesus.

141 Fat cat fate

How far ahead do you plan? In the next few chunks of Luke's Gospel, Jesus deals with matters like money, clothes and stuff. And He tells a story about a guy who planned his early retirement.

👁 Read Luke 12 v 13–21

ENGAGE YOUR BRAIN

🔘 *Jesus has been talking about how to have eternal life with Him when He returns — but what's this guy more worried about? (v13)*

🔘 *What is the man in Jesus' story most worried about? (v16–18)*

He's not just trying to put some food on the table — he's got so many possessions he has to build huge barns to put them in!

🔘 *What's he looking forward to? (v19)*

🔘 *What does God think of him? And why? (v20–21)*

🔘 *What point is Jesus making? (See end of v15.)*

Both the man talking to Jesus and the guy in the parable are focusing on storing up things for themselves for this life. What should their priority be? (v21)

THINK IT THROUGH

🔘 *How should Christians think about wealth?*

🔘 *Should our prayers focus more on asking Jesus to give us what we want, or asking Him to help us follow Him?*

PRAY ABOUT IT

Jesus, please help me to concentrate not on having money, which will buy good things now, but on having a relationship with you, which will bring me eternal life. Amen.

THE BOTTOM LINE

Make sure you're focused on the riches of eternal life which Jesus offers, not on the short-lived wealth of what this world offers!

142 Don't worry, be happy

Do you trust in God? And do you worry about stuff? Jesus says trusting God and worrying about life don't go together.

👁 Read Luke 12 v 22–31

ENGAGE YOUR BRAIN

▶ *What does God do for ravens? (v24)*

▶ *Are God's people more or less valuable to Him than birds? (v24)*

▶ *So what will God do for them?*

▶ *So, what shouldn't we do? (v22)*

▶ *What should we live for? (v31)*

The opposite of faith is… worrying! If I worry about something, I'm not trusting that God can provide, or that God knows what I need, or that God my Father loves me. Worrying shows that in my heart I trust in myself, not God — which is crazy! When I want to worry, I need to turn in trust to our amazing, all-providing God.

THINK IT THROUGH

▶ *What's one thing you worry about that you need to trust your Father God for?*

When you worry about that thing, find ways to remind yourself that God's in control, or that He knows what you need and that He loves you.

👁 Read verses 32–34

▶ *Since God gives us everything we need, including eternal life in "the kingdom" (v32), what should we do? (v33)*

▶ *If I concentrate on having eternal treasure instead of being rich now, what does that show? (v34)*

THE BOTTOM LINE

Trusting in the God who provides for us and knows us means we don't need to worry and can be generous.

PRAY ABOUT IT

Ask God to help you turn to Him in trust next time you want to worry.

143 | Get ready

Your parents leave you in an empty house. Do you...
- **throw a party and trash it?**
- **laze around and let it get really messy?**
- **enjoy it, but make sure you're ready for their return?**

👁 Read Luke 12 v 35–40

ENGAGE YOUR BRAIN

▷ *These servants have an empty house... what's the sensible thing to do? (v38)*

▷ *What will the master then do for them? (second half of v37)*

We live in Jesus' world. He's not here right now — He's in heaven. It's like having an empty house — what will we do with it?

▷ *What does Jesus, the "Son of Man", say we must do? (v40)*

▷ *Why?*

The only way to be ready for a thief (v39) is to be ready all the time — thieves don't say when they'll come! Jesus hasn't told us when He'll come back to His world, so the only way to be ready for Him is to be ready all the time.

So, how can we show we're ready?

👁 Read verses 41–48

The manager could show he was ready by looking after the other servants. We show we're ready for Jesus' return by looking after His people. We can all pray for and encourage our Christian friends.

If we're doing that, we're showing we're ready for Jesus' return to His world!

People who know Jesus' demands but do nothing will be punished more than those who don't know Jesus at all (v47).

PRAY ABOUT IT

Ask God to show you how to serve Him and care for other believers.

144 Our place in history

We live in the 21st century. In the internet age. In the postmodern era. And, much more importantly, we live between two massive markers in time…

👁 Read Luke 12 v 49–56

ENGAGE YOUR BRAIN

▶ *What did Jesus say He had come to bring? (v49)*

▶ *What did He have to do before that? (v50)*

Two strange images in those verses! The first is talking about Jesus' judgment, when He will "burn up" everything that isn't to be part of His perfect world. The second is one of the ways Jesus talked about His death on the cross.

So these are the two markers in time that we live between — Jesus dying to give His people a place in His perfect world; and Jesus returning to burn up everything that doesn't have a place there. We need to remember this and live in a way that shows it (v56).

Question is — what happens between these two markers in time?

▶ *What will there and what won't there be? (v51)*

The world, even families, will be divided between those who follow Jesus and those who don't (v52–53).

👁 Read verses 57–59

This guy needs to make friends with his enemy before he gets to court and a judgment — or he'll go to prison. Jesus has already reminded us that He will come in judgment.

▶ *Who do people need to become friends with before that day?*

PRAY ABOUT IT

We live between Jesus' death and Jesus' return — we need to make sure we're friends with God, and expect hard times, not peace. Pray for those you know who aren't Christians. And ask God to help you when people turn against you.

145 Disaster strikes

Sometimes on the news there's an earthquake or a tsunami, a war or a massacre, and we're reminded that death is real. How should we respond?

👁 Read Luke 13 v 1–5

ENGAGE YOUR BRAIN

In Jesus' day, if people died in a horrible or unfortunate way, people often responded by saying: *"Ah, they must have done something really bad. That's why they've died like that."*

▶ *What does Jesus think of that idea?*

▶ *In fact, what should another person's death remind us of? (v3, v5)*

Because we're all sinners, no one deserves to live for ever. Everyone deserves to die just as much as everyone else. The only way to live for ever is to turn back to God, to repent.

👁 Read verses 6–9

▶ *What does the owner of the useless fig tree tell the man who takes care of it to do? (v7)*

▶ *What does the man ask for? (v8)*

▶ *The fig tree represents people who won't turn back to God — what's the warning for these people? (v8–9)*

THINK IT OVER

Perhaps you've never actually repented, never turned away from living for yourself and turned back to God. Why not do that now and avoid losing eternal life?

SHARE IT

How does this help you to talk about Christianity next time your friends are talking about a terrible disaster?

THE BOTTOM LINE

Death should remind us that the only way to have life beyond our death is to have turned back to God.

146 | Jesus vs religion

TV news often ends with a happy story to cheer you up. Then a news summary. Then the commercials. The next bit from Luke shares that pattern. A miraculous story. Then a summary. (OK, so maybe no commercials.)

👁 Read Luke 13 v 10–17

ENGAGE YOUR BRAIN

▶ *How did the woman react? (v13)*

▶ *How did the synagogue leader feel, and why? (v14)*

Two different reactions. The woman who had been broken praised God for healing her; the synagogue leader was furious about broken religious rules. He was wrong. God had told His people to rest one day a week; but He'd never told them not to help people on that day!

▶ *What point is Jesus making in verses 15–16?*

Jesus reminds us that to enjoy real "rest" — the security and joy of a relationship with God — we need to let Jesus set us free from our sin, rather than thinking that we can earn that freedom by keeping rules.

Going to church, trying to be good — none of it will gain us eternal life. Only Jesus can give it to us.

👁 Read verses 18–21

▶ *What's Jesus talking about? (v18)*

▶ *How big does a mustard seed start?*

▶ *What does it go on to become? (v19)*

▶ *What happened to the yeast in the dough? (v20–21)*

▶ *At the time Jesus was speaking, the kingdom of God on earth numbered a few dozen people. What would happen to it?*

▶ *What should we expect to see happening to the kingdom of God in our day?*

PRAY ABOUT IT

Thank God that Jesus heals the broken so they can praise God. Ask God to grow his kingdom.

THE BOTTOM LINE

Only Jesus can give us the "rest" of eternity with God. We can't earn it.

147 Best party ever!

The most incredible party's about to start — but will you even get through the door to enjoy it?

👁 **Read Luke 13 v 22–30**

ENGAGE YOUR BRAIN

▷ Where is Jesus going? (v22)

▷ What will happen there? (Flick back to Luke 9 v 22.)

▷ There's a party on — but what will happen to "many"? (v24–25)

▷ These people assume they're the houseowner's friends — but what does he say? (v27)

▷ Verse 28 tells us what the "party" is. Where will Abraham, Isaac, Jacob and the prophets be?

You can't just assume you're Jesus' friend. Many people think if they go to church, or pray, or come from a Christian family, Jesus will let them into God's kingdom. They're in for a shock when He returns and closes the door on them!

Jesus says instead of assuming you're His friend, "Make every effort to enter through the narrow door"

(v24). OK! Err... what does that actually mean?

▷ Remember verse 22. Jesus is walking towards His death. How easy will it be to be one of His followers?

Following Jesus leads to a place in God's kingdom — but it will sometimes mean being "last" in life (v30). We need to make "every effort" to keep going.

THINK IT OVER

▷ Have you repented and turned to Jesus for forgiveness?

▷ Know anyone who thinks they're all right with God but haven't faced up to their sin?

▷ What can you say to them?

▷ What will you pray for them right now?

148 Fox and hens

OK, so the way to perfect, eternal life is to follow Jesus through the narrow door. So everyone will fall into line behind Him. Won't they?

👁 Read Luke 13 v 31–33

ENGAGE YOUR BRAIN

▶ *What do some Pharisees come to warn Jesus about? (v31)*

▶ *Is Jesus willing to change His plans just because Herod doesn't like Him? (v32)*

▶ *What does this tell us about Jesus?*

👁 Read verses 34–35

▶ *Who is Jesus now talking to? (v34)*

▶ *This was the capital city of Israel, where God's people, the Jews, lived. What does Jesus long to do? (v34)*

He wants to pick them up and carry them through the narrow door!

▶ *Why doesn't He? (end of v34)*

▶ *So what will happen to them instead?*

THINK IT THROUGH

You'd expect the Jews, God's people, and Herod, a king of God's people, to be the first in line to follow Jesus through the narrow door. But they're not willing — they'd rather kill God's messengers than humbly listen to them.

▶ *How's this a warning to us today?*

PRAY ABOUT IT

Lord Jesus, thank you that you gather your people together and lead them through the narrow door to eternal life. Help me to be humble enough to be willing to let you do this for me, and never to think I know better than you.

THE BOTTOM LINE

God's true people are those who humbly listen and closely follow Jesus.

149 Food for thought

The Pharisees think Jesus won't fit through their narrow door. But when they invite Him to a dinner party, they soon realise the shoe is on the other foot.

👁 Read Luke 14 v 1–9

Jesus is being "carefully watched" (v1) by His enemies. But they won't change His plans — He'll still heal people (v2–4). When Jesus notices how people position themselves and try to look good (v7), He tells them how those who are following Him through the narrow door should behave.

👁 Read verses 10–14

ENGAGE YOUR BRAIN

▶ *Where does Jesus tell these important religious leaders to sit? (v10)*

▶ *Why? (v11)*

▶ *What does He say to the host about who he should invite? (v13)*

▶ *When will they be rewarded? (v14)*

▶ *If you spend your time doing things for important and wealthy people, when do you get your reward? (v12)*

▶ *The world says we need to put ourselves forward and make sure we gain rewards in life. What does Jesus say?*

The "resurrection of the righteous" is talking about when Jesus returns to raise all believers to eternal life with Him. We shouldn't look for rewards now, God will reward us eventually. And we should value everyone, not just the richest, coolest or most important people. We should live for our eternal life to come, not for small rewards and popularity now.

PRAY ABOUT IT

Ask God to show you how you can serve those in need. Ask Him to give you the humility not to look for a reward now. Ask Him to give you an eternal perspective on life.

150 RSVP

We've seen that some people won't get through the narrow door and will be shut out of God's kingdom. Why?

👁 **Read Luke 14 v 15–24**

ENGAGE YOUR BRAIN

▷ *Any ideas what this guy means? (v15)*

▷ *What does God want? (v16-17, v23)*

▷ *What happens when God invites people into His kingdom? (v18–20)*

▷ *How good are these excuses? (v18–20)*

Just take the first excuse in verse 18. It's rubbish! If you buy a field, you look at it *before* you buy it, not after! And if you want to see it again, it'll still be there tomorrow; it won't move!

▷ *How does God respond to people turning down His free invitation to come to His banquet in His kingdom? (v21)*

▷ *What is the result of them making excuses? (v24)*

God invites us to His kingdom — His Son Jesus offers to take us there through the narrow door. But not everyone goes. Many people turn down the invitation.

▷ *What excuses have you heard for rejecting Jesus?*

PRAY IT THROUGH

Thank God for His invitation to His kingdom. If you've not yet responded to His invitation, now is the time. Pray for friends who keep making excuses.

151 Acts – Message unstoppable II

Time to get back to Acts to see how the first Christians are doing. Breaking out of prison normally requires months of planning, ingenuity, and luck. Not when you've got God on your side...

👁 Read Acts 5 v 12–21

ENGAGE YOUR BRAIN

▶ How do the high priest and his allies react to the miracles and growth of the church? (v17–18)

▶ How does God respond? (v19)

▶ What is God's purpose in doing this? (v20)

▶ How do the apostles respond, and why is this courageous? (v21)

👁 Read verses 21–27

▶ When the religious leaders hear about what's happened, what's their reaction? (v26–28)

THINK IT THROUGH

▶ What does God want His people to do? (v20)

▶ What do God's enemies try to do, despite all the evidence they're on the wrong side?

It's impossible not to be inspired by the early Christians. No matter how much intimidation or pressure they face, they will not shut up about Jesus. Even when they've been imprisoned, as soon as they're released they immediately get back to spreading the message of Jesus. What an example for us!

PRAY ABOUT IT

Father, please give me chances to tell people about Jesus, and through your Spirit please give me the courage to take those chances, even when it's hard or risky. Amen.

THE BOTTOM LINE

Tell the people the full message of this new life (v20).

152 | Privilege not problem

Every now and then there's an amazing Bible verse that just makes you sit up and think about things in a whole new way. There's one of those today.

👁 Read Acts 5 v 27–32

ENGAGE YOUR BRAIN

▶ *What did the religious council (Sanhedrin) want the apostles to stop doing? (v28)*

▶ *How do the apostles answer them?*

▶ *What does Peter say about Jesus? (v30–32)*

👁 Read verses 33–40

Things are hotting up. It looks as if Jesus' apostles are heading for death sentences (v33). But there's a voice of reason — Gamaliel, who convinces the Jews not to kill them. Instead they're flogged (v40) — whipped across their bare backs 39 times. Then they're ordered not to talk about Jesus. Maybe now the apostles have felt serious pain, they'll shut up.

Here's the amazing verse…

👁 Read verses 41–42

▶ *Why are the recently tortured apostles rejoicing? (v41)*

▶ *Why is this amazing and challenging?*

▶ *Do they shut up? (v42)*

THINK IT THROUGH

Naturally we see suffering as a problem, including suffering for being a Christian. But it's not! It's a privilege to be allowed by God to serve someone as wonderful and powerful as Jesus. He suffered for us, even to the point of death; it's great to have the opportunity to suffer for Him.

PRAY ABOUT IT

Ask God to change you through His Spirit so that you increasingly see suffering for being a Christian as a privilege, not a problem.

153 The magnificent seven

Lots of work goes into keeping a church running. There's the admin... the website... visiting the sick... the accounts... oh, and some Bible teaching, too.

👁 Read Acts 6 v 1–4

ENGAGE YOUR BRAIN

▷ *What's the problem? (v1)*

▷ *What do the twelve apostles decide isn't the solution? (v2)*

▷ *What's the right solution? (v3–4)*

▷ *What qualities do these seven need to have? (v3)*

THINK IT THROUGH

▷ *What should church members who are involved in teaching God's word be focusing on? (v2)*

▷ *Is the practical organisational stuff unimportant? (v1)*

▷ *What's noticeable about what's required for anyone involved in running a church? (v3)*

GET ON WITH IT

If you're involved with any Bible teaching, make sure you give it the time and prayer it needs; don't let other stuff get in the way. If you aren't involved with Bible teaching, what practical things can you be doing to support those who are?

PRAY ABOUT IT

Pray for those who serve at church — that the Holy Spirit will enable them to do their work well and wisely.

👁 Read verses 5–7

The church likes the idea, and chooses and prays for seven men to oversee the practical stuff.

▷ *What's the outcome of good Bible teaching and good organisation? (v7)*

THE BOTTOM LINE

Managing the church must not take over from teaching the church; but managing the church is vital for the church to grow.

154 | Going gets tough

Stephen was an ordinary guy, helping out with practical stuff at his church, and trying to tell people he knew about Jesus. But Stephen was also an extraordinary guy...

👁 **Read Acts 6 v 8–15**

ENGAGE YOUR BRAIN

▶ *What do we already know about Stephen? (v5)*

▶ *What else do we find out? (v8, v10, v15)*

Ordinary guy — just a normal church member. Extraordinary guy — full of grace and power. But some of the local Jews really don't like what he does or says (v9).

▶ *What do they do? (end of v9)*

▶ *This doesn't work (v10); so what do they do next? (v11–12)*

They can't argue with Stephen (because the Spirit helps him win!); so they slander Stephen, making things up to get him into trouble (v11). Arguing becomes slandering; slandering becomes violence.

By verse 15, Stephen's been hauled up before the religious leaders, the Sanhedrin. Notice the charges in

verses 13–14: Stephen is accused of saying Jesus will destroy the temple ("this holy place"), and get rid of the law God had given through Moses.

Look back at Mark 14 v 57–59; the charges Stephen faces are very similar to those Jesus had faced.

Based on what's happened so far in Acts (and without reading on!), predict...

a) what Stephen will do in the Sanhedrin.

b) what the Sanhedrin will do about Stephen.

THINK IT THROUGH

What's the main encouragement and challenge for you from this section?

THE BOTTOM LINE

As the Holy Spirit speaks through Christians, they face arguments, slander and violence.

155 Where's God?

As Stephen defends himself at his trial, he reveals loads about what God's like and also what people are like.

👁 Read Acts 6 v 13–14

Stephen is on trial for saying Jesus will destroy the temple and change the law of Moses. This is serious; the temple was the place God had been present among His people, and the law was the way God wanted His people to live.

👁 Read Acts 7 v 1-8

▶ What did God do and where? (v2)

God did this hundreds of years before the temple was built, hundreds of miles from Jerusalem.

👁 Read verses 9–16

▶ A few generations passed, until Joseph's time. Where was Joseph, and what did God do? (v9–10)

God did this hundreds of years before the temple was built, hundreds of miles from Jerusalem.

👁 Read verses 44–50

Centuries later, Solomon *"built a house"* (the temple) for God in Jerusalem. So now it's all about the temple, right?

▶ What do verses 48–50 tell us about God?

THINK IT THROUGH

God can't be contained by any building. In Mesopotamia (Iraq) and Egypt, He was with His people, blessing and rescuing them. God's at work in His people, not in a building. But the Jews had forgotten this; they thought it was all about the temple. For temple then, read church buildings today.

▶ How do people make the same mistake now as they did then?

THE BOTTOM LINE

God's not contained by a building; He's at work wherever His people are.

156 Rejected leader

Stephen continues to teach us how God works — here by zooming in on a famous Old Testament hero, Moses. We're in about 1400BC, with Abraham's descendants, the Israelites, living as slaves in Egypt.

👁 Read Acts 7 v 17–36

ENGAGE YOUR BRAIN

▶ What did the Israelites think of Moses, at first? (v35)

▶ But how did God use him? (v35–36)

👁 Read verses 37–43

▶ What did God give Moses to pass on to the people? (v38)

▶ How did they treat Moses? (v39)

▶ How did they treat God? (v40–41)

Moses was God's chosen leader, but the Israelites challenged his authority, ignored his message, and turned away from his God.

▶ What did Moses tell them God would do? (v37)

Moses was talking about Jesus, God's ultimate leader and messenger!

THINK IT THROUGH

▶ What are the similarities in how Moses and Jesus were treated?

▶ What point is Stephen making to the religious leaders of Israel?

▶ Did Israel's rejection of Moses stop God's plan?

▶ What does that tell us about God?

It shouldn't be a surprise to us that Jesus was challenged, ignored and rejected — it had already happened to Moses. But it wouldn't stop God's plans to rescue His people.

157 Neck problems

Why are these men, who are so religious, so anti-Christianity? Stephen explains it to them. Very bluntly!

◉ Read Acts 7 v 51–53

ENGAGE YOUR BRAIN

▷ What had Stephen's judges done with God's law? (v53)

▷ What had they done with God's Son, "the Righteous One"? (v52)

▷ What was their response to the Holy Spirit? (v51)

▷ In those days, to acknowledge someone was in charge, you bowed your head to them. So, what does being "stiff-necked" towards God mean?

These men were circumcised and thought that made them part of God's people; but their *ears* weren't circumcised — they wouldn't listen to God. Nor were their *hearts* — they didn't love God.

Stephen's on trial, but it's his judges who are guilty. Guilty of disobeying God the Father, killing God the Son and resisting God the Spirit. Yet they're very religious, very serious about God, very confident they're part of God's people.

That challenges us: just because you're from a Christian family / you're baptised / you read your Bible, doesn't mean you're part of God's people. What matters is this: have you welcomed Jesus into your life, do you bow to Him, love Him and listen to Him?

PRAY ABOUT IT

Do you need to speak to Jesus to truly welcome Him into your life and bow to Him?

Do you need to bow to Jesus in a particular area of your life, where you've not been listening to or obeying Him?

158 Dead right

First, the authorities told the Christians to shut up about Jesus. Then they flogged them. What will they do next to silence Jesus' followers?

👁 **Read Acts 7 v 51–60**

ENGAGE YOUR BRAIN

▶ *What happened to Stephen?*

▶ *Why did it happen to him — why were the court so furious? (v51–54)*

This isn't just a story — this is history. It really happened. And it still happens around the world today. More Christians were martyred (killed for their faith) in the 20th century than in any other century. Stephen was the first of many.

▶ *What did Stephen see? (v55–56)*

Jesus, the Son of Man, was waiting to welcome him into heaven!

▶ *How does Stephen's vision in verse 56 give a different perspective to his death?*

Look how loving Stephen is. Even as they were stoning him to death, he prayed that they'd be forgiven (v60) — just as his Lord, who he gave his life for, had done as He was dying (Luke 23 v 33–34).

THINK ABOUT IT

▶ *As you think back over Stephen's trial and his defence speech, how can we follow his example?*

▶ *As you look at Stephen's death, what's the encouragement?*

GET ON WITH IT

Is there someone who you need to talk to about Jesus, even though there may be a cost to doing so?

PRAY ABOUT IT

Lord Jesus, Thank you that you stand ready to welcome me to heaven. Help me to stand up for you and talk about you, whatever the cost, until I join you there. Amen.

159 Showdown

So far in Acts, the Christians have done loads of miracles and many have believed their message. But what'd happen if they came up against someone else who could do amazing things? Let's find out...

👁 Read Acts 8 v 4–13

ENGAGE YOUR BRAIN

▶ Where did Philip go, and why did people listen to him? (v4–8)

▶ In verse 9 we meet Simon. Who did the people think he was, and why? (v10–11)

Both guys can do amazing things. Will people keep following Simon, or will they be swayed by Philip and become Christians?

▶ What did Philip do that made the difference? (v12)

And even Simon believes! (v13)

THINK ABOUT IT

▶ How's this encouraging for those of us who've never done "miraculous signs"?

Whoever we are, we can do what Philip did in verse 12, and pray for the same results!

👁 Read verses 14–25

Peter and John came down to Samaria, and they prayed and placed hands on the new Christians, who received the Holy Spirit (v15–17).

▶ How did Simon react? (v18-19)

▶ What did Peter say this revealed? (v21)

Simon was thinking in terms of fame and money. He thought he could buy God's gifts (v20). But Christian ministry is about serving others humbly, not seeking fame selfishly. We're not told what happened to Simon; but we're being warned not to make the same mistake.

THE BOTTOM LINE

It's the good news about Jesus that really makes the difference.

160 Who's the man?

Yesterday we saw people in Samaria become Christians — the first people outside of Judea. Now the gospel goes further... to Africa.

👁 Read Acts 8 v 26–34

ENGAGE YOUR BRAIN

▶ *Who did Philip meet (v27)?*

▶ *What was he doing? (v30)*

▶ *Why was Philip there? (v26, v29)*

This guy's struggling to understand what he's reading (v31). It's about someone who went to his unjust death silently, someone who was being punished for others' wrongdoing. But who's the man it's describing?

👁 Read verses 35–40

▶ *So, who's it about? (v35)*

▶ *How does the eunuch respond, and what does that show about him? (v36)*

Philip knew where to go, because he listened to the Spirit prompting him; he knew what the Ethiopian was reading, because he knew his Bible; he knew the Bible is all about Jesus, so he used the book of Isaiah to talk about Jesus.

GET ON WITH IT

There are lessons for us to learn here, even if we don't know any Ethiopian eunuchs...

• Listen to the Spirit. He may prompt you to go and talk to someone.

• Know your Bible. The more we read it, the more we'll understand how each part points to Jesus.

• Use your Bible. When you're explaining about Jesus, quote what the Bible says.

• Lend your Bible. The Ethiopian was intrigued by the Bible; who could you lend yours to and encourage them to read it?

161 Psalms – Is anybody there?

Have you ever asked God why He lets bad things happen? Why He sometimes seems far away as if He doesn't care? You're not alone — the writer of this psalm had exactly the same questions.

👁 Read Psalm 10 v 1–13

ENGAGE YOUR BRAIN

▷ *Why does it seem as if God is a long way off?*

▷ *What do the wicked say or think about God? (v4, 11, 13)*

Such thoughts and questions seem reasonable. Does God notice corruption, persecution and oppression? Is there even a God at all? The world is full of lies, cruelty and murder. Will God judge? The wicked seem to succeed and get away with evil.

👁 Read verses 14–18

▷ *Find a verse to answer each of these accusations…*

- God doesn't see:

- God doesn't exist:

- God won't punish evil:

SHARE IT

Do any of your friends use these arguments? How could you answer them from this psalm and the rest of the Bible? (You might want to reflect on your answers and write them down, to help you get your head around them.)

PRAY ABOUT IT

Thank God that He does care about all the evil that goes on in this world. Thank Him that one day He will judge the world fairly. Thank Him that He will be King for ever, long after the wicked are gone.

THE BOTTOM LINE

God sees, He will judge, He is the King for ever.

162 | Run for the hills

An increasingly anti-Christian society; TV, magazines and websites which ridicule Christians; friends and family who think you're stupid for believing in Christ. Wouldn't it be better to run for the hills and avoid all the hassle?

👁 Read Psalm 11 v 1–3

ENGAGE YOUR BRAIN

▶ *What advice is David being offered? (v1b)*

▶ *Why? (v2–3)*

▶ *Why isn't he going to take it?*

Things may look hopeless — his enemies might well be deadly and destructive — but verses 4–7 explain David's reason for staying put.

👁 Read verses 4–7

▶ *Why did David have total confidence in the Lord?*

▶ *What does being "righteous" mean (there's a clue in v1)?*

▶ *What is the amazing promise for those people? (v7)*

People were telling David to run from his enemies. But David was going nowhere. He had complete confidence in the Lord. He knew that God sees into people's hearts and judges them fairly. The Lord will destroy the wicked and violent (v5–6), but those who love and serve Him — the righteous — get to know God personally (v7). Incredible.

TALK IT THROUGH

Chat to a Christian friend. How can you remind each other that God is far more powerful than the world around us? What encouragement can you take from this psalm?

PRAY ABOUT IT

Ask God to help you turn to Him when you face opposition. Thank Him for His justice, protection and the promise of eternity with Him.

THE BOTTOM LINE

Find security in the Lord.

GENESIS

Family fortunes

Does your life ever feel like a soap opera? Maybe it's not that dramatic, but take a look at Jacob and his family and you might be forgiven for thinking you'd just turned on the TV — false identities, love, hate, trickery, tearful reconciliations, dreams, sibling rivalry, jealousy, kidnapping, faked death, slavery, a woman who won't take no for an answer, and a journey from prison to prime minister. Phew!

THE BIG PICTURE

But behind the scenes, the director has a much bigger story to tell. Remember the promises God made to Jacob's grandfather, Abraham? He promised to give him countless descendants, a land for those descendants, and a huge blessing. So how will He do that through the dramas and traumas listed above?

PROMISE KEEPER

Have you ever found it difficult to keep a promise? There are plenty of films about people who make a promise, whether it's just to be home for Christmas or to return to a loved one even though war and distance separate them. Sometimes they keep their promises, but other times they can't, and the suspense is what keeps us watching. But with God there is no suspense — we already know the end of the story because He always keeps His promises.

PERFECT PLAN

Back to your life: soap opera or not, there's nothing in there that God can't handle. If you're a Christian, He has got a plan for you, just as He did for Jacob and his sons.

Check out Romans 8 v 28–30 and then get stuck into Genesis 25–50 to see just how much God can be trusted to keep His promises.

163 Double trouble

Abraham's dead, so is Sarah. Their long-promised son Isaac is married to his cousin Rebekah. So what will happen to God's promises to Abraham and his descendants? Read on...

👁 **Read Genesis 25 v 19–26**

ENGAGE YOUR BRAIN

▶ *How old was Isaac when he got married? And how long before they had children? (v20, 26)*

Just like his dad, Isaac had to wait a long time for the son God promised to give him. Isaac too is learning that children are a gift from God.

▶ *What worried Rebekah? (v22)*

▶ *What is God's explanation for this? (v23)*

Normally, the older brother would be the one in charge, taking over the family business and inheriting most of the money. But things will be different with these brothers; even the way they enter the world shows how Jacob is trying to get ahead of his elder brother.

👁 **Read verses 27–34**

▶ *How would you sum up Jacob's behaviour over the stew?*

▶ *What about Esau's?*

Esau's birthright means inheriting the amazing promises God made to Abraham and Isaac. To give that away is serious. Jacob's not much better, trying to con his brother out of what is rightfully his. But even through all this human sin, God's promise to Rebekah in verse 23 comes true.

PRAY ABOUT IT

Can you think of any other times when God brings about His plans despite or even through human sin? Think about the cross and thank God for it.

THE BOTTOM LINE

God works in us and through us despite our sin.

164 Sister act

Here we go again — like father, like son. You'd have thought Isaac might have learned from his dad's experiences… well, he has, sort of, but then again, not entirely.

👁 Read Genesis 26 v 1–6

ENGAGE YOUR BRAIN

▶ *How does God encourage Isaac?*

▶ *Does Isaac listen to God? (v6)*

So far, so good. Unlike Abraham, Isaac hasn't run away to Egypt (see chapter 12), but stayed in the land God is promising him.

👁 Read verses 7–11

▶ *Why does Isaac tell this lie?*

▶ *What does that tell us about his faith in God?*

Before we slate Isaac for not trusting God and being scared of people, ask yourself how often *you* do that.

TALK IT THROUGH

Are there times when you keep quiet about being a Christian because you are scared of what people might say?

Are you ever tempted to lie or behave in a way you know hurts God, just to avoid hassle?

You're not the only one. Chat to a Christian friend about how you could encourage each other to fear God and not people. Pray for each other.

▶ *Despite not knowing God in the way Isaac does, how does Abimelek act?*

▶ *How does this make Isaac look?*

PRAY ABOUT IT

Often as God's people we don't act in a way that honours Him. Thank God that He is patient with us and ask for His help now to do the right thing.

THE BOTTOM LINE

Fear God, not people.

165 | Well well

Despite Isaac's dodgy "She's my sister, honest!" behaviour, God blesses him — see verse 12. But that doesn't go down too well with the locals...

👁 Read Genesis 26 v 12–22

ENGAGE YOUR BRAIN

▶ *What is all the conflict about?*

▶ *What is Isaac's reaction — does he stay in the land God told him to?*

Pretty impressive behaviour! Isaac and his household just move on. He doesn't stay to squabble nor does he decide to try his luck elsewhere — check out verse 22. He knows that God will provide what He's promised and so Isaac stays in the land.

GET ON WITH IT

Do you trust God to take care of you when you face opposition? If someone spreads untrue rumours about you, do you retaliate by being just as unpleasant? Jesus spoke about turning the other cheek and loving your enemies (it's in Matthew 5 v 38–48). Pray for the strength to do that today.

👁 Read verses 23–35

▶ *So what does God promise Isaac now and in the future? (v24)*

▶ *How does Isaac respond?*

Despite Isaac's sin and lack of trust, God tells him not to be afraid and reassures Isaac that He is with him. And Isaac can't take the credit for succeeding in life when things do go well either. Even the pagan king Abimelek can see that it's the Lord who has blessed Isaac (v28–29).

PRAY ABOUT IT

Thank God for things that are going well in your life and say sorry for when you mess up.

THE BOTTOM LINE

Anything good we have or do comes from God.

166 Tricky business

Things start getting messy now. It seems that no one in Isaac's family is up-front and honest. Try to keep track of who's tricking who.

👁 **Read Genesis 27 v 1–29**

ENGAGE YOUR BRAIN

▷ *Bearing in mind that Isaac would have known about God's prophesy to Rebekah (25 v 23) and that you needed witnesses back then to give a blessing like this, who is Isaac trying to trick?*

▷ *What about Rebekah?*

▷ *What risks does she take? (v13)*

▷ *Who does Jacob try to trick?*

▷ *What two lies does he tell? (v19–20)*

Poor old Isaac. If he hadn't been so sneaky, there's no way Jacob could have tricked him as there would have been witnesses to check his son's identity. Blind in more ways than one!

It's all such a mess. Everyone is trying to get their own way, with no attempt at God's way of doing things or considering the feelings

of anyone else. But God's words to Rebekah still come true despite all the scheming and deceit.

▷ *What does Isaac's blessing involve? (v28–29)*

Remember that Isaac is passing on the promises of God which he inherited from Abraham — can you spot any of them?

PRAY ABOUT IT

God's plans always work out. His promises always come true. When Jesus was executed by the Jerusalem authorities it looked like human plotting had triumphed, but God was perfectly in control. Praise and thank Him for that.

THE BOTTOM LINE

God is bigger than our sin.

167 | Trouble and strife

Jacob lies, then Esau cries; Isaac's irate, Esau hates;
then Rebekah fears what she hears...

👁 Read Genesis 27 v 30–46

ENGAGE YOUR BRAIN

▶ *So Jacob's got the blessing but what is Esau promised? (v39–40)*

▶ *What does he promise himself he'll do to Jacob? (v41)*

▶ *What's Rebekah's fear? And her solution?*

▶ *What reason does she give her husband, Isaac? (v46)*

Not entirely a lie — look back to 26 v 34–35. Abraham didn't want his son to marry Canaanite women either (24 v 3), so Rebekah used it as a good excuse to get Jacob out of harm's way.

👁 Read Genesis 28 v 1–9

▶ *What is Isaac's parting blessing to Jacob? (v3–4)*

▶ *What might be encouraging about this, bearing in mind that he's about to travel 500 miles away?*

God's promise to Abraham, Isaac and now Jacob still stands (v4); his family will inherit the land one day. And so off he goes to visit Uncle Laban… more of that later. Note Esau's dozy reaction – *My parents aren't happy with my two pagan wives, so hey, I'll marry another one!* Not exactly the sharpest tool in the box.

PRAY ABOUT IT

Two brothers, one with murder on his mind. Where have we seen that before? Are we any better? Jesus said that being angry with someone is just as bad as murder (Matthew 5 v 21–22). Ask God's forgiveness for specific times when you've lost your temper with someone.

168 From pillow to pillar

If you dream about dogs, some analysts say it's because you're worried or you like maths or something. Nothing to do with the fact Bonnie sleeps on your bed. Jacob's about to have a dream that really does mean something.

👁 Read Genesis 28 v 10–15

ENGAGE YOUR BRAIN

▶ *How does God introduce Himself to Jacob? (v13)*

▶ *What does the Lord promise him?*

God is really gracious to Jacob, appearing to him personally and confirming the promises He'd made to his dad and grandad.

👁 Read verses 16–22

▶ *How does Jacob react when he wakes up? (v16)*

▶ *How does he feel? (v17)*

▶ *What does he do? (v18–19)*

The most common reaction to meeting God in the Bible is fear. When sinful people meet the holy God, they realise how great He is and how utterly rubbish they are. Jacob begins to see that here. But…

▶ *How does Jacob's vow compare with God's generous promises?*

Jacob still wants things on his own terms. He wants evidence first before he'll fully trust God (v20). He's still got a lot to learn about the Lord.

PRAY ABOUT IT

"If you get me through these tests, Lord, then I'll trust you." Do you ever treat God like this? Remember who it is you're talking to. Spend some time now thinking about who God is and what He's done in creating you and sending His Son to rescue you. What do you want to say to Him now?

THE BOTTOM LINE

God is awesome and to be feared.

169 Love at first sight

Jacob's long journey is almost over. But he's far away from the land God has promised him, and there's no sign of those zillions of descendants yet either. But God is still at work, and love is in the air.

👁 Read Genesis 29 v 1–20

ENGAGE YOUR BRAIN

▶ Who does Jacob meet at the well? (v9–10)

▶ What sort of welcome does Jacob get from Laban? (v13–14)

▶ Jacob agrees to work for Laban. In return for what?

Awww, how sweet, those seven years seemed like only a few days. Bet the second seven didn't!

👁 Read verses 21–30

▶ How does Laban trick Jacob?

Remember how in chapter 27 Jacob disguised himself as the firstborn son? Well, now Laban has beaten him at his own game by pretending that his firstborn daughter was the wife Jacob had requested. Jacob the deceiver is deceived.

GET ON WITH IT

Jesus said: "So in everything, do to others what you would have them do to you, for this sums up the Law and the Prophets" (Matthew 7 v 12). Jacob experiences the flip side of that.

▶ How can you apply Jesus' words to your life this week?

Trickery, polygamy, favouritism. It's not looking great for Jacob. But God will use this dodgy character and his dysfunctional family to build a nation for Himself. His promises to Jacob do come true. That's amazing grace.

THE BOTTOM LINE

Grace is when God gives us great things we don't deserve. *Mercy* is when God doesn't give us the punishment we do deserve.

170 Jacob and sons

God promised Jacob loads of descendants. That starts looking a lot more likely in the next few verses. But things start getting ugly in Rachel and Leah's race to have Jacob's children.

👁 **Read Genesis 29 v 31 – 30 v 24**

ENGAGE YOUR BRAIN

▷ *Who was responsible for Leah having children? (v31)*

▷ *Why didn't Rachel have any kids?*

Just like Abraham and Sarah and Isaac and Rebekah, Rachel learns that children are not an automatic right but a gift from God, given in His time.

Names in biblical times often had significant meanings — jot down the meanings of Jacob's children (see notes at the bottom of the page in your Bible):

Reuben –
Simeon –
Levi –
Judah –
Dan –
Naphtali –
Gad –
Asher –
Issachar –
Zebulun –
Joseph –

▷ *What do these names tell us?*

Jacob's twelve sons eventually become the twelve tribes of Israel, but it's not a very promising start. Rachel and Leah's rivalry is not pretty, especially when they drag their maids into it, and Jacob's favouritism doesn't exactly help matters.

▷ *Mandrake roots (v14) were a superstitious fertility drug. What does this tell us about Rachel and Jacob's attitude to God?*

▷ *How does Rachel actually end up pregnant (v22)?*

PRAY ABOUT IT

Ask God to help you trust Him more and not take matters into your own hands, as Rachel and Jacob did.

171 | Sheep and cheerful

After 14 years hard work, Jacob wants to go home and he wants some wages. Fair enough? Well, Laban's not about to let a nice little earner disappear and his sons aren't too happy either. Fortunately for Jacob, God is on his side.

👁 Read Genesis 30 v 25–43

ENGAGE YOUR BRAIN

🔘 *What deal does Jacob make with Laban regarding his wages? (v32)*

🔘 *How does Laban attempt to cheat Jacob? (v35–36)*

🔘 *How does Jacob get around this?*

🔘 *What's the outcome (v43)?*

Despite Jacob's crazy superstitions — as if a few twigs can determine the colour of an animal! — he ends up very rich. How do you think that will go down with Laban and his sons?

👁 Read Genesis 31 v 1–13

🔘 *What lies do Laban's sons tell?*

🔘 *How does Laban treat Jacob?*

🔘 *What is the real reason for Jacob's success (v5, v7, v9)?*

Do you take the credit for things going well in your life? Is it down to your brains, your skill, or your family? Or do you know that God is behind everything good?

👁 Read verses 14–21

🔘 *How did Jacob and Rachel mess up? (v19–21)*

Do we only obey God when it fits in with our own plans? Jacob's come a long way but he still does a runner rather than trusting God to sort things out with his father-in-law.

PRAY ABOUT IT

Thank God for some of the good things in your life. And ask Him to help you please Him with the way you treat other people.

172 Cover up

So Laban finally finds out that Jacob has cut and run. And despite his terribly sentimental reasons in verse 28, he's not just chasing after them so he can kiss his grandchildren goodbye. Laban is not happy.

👁 Read Genesis 31 v 22–35

ENGAGE YOUR BRAIN

▶ What does God say to Laban?

▶ What do you think Laban was planning to do to Jacob (v29)?

▶ What did Rachel do? (v34–35)

Jacob has been a deceiver all along, but now Rachel seems to have caught the disease from her husband. It's so tempting to lie to cover our tracks, especially when we know we're in the wrong. Ask God for the strength to do the right thing and tell the truth.

👁 Read verses 36–55

▶ How do they settle things?

▶ How do Jacob and Laban talk about God? (v42, 53)

"I'm the good guy here. I worked my guts out for you and God has rewarded me for it. You'd better watch out or He'll get you!"

"Actually, everything you've got is mine in the first place, but God is watching us, so don't step out of line, mate!"

Although both men realise they need to take God into account, Jacob is still twisting things to his own advantage. He's still referring to God as his father Isaac's God rather than his own Lord.

PRAY ABOUT IT

Is the Lord, the God of Jacob, your God? Not just your parents' or your friends' God? Talk to Him honestly about what He means to you.

THE BOTTOM LINE

God's in charge. Is He in charge of your life?

173 | Caught in two minds

Jacob's finally heading home, and he's worried Esau is still out to kill him after 20 years. But will Jacob trust God to protect him or rely on his own cunning? What do you reckon?

👁 Read Genesis 32 v 1–21

ENGAGE YOUR BRAIN

▷ How does God encourage Jacob as he heads home? (v1)

▷ How is Jacob feeling? (v6–7)

▷ What are Jacob's two cunning plans to win over his brother?

▷ What good move does Jacob make? (v9–12)

Jacob was terrified of Esau. He came up with two crafty plans to stay safe. But in the middle of his plotting, he asked God to help him.

THINK IT THROUGH

Is prayer your first line of defence or a last resort?

Let's take a look at Jacob's prayer…

▷ What does he recognise about God? (v9, v12)

▷ What does he admit about himself? (v10)

▷ What does he ask for? (v11)

PRAY ABOUT IT

Are your prayers like this? Or are they just asking for things? Talk to God now — thank Him for His promises and His character, admit your own unworthiness, and then ask for His help with whatever's troubling you — exams, parents or friendship problems.

THE BOTTOM LINE

Prayer shows we rely on God.

174 Cling on

Extreme wrestling, Old Testament style. Jacob's about to face an incredible opponent. And he'll come out of the bout changed — physically and spiritually. He'll even get a new name.

👁 Read Genesis 32 v 22–32

ENGAGE YOUR BRAIN

▶ *His opponent wins the wrestling match with some clever tactics, but Jacob doesn't give up. What does he want? (v26)*

▶ *What does this tell us about his attitude?*

This strange supernatural wrestling match makes Jacob cling to God. He finally recognises his total dependence on God. He's come to the point of trusting God. At last. So God blesses him and gives him a new name.

Israel the man would eventually become Israel the nation as God continued to keep the promises He made to Abraham's descendants. God is faithful to His people.

▶ *What two things does Jacob realise have happened? (v30)*

▶ *Why are they amazing put next to each other? What might sinful Jacob have expected after seeing God face to face?*

▶ *What does this tell us about God?*

It took 20 years for Jacob to hand over control of His life to God. He didn't change overnight. Christians have a "work in progress" sticker on them. God continues to change us so that we become more like Him.

PRAY ABOUT IT

God deals personally with us. He breaks down our defences. Breaks down our pride. Brings us to the point where we have to admit: *God, you have every right to run my life your way. Please do that.*

THE BOTTOM LINE

We need to cling to God and completely depend on Him.

175 | Oh brother

Time for the big reunion. 20 years ago Jacob tricked Esau, and Esau promised deadly revenge. What will happen now? Should we expect hugs and tears or an even more violent wrestling match than yesterday?

👁 **Read Genesis 33 v 1–20**

ENGAGE YOUR BRAIN

▶ *How has Jacob changed? (see v3, v5, v8, v10-11)*

Jacob even goes out first to meet Esau (v3). He's putting his money where his mouth is and trusting God at last. But the old Jacob is still in there…

▶ *Esau has changed too. What might we expect from him?*

▶ *How does he actually behave?*

It all seems very lovely — the two brothers reunited at last, swapping presents and making up for their bad behaviour. But it's not all sweetness and light: Jacob flatters Esau (v10) and then pretends he'll follow Esau to Seir before heading in a different direction. Old habits die hard — Jacob is still a deceiver.

▶ *Jacob should have headed to Bethel, where he first met God. Where does he go instead? (v18)*

▶ *What name does he give the altar he sets up to honour God?*

Jacob calls the altar "Mighty is the God of Israel". He's saying: *God's been good to me, I'll follow Him.*

But lingering in Shechem doesn't turn out to be a good idea as we'll see tomorrow. Jacob's still a work in progress.

PRAY ABOUT IT

All Christians are a "work in progress". Thank God that He kept going with Jacob, and will keep working in you too.

THE BOTTOM LINE

God's at work in us, changing us.

176 Daughter slaughter

Chapter 33 ends with God and chapter 35 begins with God, but there's no mention of Him at all in chapter 34. It's a story of people acting with no thought for God — with dreadful results.

Read Genesis 34 v 1–31

ENGAGE YOUR BRAIN

▷ What crime does Shechem commit?

▷ How do Dinah's brothers and the author of Genesis see this crime? (v7)

▷ What does Hamor really want from the marriage deal? (v21–23)

As head of the family, Jacob should have been the one to reply to Hamor and his son. But instead his sons do (v13) and surprise, surprise, they're just as crafty as their dad and plan to deceive the Shechemites.

▷ What do Jacob's sons do in revenge?

▷ What does Jacob seem most concerned about? (v30)

It's a pretty gruesome story — rape, greed, deceit, mass murder, looting and plundering. Yes, it's a horrible crime, but Jacob's sons don't exactly come out of it well either. One sinful action has snowballed into a disaster affecting every family in the area.

THINK IT THROUGH

Do you ever catch yourself thinking "It's just a little sin, it won't go any further"? Watching that dodgy late-night film, reading that book or magazine you know wouldn't please God, lying about your coursework to get out of a tight spot… sin snowballs.

PRAY ABOUT IT

Say sorry to God for times you've failed and ask His help to avoid those sins you really struggle with.

THE BOTTOM LINE

One sin leads to another.

177 House of God

After the godlessness and horror of chapter 34, God is back on the scene. He speaks to Jacob again and reminds him of something important.

👁 **Read Genesis 35 v 1–15**

ENGAGE YOUR BRAIN

▶ *What does God command Jacob to do?*

▶ *What was so significant about Bethel (look back at 28 v 15, 19 and 31 v 13)?*

▶ *What do Jacob and co need to do first? (v2)*

Rachel, in particular, had been hanging onto her father's idols, but there's no room for anyone else in this relationship. God demands Jacob and his family's obedience and worship.

GET ON WITH IT

Do you follow God whole-heartedly or are you two-timing Him with popularity, success or possessions? Get rid of other gods in your life.

▶ *Remind yourself what Jacob was scared of in 34 v 30. How does God deal with that? (v5)*

▶ *How does God encourage Jacob? (v10–12)*

God reminds Jacob of the time he wrestled with God and was given a new name. Back then, Jacob asked his opponent's name. This time, God tells him (v11). He also gives Jacob a new blessing, which includes the ones God gave Abraham and Isaac.

▶ *How does Jacob respond? (v14–15)*

PRAY ABOUT IT

Think about all the amazing promises God has made to you in the Bible — forgiveness through Jesus' death; eternal life with Him; His Spirit to live in you and help you. How are you going to respond to Him now?

THE BOTTOM LINE

Our great promise-keeping God is the only true God.

178 Beginnings and endings

The end of one era and the beginning of the next. A lot of deaths — Deborah (back in verse 8), Rachel and Isaac. And more bad behaviour from Jacob's sons. But in the middle of all this, God's plan keeps unfolding.

👁 Read Genesis 35 v 16–29

ENGAGE YOUR BRAIN

Rachel had wanted another son (30 v 24), but sadly died giving birth to him. She called him Ben–Oni ("Son of my trouble") because of the pain she went through. But Jacob renamed him Benjamin ("Son of my right hand"). He and Joseph became Jacob's favourite sons.

▶ *What did Reuben do wrong? (v22)*

Years later, Jacob remembered Reuben's sin against him and Reuben lost the rights of being the firstborn son (49 v 3–4). What goes around comes around.

👁 Read Genesis 36 v 1–8

▶ *Where do Esau and his descendants end up?*

▶ *Look back and read 27 v 39–40. What has happened?*

Look back over chapters 28–36 of Genesis and answer these big questions:

▶ *What have you found out about God in these chapters?*

▶ *What have you realised about human behaviour?*

▶ *Is there anything you've learned about yourself and your relationship with God?*

PRAY ABOUT IT

Talk to God about your thoughts.

THE BOTTOM LINE

God's plans never fail.

179 Luke – Walking with Jesus

Back on the road with Jesus. Despite the opposition to Jesus, there's still a large crowd travelling with Him. It's time for Jesus to give them (and us) a reality check...

👁 Read Luke 14 v 25–35

ENGAGE YOUR BRAIN

▶ *Compared to how they feel about Jesus, how must his followers feel about their families and themselves? (v26)*

▶ *What do real disciples do? (v27)*

▶ *What does that mean?*

Jesus isn't saying to hate your relatives. He's saying you can't follow Him half-heartedly. Either He's your number one, and you're willing to suffer for Him, or you're not. Either you're a 100% follower, or you're no follower.

▶ *If you want to build a tower, what do you do before starting? (v28)*

▶ *Otherwise, what'll happen? (v29–30)*

▶ *What is Jesus encouraging people to do before they start following Him?*

Following Jesus is like running a marathon; it's the finishing that counts, not the starting. Before you start, you must decide to keep going to the finish even when it hurts. Same with following Christ! Still, it's better to be on Jesus' side than opposing Him — just as it's better for a king to be at peace with a stronger king instead of getting slaughtered by him (v31–32).

THINK IT THROUGH

▶ *If you're considering becoming a Christian... what's Jesus telling you to do first? (v28–30)*

▶ *If you're already a Christian... what's Jesus telling you following Him will be like? (v27)*

PRAY ABOUT IT

I'm guessing you've got loads to talk to God about today.

180 | Get ready to party

Everyone likes a good party. Birthdays, end of exams, weddings, or just because you fancy it. But when does heaven have a party?

👁 **Read Luke 15 v 1–2**

ENGAGE YOUR BRAIN

🔸 *What type of people want to listen to Jesus? (v1)*

🔸 *How do the Pharisees feel about that? (v2)*

So Jesus tells these religious leaders a couple of stories to make a point.

👁 **Read v 3–10**

and draw what happens in them:

🔸 *What prompts heaven to throw a party? (v7, v10)*

GET ON WITH IT

🔸 *What do these two parables tell us was Jesus' priority on earth?*

🔸 *If you're a follower of Jesus, what should your priority be?*

🔸 *What should you most rejoice about in life?*

PRAY ABOUT IT

Think of a couple of people you know who are "lost". Pray for opportunities to tell them about how Jesus offers them eternal life, and pray that Jesus would find them so that you and everyone in heaven can celebrate.

THE BOTTOM LINE

Jesus' priority is to find and rescue sinners; and heaven has a party when sinners turn to God.

181 Two ways to get it wrong

Jesus is in story-telling mode — here's another famous parable. Get this, and you get Jesus' mission, so we'll spend two sessions on it.

👁 Read Luke 15 v 11–32

ENGAGE YOUR BRAIN

▶ What does the younger son say and do? (v12–13)

▶ Where does living this way get him? (v14–16)

By verse 16, the younger son's away from his father's house and his life is ruined! So he decides to go back (we'll get to that next time). But now let's meet the older brother...

▶ When his father welcomes the younger son back into his house, how does the older brother react? (v28)

▶ He's been "slaving" for his father — what was he hoping his dad would give him? (v29)

The older son didn't seem to be working hard out of love for his father — he was in it for the reward. And he ends the story outside his father's house, refusing to go in.

The first son ignored his father and took his gifts; the second son was being good so he could earn rewards from his father. Jesus is saying everyone's like that with God; you're either a "sinner" (v1), who has taken God's good gifts and ignored Him, or you're a "Pharisee" (v2), who only obeys God's rules to try to earn eternal life. Neither of these attitudes shows love to God; neither brings us to God's house — eternal life in His kingdom.

PRAY ABOUT IT

Pray for people you know who are like either of the brothers. Pray that they will understand the only way to eternal life — through Jesus Christ.

THE BOTTOM LINE

Ignoring God completely or trying to be good enough both leave us outside God's kingdom.

182 Thanks, Dad!

The younger son took his father's gifts, ignored his father, and ruined his life. But then he came to his senses...

👁 **Read Luke 15 v 11–32**

ENGAGE YOUR BRAIN

▶ *The son was hoping he could work for his father (v19) — but when the father saw him, what did he say? (v22–24)*

From starving in a pigsty to a massive party in his father's house — the son's life is so much better with his father than on his own.

▶ *What did the father do when he saw his son in the distance?*

For a man in that society, this would have involved total humiliation. To meet the son and welcome him home, this father had to leave his house and shame himself.

👁 **Turn to 2 Corinthians 8 v 9**

▶ *What did Jesus do to welcome people into the riches of heaven?*

God left heaven, became a man, and was humiliated in death — just to meet us and welcome us to His heavenly party. Incredible.

PRAY ABOUT IT

While the younger son enjoyed the party, the older son finished the story outside, refusing to go in (Luke 15 v 28).

▶ *Which son are you?*

▶ *Do you need to thank God for welcoming you in so you can enjoy life with Him?*

▶ *Or do you need to ask God to welcome you in today so you can begin life with Him?*

THE BOTTOM LINE

Life's indescribably better with God than on our own; and God welcomes us into eternal life even though we don't deserve it.

183 Money money money

This is one of Jesus' stranger parables — but basically it's all about how we use money.

👁 **Read Luke 16 v 1–9**

ENGAGE YOUR BRAIN

▶ *The manager had influence and wealth — what did he use it to do? (v4)*

He's sensible — he wants people to still welcome him when he no longer has a job.

▶ *What does Jesus tell His followers to do with their worldly wealth? (v9)*

▶ *Why? (end of v 9)*

Jesus isn't saying it's ok to cheat. The point He's making is this: use whatever you've got now to serve God — and you'll find a bunch of friends who last beyond death.

Wouldn't it be great if you gave money to a missionary organisation and someone you'd never met welcomed you into eternity, because your money had enabled someone to tell him about Jesus?

👁 **Read verses 10–15**

Notice verse 13 — we're to devote our money to God, not devote ourselves to money as our god.

GET ON WITH IT

▶ *Are you mainly using your worldly wealth for yourself, to have friends now, or for God, so you're welcomed in eternal life?*

▶ *How can you use your money and possessions to serve God?*

PRAY ABOUT IT

Ask God to show you how you could usefully use what He's given you.

184 A serious warning

You're about to be hit by a car when someone shouts: "Get out of the way!" They're doing that to help you, not shock you — and that's why Jesus talks about hell...

👁 Read Luke 16 v 19–26

ENGAGE YOUR BRAIN

▶ In the parable, what happens to the rich man? (v22–23)

▶ How is hell described? (v23–24)

▶ What else does Jesus reveal about hell? (v26)

Jesus is warning people not to ignore God and end up in hell. But hang on, what gives Jesus the right to tell people about hell?

👁 Read verses 27–31

▶ What does the rich man want to happen, and why?

▶ But they haven't listened to Old Testament teaching — would anything convince them? (v31)

Jesus has authority to warn us about hell because He's the One who would rise from the dead. He's warning us, not to shock us but to help us.

He wants us to listen to God's word, to repent (turn back to God and ask for forgiveness), and to enjoy eternal life with Him, rather than ignoring Him and experiencing hell.

PRAY ABOUT IT

▶ Do you need to repent and ask God to forgive you?

▶ Do you need to ask God to give you opportunities to tell your family and friends about heaven and hell?

THE BOTTOM LINE

The risen Jesus has the authority to tell us about hell — and He says it's real, painful and final.

185 Your problem, my problem

"No man is an island", a poet once wrote. We live among other people and our lives affect theirs. How much do you care about Christians you know who are sinning? What do you do about it?

👁 Read Luke 17 v 1–4

ENGAGE YOUR BRAIN

- *Who does Jesus say "woe", or trouble, will come to? (v1)*
- *How serious is He? (v2)*

Lesson 1 — We must not cause others to sin

- *If a Christian we know sins, what should we do? (middle of v3)*
- *Why is this so amazingly hard?*

Lesson 2 — We must rebuke Christians when they sin

That doesn't mean shouting at people. It means gently but firmly telling someone that what they've done is wrong.

- *If a Christian repents (accepts they were wrong and turns back to God), what should we do, even if they've hurt us? (v3–4)*
- *Why is this so hard?*

Lesson 3 – We must forgive Christians when they repent

Jesus isn't asking us to do anything He didn't do. He never caused others to sin; He always gently rebuked those who were sinning; He forgave His followers when they repented.

GET ON WITH IT

- *How do your words or actions encourage others to sin?*
- *Is there anyone you need to help face up to their sin?*
- *Or anyone you need to forgive?*

PRAY ABOUT IT

Pray you'll help your Christian friends in these three ways.

186 Who's on whose side?

**Should God be thankful we're on His side?
Or should we be grateful He's on ours?
Or is it both?**

👁 Read Luke 17 v 5–6

ENGAGE YOUR BRAIN

▶ *What can even a small amount of faith in God achieve?*

Jesus is telling us something really important about faith here. The power of faith doesn't come from its owner (you) but from its object — who you've got faith in. A lot of faith in your school soccer team to win the World Cup is no use — the faith is in the wrong team. A small amount of faith in the Creator God to do whatever He likes is massively powerful. So if a Christian does something great, it's not them doing something great because they have lots of faith; it's God doing something great because God is amazingly powerful.

👁 Read v 7–10

▶ *If a servant just does what it's his job to do, does he deserve thanks? (v9)*

▶ *When a servant of God has done what He asks, do we deserve loads of thanks? (v10)*

Christians are privileged to be God's servants. When we do things for Him, it's only what He deserves — we have no right to think that He owes us.

PRAY ABOUT IT

Thank you for…

Please help me to remember…

THE BOTTOM LINE

When we do great things, it's actually God doing them through us; when we work for God, it's only what God deserves.

187 | Thanks, God!

My god-daughter is three, and she's just learned to say "Thank you" when someone does something for her. She could teach these guys a thing or two!

👁 Read Luke 17 v 11–14

ENGAGE YOUR BRAIN

▶ *Who does Jesus meet, and what do they want? (v11–13)*

Anyone with leprosy was considered unclean, and so had to be cut off from God's people, the Jews.

▶ *Jesus heals them in verses 13–14. How should they respond?*

👁 Read v 15–19

▶ *How many of them do say "thank you"? (v15–16)*

▶ *What else do we learn about the thankful man in verse 16?*

Nine of the men don't return to thank Jesus. Only one shows true faith. This was another example of God's people ignoring Jesus' message. So Jesus would take His message and healing to other nations, as shown by this Samaritan.

▶ *How did this guy respond to being cured? (v15, v18)*

▶ *What does Jesus tell him has made him well? (v19)*

This guy leaves not just with his leprosy cured, but with his heart cured. He leaves as a friend of God. True faith is seen in people thanking and praising God for saving them.

PRAY ABOUT IT

Has God cured your sin disease? Do you praise and thank Him? Will you do so right now?

THE BOTTOM LINE

Don't take Jesus saving you for granted; thank Him for it.

188 | Jesus: the return

Young kids and long car journeys are a bad mix. "Are we nearly there yet?" they constantly yell. Jesus has already said He'll return to the world. But the Pharisees want to know when. Are we nearly there yet?

👁 Read Luke 17 v 20–25

ENGAGE YOUR BRAIN

▷ What will Jesus' return be like? (v24)

▷ Will everyone know it's happening?

▷ But what must happen first? (v25)

👁 Read v 26–30

▷ In Noah's time, how much warning was there that God was sending a flood? (1 Peter 3 v 20)

▷ So, what do we know it will be like when Jesus, the Son of Man, returns? (Luke 17 v 26)

👁 Read v 31–37

Jesus' return will divide people — some will be left to live in His perfect kingdom: others will be shut out (v34–35).

▷ When Jesus returns, what shouldn't Christians do? (v31)

When Jesus returns, Christians will live in His perfect world. So we should be looking forward to His return more than anything else! More than holidays, or falling in love, or getting our dream job, or making money — more than anything! If we're not looking forward to it, we haven't understood how great it'll be for Christians when Jesus returns. If we understand that, then we'll realise that verse 33 is true!

GET ON WITH IT

How do you need to change your thinking and attitudes, based on Jesus' words here?

PRAY ABOUT IT

Lord Jesus, Thank you that you will return. Help me to be ready for that day by trusting in you; help me to look forward to that day more than anything else.

189 Do something, God!

There's so much wrong in this world, so much God doesn't like. Should we just ignore it? Is there anything we can do? Why doesn't God seem to do much about it?

👁 Read Luke 18 v 1–5

ENGAGE YOUR BRAIN

▷ *What's Jesus saying in this parable?*

👁 Read verses 6–8

▷ *If even this unjust judge was willing to give justice, what will the perfect God definitely do for His people? (v7–8)*

▷ *So, can we ask for justice confidently?*

▷ *When will we ultimately see this happen? (end of v8)*

▷ *So, will we always see God's justice immediately?*

Verse 8 is confusing. Will God's justice come quickly or will we have to wait? Well, God answers our prayers quickly. Sometimes the answer may be "No" or "Wait", but He does answer. His ultimate and final justice will come when Jesus returns.

Around the world today, God's people will be unfairly treated because they're Christians. Some (maybe you) will be laughed at; others will be tortured; some will die. God will bring justice for His persecuted people when His Son Jesus returns. So we can pray confidently; we must pray patiently; we should pray persistently.

PRAY ABOUT IT

Why not visit www.opendoorsuk.org

Pray for a particular group of persecuted Christians — that God would bring His justice for them. And thank Him that He will bring perfect justice when Jesus returns.

THE BOTTOM LINE

Jesus will return and bring God's justice — so pray for it and don't give up praying for it!

190 Compare and contrast

Who do you compare yourself to? Are you a good person? A clever person? A successful person? Is there anyone you're glad not to be like? Anyone you look down on?

👁 Read Luke 18 v 9–14

ENGAGE YOUR BRAIN

▶ Who went to the temple to pray?

▶ Who does the Pharisee compare himself to? (v11–12)

▶ Why does he think he's better than them?

Here's a very good, very religious man. Compared to others he's great, and he knows it! And he clearly thinks that his goodness makes him right with God.

▶ How does the tax collector describe himself? (v13)

He doesn't compare himself to others: he compares himself to God. He knows he's not good — he's a sinner.

▶ So what does he ask God for?

So, we've got a Pharisee who compares himself to others and thinks he's really good… and a tax collector who knows he's not good because he compares himself to God.

▶ Which of these guys goes home "justified" — put right with God?

👁 Read verses 15–17

▶ Tricky question — how does what Jesus says in verses 15–17 reinforce His parable in v 9–14?

That tax collector was like a child. He came to God not offering Him anything, or thinking he deserved anything, but simply asking for mercy.

PRAY ABOUT IT

Write your own prayer based on today's Bible bit.

THE BOTTOM LINE

Compare yourself with God instead of others, and you'll see that the only way into His kingdom is to ask Him for mercy, not by trying to be good enough.

191 All you need

Time for a big big question. How can we have a good life now and eternal life in the future?

👁 **Read Luke 18 v 18–30**

ENGAGE YOUR BRAIN

▶ It's a great question in verse 18 — how does Jesus answer in verse 19?

Here's a reminder of what we saw yesterday — only God is totally, utterly, perfectly, good.

▶ How does Jesus answer in verse 20?

And so to do enough to inherit eternal life, you need to keep every single one of God's commandments.

▶ How well is this guy doing? (v21)

What a claim! But Jesus knows the man's heart and so challenges him to give up his wealth and get on with following Him (v22).

▶ How does this guy react? (v23)

It's impossible for anyone to live a life good enough for God. No one can earn eternal life.

▶ But what's the great news? (v27)

▶ Who does God give eternal life to? (v28–30)

Did you notice in verse 30 that it's not just after we die that Jesus' followers receive a better life — it's "in this age" as well!

GET ON WITH IT

▶ What kind of things do people say you need to have a good life?

▶ What kind of things is it easy to think you need to do to deserve eternal life?

Remember, all you need to do is trust in Jesus. Nothing else! Being good and being rich doesn't bring full life, now or in eternity — only following Jesus does.

192 Blind faith

We've been following Jesus through Luke's Gospel for a while now. Everything we've seen so far is now drawn together in one episode. So listen very carefully...

👁 Read Luke 18 v 31–34
ENGAGE YOUR BRAIN

Jesus reminds His followers He's going to Jerusalem. There He'll be rejected, die, and rise back to life (v32–33). The disciples don't get it (v34), but someone shows them what it's all about...

👁 Read verses 35–43

▶ *What does he call Jesus? (v38–39)*

David had been God's people's king. God promised that one of David's descendants would be God's promised, eternal King, His Christ. This blind guy can see who Jesus is!

▶ *What does he want? (v38, v41)*

▶ *Why does Jesus heal him? (v42)*

▶ *What two responses does he make? (v43)*

Remember, Jesus is on the way to rejection and death. Following Him won't be easy — but this man happily follows Jesus, the Son of David, who has healed him and saved him.

GET ON WITH IT

▶ *Do you need for the first time to ask Jesus to heal you, to give you eternal life?*

▶ *Do you need to get on with following Jesus and praising God even when that brings difficulty and rejection?*

PRAY ABOUT IT

Turn your answers into a prayer.

THE BOTTOM LINE

This blind beggar shows what Christianity's about: recognising Jesus, being saved through faith, and following Him even though it's hard.

193 Psalms – Speak no evil

"It's only a little white lie."
"I was being economical with the truth."
"What they don't know won't hurt them."

Read Psalm 12 v 1–4

ENGAGE YOUR BRAIN

▶ *According to David, what is the big problem with the world?*

▶ *What are the different ways in which this problem shows itself?*

GET ON WITH IT

Ask yourself honestly if verse 2 applies to you.

- Do you talk about other people behind their backs?

- Is it easier to say what others want to hear than speak the truth?

- Would you lie to get out of trouble?

- Do you like to make yourself sound better than you really are?

Remind yourself of the truth of verse 3 and ask for God's help to change.

Read verses 5–8

▶ *In contrast, what are God's words like? (v6)*

▶ *What is God's response to human wickedness? (v5, 7)*

▶ *What is the world's response?(v8)*

God's words are pure, perfect and completely trustworthy. So when He says He'll protect the weak and needy from the wicked, we can believe Him. God's people may get treated badly in this world, but one day they will be safe with God for ever in eternity. And the wicked will be punished.

PRAY ABOUT IT

Thank God that He never lies, is totally trustworthy, and will keep His people safe for ever.

THE BOTTOM LINE

Jesus is King!

194 | More than a feeling

In these next two psalms, David pours out his innermost feelings to God: helplessness, stupidity, fear, awe, amazement, anger and praise. Felt any of those recently?

👁 Read Psalms 13 v 1–2

ENGAGE YOUR BRAIN

▶ *How did David feel about God?*

▶ *Ever felt that God's out of reach?*

David was feeling frustrated. He feared he'd be killed by his enemies, and he just couldn't get through to God. It felt as if God had forgotten about him.

👁 Read verses 3–4

▶ *What do the words "LORD my God" tell us about David's relationship with God?*

▶ *How is David an example to us in tough times?*

Even when it appeared that God had abandoned him, David's faith held firm. So he prayed, asking God to help him out.

👁 Read verses 5–6

▶ *What top truths did David remember about God?*

Even at this low point, David could hold on to three truths about God — His unfailing love, His great rescue and His goodness. Even in dark times, David's hope for the future was based on what God had done in the past.

GET ON WITH IT

Make a list of times when you've seen God's love, His rescue and His goodness to you. Pull out the list when you feel at rock bottom and when God seems distant.

PRAY ABOUT IT

Thank God for those times in the past. Now, like David, be honest with God about how you feel about life and how you feel about Him.

195 Fool proof

"There is no God." "I look after number one, because no one else will." Ever heard friends say something similar? It's heart-breaking when people come to conclusions like that.

Read Psalm 14 v 1–3

ENGAGE YOUR BRAIN

How do people who refuse to believe in God usually act? (v1)

David isn't holding back in this psalm. "It's dumb to say there's no God," he says. "Look where it's got them" (v1). The person who refuses to let God rule his life makes himself boss. But the results are dreadful — corruption, disgusting deeds, selfishness.

What conclusion does David come to? (v3)

"You say there's no one who does good? But yesterday I helped an old lady…" Big deal. When it comes to matching God's perfect standards, we fall far short. Left to ourselves, we're self-serving, not God-serving.

Read verses 4–7

What will happen to those who oppose God? (v5)

What about people who call to God for help? (v5–6)

God will live with those who cry to Him for help. He'll protect them. And God's enemies will run for cover. David looks to the future by asking God to rescue His people again, as He'd done before.

THE BOTTOM LINE

There is a God. A God who deserves our respect and worship. A God who acts. A God who has made Himself known to His people. Only a fool refuses to recognise that.

PRAY ABOUT IT

Pray that God would help you live in a way that shows you believe in Him and shows He's with you.

Pray for your friends who live as if God doesn't exist.

ACTS

To be continued...

To be continued...

How do those words make you feel? Excited? Exasperated? Eager to see what happens next or annoyed by a cop-out cliffhanger? Well, Acts is all about "to be continued".

So far in chapters 1–8 of Acts, we've seen "all that Jesus began to do and to teach" continuing, with the exciting birth of the church at Pentecost and its growth mainly in Jerusalem and Judea and Samaria. But what about the "ends of the earth" where Jesus also sent them (Acts 1 v 8)?

TURNING POINT

Chapters 9 and 10 mark a turning point in the mission of the early church. First, we see a major persecutor of Christians become a believer who's sent out spreading the news. Second, we see God's ground-breaking revelation to Peter that the Gentiles, far from being "unclean", could now be part of God's new people.

By the end of the book, the Christian message had reached the heart of the then-known world, Rome itself, and as we leave Paul, we get that "to be continued" feeling again.

MARCHING ON

Of course, in the centuries that followed Acts, the gospel continued to be preached across the world, until it reached you, wherever you live!

God's mission is still active today, as there are still people and sadly, whole countries, who haven't heard about Jesus' death and resurrection, and the forgiveness and eternal life He offers. But God is still working! His Spirit works in us to get His message out there. Yes, that includes you.

To be continued...

196 Transformer

Today's section is one of the most famous moments in the book of Acts, and another example of God's transforming power. Remember Saul? It features Saul, who had helped imprison, torture and even kill Christians.

👁 Read Acts 9 v 1–19

ENGAGE YOUR BRAIN

▶ *Sum up Saul's attitude and behaviour towards Christians in verses 1–2. (The Way = Christianity)*

▶ *How does Jesus describe Saul's behaviour? (v4–5)*

Notice the way Jesus identifies Himself with His people. It's Him Saul is persecuting — not just Christians.

PRAY ABOUT IT

Pray for Christians who are suffering persecution right now. Pray that they'd know the wonderful strength and comfort of being united to Jesus even while suffering.

▶ *What is Ananias' initial reaction to God's command? (v10–14)*

▶ *What is God's answer?*

In case you're wondering, verse 16 came true. Read 2 Corinthians 11 v 24–29 to see how Saul/Paul suffered for Jesus' name.

▶ *What's so amazing about Ananias' first words to Saul, considering Saul's past?*

The good news about Jesus turns enemies into brothers, makes the blind see and transforms persecutors into believers!

PRAY ABOUT IT

Thank God that although you were once His enemy, Jesus' death and resurrection have made it possible for you to be His friend.

THE BOTTOM LINE

The gospel transforms God's enemies into His friends.

197 | Go, Saul, go!

Saul's transformation has immediate effects — joy and excitement, along with spreading the message and the persecution that comes with it.

👁 Read Acts 9 v 19–31

ENGAGE YOUR BRAIN

▶ What is Saul's immediate reaction to God's grace? (v20)

▶ What does he preach about Jesus? (v20 and v22)

▶ Does God's grace have the same effect on you?

GET ON WITH IT

A wise man once said that the reason we don't tell others the good news about Jesus is because either we don't really believe it or we don't care about them. If we've received the gift of God's amazing grace, surely we'll want to share it?

▶ How do the Jews in Damascus (and Jerusalem) react to Saul's transformation? (v23 and v29)

▶ Why is this not surprising? (Acts 9 v 15–16, Luke 9 v 21–23, John 15 v 18–20)

▶ What's the reaction of the church in Jerusalem to Saul? (v26)

But, as in Damascus, fearful former enemies soon become brothers who care for and protect Saul (v27–28).

PRAY ABOUT IT

Think about your church, CU or youth group. The relationships that exist not because of similar interests but only because of a shared love for Jesus are a wonderful sign of God's grace and power. Thank Him for them.

THE BOTTOM LINE

God grows His church in times of both peace and persecution.

198 Saints and sinners

Luke wrote Acts. In the first verse of Acts, he talks about his first book (Gospel of Luke), which was about "all that Jesus BEGAN to do and teach". The book of Acts simply carries on the story of Jesus' actions through His church.

👁 Read Acts 9 v 32–43

ENGAGE YOUR BRAIN

▶ *Depending on which Bible version you use, verse 32 will either describe believers as "the Lord's people" or as "saints"? Do you think of yourself as a saint?*

The great thing about being a Christian is that God counts us as washed clean of our sins by Jesus' blood. Our status is one of "saints", God's holy people. Not because of our "saintly" deeds, but because of the cosmic swap that took place on the cross; our sins for Christ's righteousness!

PRAY ABOUT IT

Thank God for that wonderful truth now! Ask Him to help you to live up to your calling — to be what you are.

▶ *What miraculous act does Peter perform in verse 34?*

▶ *In whose name / under whose authority?*

▶ *Can you think of any similar miracle performed by Jesus? (eg: Luke 5 v 18–26)*

▶ *What miraculous act does Peter perform in verses 36–40?*

▶ *Remind you of anything? (eg: Luke 8 v 49–56)*

Jesus may have left the disciples but His Spirit is still with them, working through them. We may not have healed anyone or raised anyone from the dead personally, but it's no less true that God's Spirit is with us today if we are Christians.

TALK IT OVER

Chat with an older Christian about what it means to have the Holy Spirit in our lives. Good Bible bits to start with are Romans 15 v 13, 1 Corinthians chs 12–14, Galatians 5 v 22–23.

THE BOTTOM LINE

Jesus is still at work today.

199 Belly vision

A major shift is about to take place. With a few exceptions, the gospel (the good news about Jesus) has only been shared with the Jews, God's historic chosen people. But all that is about to change!

Read Acts 10 v 1–8

ENGAGE YOUR BRAIN

▷ Who are the main characters in this section?

▷ What do we know about each of them?

Read verses 9–23

▷ What is the issue Peter faces in this vision?

▷ As Peter ponders the meaning of the vision, how does God provide the answer? (v17)

In the Old Testament, God commanded His people to be separate from the nations around them. One way this was displayed was in what they did and didn't eat — what was "clean" and "unclean". By New Testament times, this extended to seeing non-Jewish people as "unclean" too. In Peter's vision, God was saying those boundaries no longer existed.

TALK IT OVER

We may not go so far as to call non-Christians "unclean", but do we still have distinctions and prejudices in our heads. Do we really believe that the gospel is for all people? The Muslim, the Sikh, the Hindu? The atheist? The rapist, the paedophile or the murderer?

PRAY ABOUT IT

Pray about all the people you come into contact with. Are there any you probably wouldn't share the gospel with? Ask for God's forgiveness now and ask Him to give you a love for them and opportunities to share Jesus with them.

THE BOTTOM LINE

God breaks down boundaries.

200 | No favourites

Things are defrosting between Peter and the Gentiles. He's invited them to be his guests (he's already staying with a tanner who deals with unclean animal skins) so things are thawing nicely. What will happen next?

Read Acts 10 v 23–35

ENGAGE YOUR BRAIN

▶ *How eager was Cornelius to hear from Peter? (See his preparations in verse 24.)*

PRAY ABOUT IT

It's great when people are so eager to hear about Jesus that they invite their friends along to hear too! Pray for any outreach events your church or youth group might be planning — that people would be eager to come along and listen, and that they'd bring their friends too.

▶ *What mistake does Cornelius make at first? (v25)*

▶ *How has God been at work behind the scenes of this historic meeting? (See v28, v31, v33)*

▶ *Has Peter understood what God is doing now? (v28)*

▶ *How do his actions show that?*

▶ *In what way does God not show favouritism? (v34–35)*

Despite all of Cornelius' prayers and gifts to the poor, he still needs Jesus. It's not until he hears the gospel message that Peter is about to share with him that he receives the Holy Spirit and becomes part of God's family.

SHARE IT

Often we find that some non-Christians are nicer, kinder and seem more "Christian" than we are. But it's not being good that saves you — it's being *forgiven*. Can you share that surprising truth with someone today?

THE BOTTOM LINE

God doesn't show favouritism.

201 Crunch time

After all this build up, we finally hear the message. How will Cornelius and co react? After all God has done so far, it's going to be pretty important...

👁 **Read Acts 10 v 34–48**

ENGAGE YOUR BRAIN

▷ *How does Peter explain the good news about Jesus to Cornelius (v34–43)? Jot down his key points:*

•

•

•

•

•

•

SHARE IT

Could you use Peter's summary to help you explain the gospel? Practise it in your own words and pray for an opportunity to share it this week.

▷ *How do Cornelius and his family and friends respond?*

▷ *How amazing is this turn of events? (See Peter's companions' reaction in verse 45.)*

PRAY ABOUT IT

Thank God for saving Cornelius' family and friends, and pray that He might show the same grace and mercy to people you know. Pray for them by name. Remember Jesus is Lord of all, He is Judge of all, and everyone who believes in Him receives forgiveness of sins.

THE BOTTOM LINE

Jesus is Lord of all.

202 | Suspicious minds

After the exciting events of chapter 10 you might have expected the church in Jerusalem to be buzzing. Hmmm, not quite.

👁 Read Acts 11 v 1–18

ENGAGE YOUR BRAIN

▶ *What is the issue the circumcised believers have? (v2–3)*

▶ *Is their criticism fair?*

▶ *How does Peter defend himself/ God? (v5, v9, v12, v13, v15, v17)*

▶ *What is his key point? (v17)*

▶ *How do the circumcised believers then respond? (v18)*

God doesn't necessarily always do things the way we expect or want. Initially, the Jews were privileged to be God's chosen people. But now God is including all people in His offer of "repentance that leads to life" (v18). Of course this is nothing new, but maybe these Jews had forgotten Genesis 12 v 3.

PRAY ABOUT IT

Thank God that from the beginning He planned that all peoples on earth would be blessed through Abraham and his descendant Jesus. Pray for countries where there is no strong Christian presence — that the good news about Jesus would reach people there.

SHARE IT

Do you sometimes forget that saving people is God's work? He will do all He has said He'll do and He can save anyone. We don't have to have all the answers, but amazingly God does use us to get His message out. Ask Him now to help you talk about Jesus to someone this week and ask Him to be at work in them.

203 | Ready steady grow

If you've got a new plant, how do you encourage it to grow? What would you do for it? And what about a new church? How would you encourage that to grow?

👁 Read Acts 11 v 19–30

ENGAGE YOUR BRAIN

▶ *What's the unexpected effect of persecuting the early church? (v19–21)*

▶ *Who gets to hear the message? (v19–20)*

▶ *Is this part of God's plan? (v21)*

Despite the lesson they'd learned from Peter's encounter with Cornelius, the church in Jerusalem is still wary of these Gentile Christians, so they send Barnabas to check out what's going on. Barnabas' name means "son of encouragement".

▶ *What's Barnabas' reaction? (v23)*

PRAY ABOUT IT

See how Barnabas is described in verse 24. Wouldn't you love to be described that way? Pray that God would help you to see the good in situations rather than always being critical. Pray that God would help you to love and encourage other believers.

▶ *What does Barnabas do to help the church at Antioch grow? (v25–26)*

▶ *What happened between the Jewish believers and Gentile Christians? (v27–30)*

This breaking down of boundaries wasn't just a one-way thing. Bitter enemies become brothers. We've seen it with Saul and now between Jews and Gentiles.

GET ON WITH IT

What can you do to love and encourage other Christians today? A word, an email, a text? Turning up to a Christian meeting to encourage others? Will you love the whole family of believers, not just the ones you'd naturally get on with?

THE BOTTOM LINE

Faith brings with it a family.

204 | Peter, prayer and persecution

After the gospel explosion of chapter 11, was everything now nice and cosy, sweet and rosy? Nope. Persecution of Christians became very popular. Only this time you'd pay for being a Christian with your life.

👁 Read Acts 12 v 1–19

ENGAGE YOUR BRAIN

▷ *What does Herod do and why? (v1–3)*

▷ *What does he try to do next? (v4)*

▷ *How does the church respond? (v5, v12)*

You might remember that Jesus had warned James and his brother John they would "drink the same cup" that Jesus did, and sure enough James goes on to face execution like his master. Remember too what Jesus told Peter about his future? (See John 21 v 18–19 for a reminder.)

TALK IT OVER

Jesus told His followers that if they wanted to be His disciples, they should take up their cross and follow Him. For most of us, being a Christian won't mean dying for our faith. But for lots of people today it does, and one day it might for you.

Have you faced that truth? Chat and pray it over with another Christian.

▷ *What does Peter initially think is going on when the angel shows up? (v9)*

▷ *What does he eventually realise God has done? (v11)*

Things look pretty hopeless in verse 1 — a godless king threatening God's people. But God is the true King, as His rescue of Peter demonstrates. More on this in the next study.

▷ *Despite all their prayers, how do the believers respond to Peter's appearance? (v14–16)*

▷ *How does Herod react? (v19)*

PRAY ABOUT IT

Prayer changes things. God can and will act. Will you let that affect how you pray now?

205 | Herod humbled

King Herod is still throwing his weight around in these next few verses. But he's forgotten who the real King is...

👁 Read Acts 12 v 19–24

ENGAGE YOUR BRAIN

▷ How important do you think Herod felt on his diplomatic visit? (v19–21)

▷ List the things that might have made him feel this way.

▷ How do the people flatter him? (v22)

▷ How does God respond to this nonsense? (v23)

▷ What is the stark contrast in v23–24?

▷ What did Herod set out to do in the early verses of chapter 12?

▷ Did he succeed?

GET ON WITH IT

Are you ever tempted to think too highly of yourself? Read what the apostle Paul said of himself in 1 Timothy 1 v 12–16.

As Christians we can relate to his words if we've ever thought honestly about our own sin. Do you need to correct the way you think about yourself today?

PRAY ABOUT IT

Thank God that His plans for the gospel message to spread are unstoppable. Pray for that message to spread in your school, college, workplace, community, town, country and world!

THE BOTTOM LINE

God is the King!

206 Genesis – Dreams and drama

You might be familiar with Joseph and his exploits thanks to a certain musical, but these chapters in Genesis aren't about shiny song-and-dance numbers. They're about how God keeps His promises to Jacob's descendants.

👁 Read Genesis 37 v 1–11

ENGAGE YOUR BRAIN

- ▶ *What made Joseph's brothers angry? (v1–4)*

- ▶ *What do Joseph's dreams tell us about him and his brothers?*

- ▶ *How would you describe the feelings of the brothers towards Joseph? (v4, v8, v11)*

Jealousy is an emotion we've all experienced at one time or another. Perhaps it's provoked by blatant favouritism, like that shown by Jacob. Or maybe it's our own pride that hates other people having more than us or doing better than us. Whatever the reason, it's a dangerous thing. The book of James tells us that jealousy leads to arguments, conflict and even murder (James 4 v 2).

There is no direct mention of God in ch 37 of Genesis, but there's a hint of His involvement in Joseph's dreams.

- ▶ *What is Jacob's reaction to these dreams?*

Verse 11 tells us that Jacob kept these things in mind. Remember that Jacob himself had experienced a strange dream, and perhaps he thought that God might be behind Joseph's dreams too.

PRAY ABOUT IT

Talk to God about any jealousy you have. Pray that God would teach you to be humble and peace-loving without a trace of favouritism or hypocrisy (James 3 v 17).

THE BOTTOM LINE

Jealousy is dangerous.

207 Brothers and cisterns

Things don't get any better between Joseph and his brothers, and that's an understatement. But in the middle of all the scheming and cover-ups, God is at work behind the scenes.

👁 Read Genesis 37 v 12–28

ENGAGE YOUR BRAIN

🅳 *What do the brothers do when they see Joseph? (v18)*

🅳 *How does Reuben (the eldest) prevent his brothers from killing Joseph? (v22)*

Sadly, Reuben's plan to come back and rescue Joseph later doesn't work, as Judah has a bright idea…

🅳 *What is Judah's scheme? (v26-28)*

PRAY ABOUT IT

Can you think of another occasion when someone is sold for a few pieces of silver (Matthew 26 v 14–16)? Jesus' death on the cross is the ultimate example of God bringing good out of something evil, just as He will with Joseph. Thank Him now for being at work behind the scenes in everything.

👁 Read verses 29–36

🅳 *How does Reuben respond when he returns?*

🅳 *What is Jacob's reaction when the brothers tell him their story?*

Poor Jacob. He'd lost the child he loved the most, son of the dead wife he loved the most. And despite his favouritism, you have to feel sorry for him. Maybe his other children felt a bit guilty — verse 35 shows they tried in vain to cheer him up.

🅳 *Where does Joseph end up? (v36)*

More of that later…

THE BOTTOM LINE

God is at work behind the scenes in everything.

208 Private lies

Time out: we'll take a bizarre and not too flattering excursion into Judah's private life. We'll find out what happened to Joseph tomorrow, but meanwhile, there's some nasty business back home.

👁 Read Genesis 38 v 1–10

ENGAGE YOUR BRAIN

Judah marries the daughter of Shua while staying with his mate Hirah.

▶ *List his three children:*

▶ *What happens to the first two? (v7, v10)*

▶ *Why?*

If a married man died childless, then it was his relatives' duty to provide his widow with children to inherit the dead man's property. Onan is trying to duck out of this important responsibility, which is why what he does is so bad.

👁 Read verses 11–30

▶ *How had Judah failed in his duty to Tamar? (v14)*

Things now get really messy, as Tamar tricks Judah, Judah sleeps with his daughter-in-law, and then… she gets pregnant! Judah, as head of the family, has to punish Tamar for sleeping around (v24) but she pulls the rug out from under him when she reveals the identity of the man who got her into trouble (v25)!

▶ *What does Judah recognise? (v26)*

▶ *What are Tamar's twins called?*

Perez was an ancestor of Jesus (see Matthew 1 v 1–16). Despite the sin in this family, God still used them in His perfect plans.

PRAY ABOUT IT

We frequently make a mess of things but God's plans can't be stopped. If you're a Christian, God has promised to make you more like Jesus. Despite your mistakes and sins. Thank Him for that now and ask Him to help you live up to that promise.

209 Poti' training

Back to Joseph, who's facing more than his fair share of ups and downs. Just when things are starting to look up, something else bad happens — but crucially God is with him through it all.

👁 Read Genesis 39 v 1–12

ENGAGE YOUR BRAIN

▶ *Sold into slavery, but what is the big encouragement for Joseph? (v2)*

▶ *But what temptation does Joseph face? (v7)*

▶ *How does he respond? (v8-9)*

▶ *What extra steps does Joseph take to avoid temptation? (v10 and v12)?*

👁 Read verses 13–23

Poor Joseph gets thrown in jail, but it's not the worst one available (v20) and even better, God is still with him (v21–23).

▶ *How does God bless Joseph even in prison?*

GET ON WITH IT

▶ *How do you respond to temptation?*

▶ *What can you learn from Joseph?*

Think about times when you're tempted to sin — at home, at school, out with friends. How can you run from temptation? Perhaps take a Christian friend to a party to keep an eye on you. Or don't even use your phone or computer if you know you'll end up sinning.

PRAY ABOUT IT

Talk to God about what you need to do to avoid regular temptations. Ask Him to help you do it.

THE BOTTOM LINE

Run from temptation and stick close to God.

210 Sweet dreams

Joseph is behind bars, but it's not as bad as it could have been. God is with him and has given him success in everything he does. So much so that he's in charge of part of the prison, which is when two new inmates arrive...

Read Genesis 40 v 1–23

ENGAGE YOUR BRAIN

- Why are the baker and cupbearer so distressed in verses 6–8?

- Describe Joseph's attitude towards God. (v8)

- How does Joseph feel about his current situation? (v14-15)

Joseph knows he's been treated unfairly, yet he still recognises that God is in charge.

TALK IT THROUGH

Do you expect life to be easy or difficult for Christians? Talk over this issue with a Christian friend, looking at Mark 8 v 34–35.

- What's the interpretation of the two dreams?

Cupbearer's dream:

Baker's dream:

- How accurate are these interpretations? (v20-22)

- What happens to Joseph? (v23)

No quick fix for Joseph. He has to wait another two years before getting out of jail, but God is still with him.

THE BOTTOM LINE

God is with us even when life's hard.

211 | Dream job

More dreams, this time from Pharaoh. Had he been eating a lot of cheese before bedtime? Or was something more significant going on? Step forward, Joseph.

👁 Read Genesis 41 v 1–32

ENGAGE YOUR BRAIN

▶ Bizarre dreams. What's the effect on Pharaoh? (v8)

▶ Can the Egyptian magicians and wise men help?

▶ Sum up Joseph's attitude towards Pharaoh and towards God in verses 14–16.

▶ Who is in charge? (v32)

So God gives Joseph the meaning — seven years of plenty to be followed by seven years of famine. And Joseph goes on to give Pharaoh some good advice on what to do next (v33–36).

👁 Read verses 33–57

▶ What does Pharaoh recognise about Joseph? (v38-39)

▶ What rewards does Pharaoh give Joseph?

▶ Who are all these things really from according to Joseph? (v50–52)

In naming his children, Joseph shows that he still knows that God is the one responsible for his present prosperity, just as it was God who helped him through tough times. But more than that, God has put Joseph in this important position in Egypt to rescue His people.

SHARE IT

When things go well for you, do you give the glory to God or keep it for yourself? When things are grim, do you moan or do you still trust God? Whatever your circumstances today, take a leaf out of Joseph's book and think about how you can let people know who's in charge of your life.

THE BOTTOM LINE

God is in charge of the good times and the bad.

212 | Spies in the family

Funny how things turn out, isn't it? Joseph's brothers probably feel as if things couldn't get any worse by the end of this chapter, but actually it's all part of God's rescue plan for Jacob and family.

👁 Read Genesis 42 v 1–7

ENGAGE YOUR BRAIN

▶ Can you spot how Joseph's first dream (37 v 6-7) comes true in verse 6?

▶ Why do you think Joseph acts the way he does in verse 7?

Maybe Joseph is worried his brothers still hate him and will want to kill him, but more importantly he wants to find out what has happened to his father and younger brother.

👁 Read verses 8–24

▶ What does Joseph want the ten brothers to do? (v15)

▶ After 13 years, how do the brothers feel about what they did to Joseph? (v21-22)

So Simeon (the second eldest) is left behind as a hostage. Perhaps Joseph felt more kindly towards Reuben, who had at least wanted to save his life. In fact, Reuben comes out of this quite well.

👁 Read verses 25–38

▶ How do they react to Joseph's generosity? (v28)

▶ How does Jacob react to what has happened in Egypt?

"Everything is against me!" wails Jacob (v36). Well, it might seem like that, but we know differently. God was working to save His people from famine and bring about a wonderful family reunion.

PRAY ABOUT IT

How often to you moan that things are against you? Remember that, if you're a Christian, God is for you even when life is hard. Remind yourself of Romans 8 v 28 — "In all things God works for the good of those who love him". Thank Him for that now.

213 | Testing time

The famine's getting worse but Jacob doesn't want Benjamin to have to go to Egypt with his brothers. Eventually he has to give in, as they face severe hunger. But what does Joseph have in store for them this time?

👁 Read Genesis 43 v 1–16

ENGAGE YOUR BRAIN

▶ *How has Judah changed in the last 13 years? (v9)*

▶ *What two things does Jacob recognise about God as he says farewell to his sons? (v14)*

👁 Read verses 17–34

Joseph's brothers received a surprise welcome back in Egypt — a feast. Then we hear a surprising comment from Joseph's foreign servant, followed by yet another surprise at dinner.

▶ *How do the brothers react to the invitation? (v18)*

▶ *How did the brothers react to the seating plan? (v33)*

Despite their confusion, it's beginning to become clear that Joseph's brothers have changed for the better. They all feel guilty about what they did to Joseph, Judah shows genuine care for Benjamin and they no longer seem to have such a problem with jealousy. But Joseph still has a final test to set, as we'll see tomorrow.

PRAY ABOUT IT

Considering how upset he is, Jacob's comments in verse 14 are amazing. He asks God for mercy but recognises that it is ultimately God's decision what to do. Ask God that you would have the kind of faith that trusts in Him, whatever the outcome.

THE BOTTOM LINE

God can be completely trusted.

214 One for all...

We've spent a lot of time looking at how God has acted powerfully in Joseph's life. But the really good news is that He's also been at work in the lives of Joseph's jealous, scheming, sinful brothers.

👁 Read Genesis 44 v 1–34

ENGAGE YOUR BRAIN

One last test from Joseph — he frames his younger brother, Benjamin, for stealing his silver cup and then waits to see the reaction.

▶ *What do the brothers promise when first accused? (v9)*

▶ *How do Joseph and his servant alter that? (v10, v17)*

▶ *How do they all respond to the cup being found? (v13-16)*

▶ *Which brother pleads with Joseph directly? Remember him?*

▶ *What does he offer to do? (v33)*

A big change here. This time round, Judah and the others are passionately concerned about the fate of their youngest brother and the effect it will have on their father. Not like last time when they were eager to murder Joseph and didn't think twice about how Jacob might feel. More than that, Judah is ready to offer himself as a substitute for Benjamin, to become a slave instead of him.

Judah's great-great-great ... lots of greats... grandson also offered himself in the place of the guilty. *Jesus* willingly took our place on the cross so that we could escape God's anger at our sin, even though He didn't do anything wrong Himself.

PRAY ABOUT IT

Thank God for His undeserved kindness to you in Christ. Thank Him too that He changes us, and makes us more Christ-like by His Spirit, even though we do nothing to deserve that.

THE BOTTOM LINE

God is unbelievably kind even though we don't deserve it.

215 | The big reveal

The moment we've all been waiting for has arrived — Joseph drops his disguise and tells his brothers who he really is. They're flabbergasted and so is Jacob. Let's see what happens...

👁 Read Genesis 45 v 1–15

ENGAGE YOUR BRAIN

▶ Why might Joseph's brothers be so terrified? (v3)

▶ Amazingly, Joseph is not angry with them — he had every reason to be! Instead, what is he like?

▶ How does Joseph describe all that's happened? (v5–8)

Take a minute to take in verses 5, 7 and 8. Obviously God didn't approve of what the brothers had done to Joseph, but incredibly, He turned their evil plot into rescue for all of His people.

👁 Read verses 16–28

▶ What offer does Pharaoh make? (v17-18)

▶ How does Jacob react when he first hears the news? (v26)

▶ How about by the end of the chapter?

From a fractured family facing starvation to a reunited family enjoying all the comforts of Egypt, God continues to bless Abraham's descendants. He had even told Abraham his descendants would end up in Egypt before they inherited the land they'd been promised (Genesis 15 v 13–16). God kept His word.

PRAY ABOUT IT

It might not seem as if God is in control sometimes, but He always is. Pray that God would teach you that truth today, and pray for anyone you know who is suffering — that they would know that God is with them.

THE BOTTOM LINE

God is always in control.

216 | Life's a journey

At long last, Jacob is reunited with his favourite son, and God's long-ago words to Abraham come true as His people head into Egypt. Get ready for some strange encounters.

👁 Read Genesis 46 v 1–7

ENGAGE YOUR BRAIN

ⓘ *How does God introduce Himself to Jacob?*

ⓘ *How does God encourage Jacob?*

ⓘ *What promises does He make?*

A huge number of Jacob's children and grandchildren make the journey into Egypt (the 70 doesn't include all the wives). God's promise of making Abraham's descendants into a great nation is coming true. And on a more personal note we see the joy as Jacob and Joseph are reunited.

👁 Read 46 v 26 – 47 v 6

ⓘ *What is Joseph's plan for his family? (v34)*

ⓘ *How does it work out? (47 v 1-6)*

So far, so good. Next up, Jacob meets Pharaoh. Considering how powerful Pharaoh is, their encounter is a bit of a strange one.

👁 Read Genesis 47 v 7–12

ⓘ *Who blesses who (v7) — would you expect this?*

ⓘ *What does that show?*

ⓘ *Why do you think Jacob talks about his life as a pilgrimage (a journey with God)?*

Pharaoh respects Jacob because of his great age (130). Yet Jacob says his years have been "few" (compared to his ancestors) and "difficult". It's been a long and hard journey through life — but God has been with Him the whole way.

PRAY ABOUT IT

Think back about your own journey with God. What have been the high points and the low points? Thank God for being with you through it all.

THE BOTTOM LINE

Life is a journey with God.

217 No food = no fun

As the seven years of famine continue, things get tougher and tougher in Egypt. But God's people are kept safe. We also hear some of Jacob's final words as he faces death at the grand old age of 147.

👁 Read Genesis 47 v 13–31

ENGAGE YOUR BRAIN

▷ What do the people of Egypt do to survive? (v16, v19, v24)

Sowing and reaping still happened during the famine, but the harvests were much smaller. Joseph shows real wisdom here and everyone seems happy with the deal.

▷ In contrast, how do the Israelites (Jacob's family) get on in Goshen? (v27)

▷ Can you see how God's promises to his people are being fulfilled?

Next, we get a death-bed scene, with Joseph making a solemn vow to his dying father — the whole thigh thing was a way of making a serious promise (see also 24 v 2).

▷ Why do you think Jacob wants to be buried in Canaan?

▷ What message would this have sent to his younger grandchildren, who might have been settling down happily in Egypt?

SHARE IT

▷ Do your friends think this world is all there is?

▷ Do they believe in an afterlife? If so, why/why not?

▷ Can you share your hope for the future with them this week?

THINK IT THROUGH

Are you at home in this world? Do you feel nice and comfortable? Or are you longing for Jesus to come back so that you can be with Him for ever? Think about your priorities — what you spend time doing, or spend your money on. Do they need to change?

THE BOTTOM LINE

Where's your home?

218 Always there

Jacob's reaching the end of his life. But he's not down about it. In fact, he's remembering how great God has been to him throughout his long long life.

👁 **Read Genesis 48 v 1–11**

ENGAGE YOUR BRAIN

▶ *What does Jacob (AKA "Israel") remind Joseph about God and about the future? (v3-4)*

Jacob then blesses Joseph's two sons, counting them as his own children in terms of their inheritance (v5) and his affection for them (v10).

👁 **Read verses 12–22**

▶ *What is unusual about the order in which Jacob blesses Joseph's sons? (v14)*

▶ *Have you seen this pattern anywhere else in Genesis? (Look back at Day 166 on page 181.)*

▶ *How does Jacob describe God? (v15)*

▶ *Can you remember the ways God has rescued Jacob?*

Shepherds didn't just cuddle their baby lambs; they led them, fed them, kept them from wandering off (with a thwack of their stick if necessary!) and protected them. Check out Psalm 23 for a wonderful picture of God as our Shepherd.

▶ *How does Jacob reassure Joseph? (v21)*

PRAY ABOUT IT

Just as God was with His people in the Old Testament, Jesus promises to be with His followers "always, to the very end of the age" (Matthew 28 v 20). Think about that for a minute and thank Him for that promise.

THE BOTTOM LINE

God will always be with His people.

219 Roar data

What will Jacob's final words to his twelve sons be? These lads' families would become the twelve tribes of Israel, (which the rest of the Old Testament tells us about), so the blessings/curses are for their descendants too.

👁 Read Genesis 49 v 1–12

ENGAGE YOUR BRAIN

▶ *Jot down what Jacob says about each of his first four sons...*

Reuben:

Simeon & Levi:

Judah:

▶ *Why did Reuben lose his status as eldest son? (see 35 v 22)*

▶ *What have Simeon & Levi got to look forward to? Remember chapter 34?*

Judah is described as a lion — the king over all the rest, and there's an amazing promise in there too.

▶ *Take a close look at verse 10 — any idea who this ruler might be who is a descendant of Judah?*

This king from Judah's family will rule all the nations one day. His family will be wealthy and successful (v11).

PRAY ABOUT IT

Philippians 2 v 5–11 tells us that one day every knee will bow before Jesus, God's King. Pray for the people you know who aren't Christians. Pray that they would come to bow to God — knowing and loving Jesus as their King, rather than being forced to do so when it's too late.

THE BOTTOM LINE

Jesus is God's promised King.

220 Son shine

What's in store for Jacob's eight other sons? A bit of a mixed bag, really. The message may be different for each son, but there's one thing that stays the same...

◉ Read Genesis 49 v 13–28

ENGAGE YOUR BRAIN

▶ *Jot down what Jacob says about the rest of his sons...*

Zebulun:

Issachar:

Dan:

Gad:

Asher:

Naphtali:

Benjamin:

Yes, I know, I've missed out Joseph.

◉ Re-read verses 22–26

▶ *Which four titles does Jacob call God? (v24–25)*

▶ *What do these names tell us?*

▶ *What has God done for Joseph so far?*

▶ *What will He do for him in the future?*

God is the same now as He was then. He has blessed us in the *past* — sent Jesus to die for us, forgiven us, brought us into relationship with Him. He is with us *now* — helping and guiding us by His Spirit, and in the *future* He will bring us to be with Him for ever in His perfect kingdom.

PRAY ABOUT IT

Thank God for what He's like, for all He has done for you in the past and for His promises to you for the future.

221 Good mourning

Jacob's time is up, but he has some very specific funeral arrangements. He's not wanting an antique wooden coffin or a hearse drawn by horses with black plumes on their heads. He's more concerned about *where* he's buried.

👁 Read Genesis 49 v 29–33

ENGAGE YOUR BRAIN

▶ *Where does Jacob want to be buried? (v29–30)*

▶ *How is Jacob's death described (v33)?*

Jacob wanted to be buried in Canaan — the land God promised to give his descendants. Jacob's death is described as being "gathered to his people".

SHARE IT

Celebrities are sometimes asked, "Where do you go when you die?" A lot of them answer, "A hole in the ground" or have some vague ideas about reincarnation. Find out what some famous people think about death and discuss their opinions with your non-Christian friends.

Do your friends agree/disagree? Why? How can you explain your view of death and what happens next?

👁 Read Genesis 50 v 1–14

Now we see national mourning and a huge funeral procession, as Joseph and his brothers set off to fulfil Jacob's dying request. Yet Joseph returned to Egypt instead of staying in the promised land.

▶ *What does that show us about his trust in God?*

Joseph knew that God would fulfil His promises in His own good time. If the events of Joseph's life had taught him anything, it was that God has everything under His control.

PRAY ABOUT IT

Talk to God now about things you're impatient about — maybe particular prayers that you long to see answered. Ask Him to help you trust that He will act when the time is right.

222 Looking forward

Joseph and his brothers have been reunited in the most amazing way. They are a family again. But now that their father Jacob has died, do they really trust the brother they sold into slavery?

👁 Read Genesis 50 v 15–21

ENGAGE YOUR BRAIN

▶ *Why did Joseph's brothers make up a story? (v15)*

▶ *What had they failed to understand? (v19-20)*

▶ *How do verses 19–20 sum up the events of Genesis 37–50?*

PRAY ABOUT IT

Verse 20 also sums up Jesus' death on the cross. All the plotting of the religious leaders and the betrayal by Judas couldn't mess up God's plan to bring something wonderful out of a horrible situation. Thank Him now for bringing forgiveness and eternal life out of Jesus' suffering.

👁 Read verses 22–26

▶ *What does Joseph focus on as he dies? (v24–25)*

Jacob looked forward to the life to come. Joseph looked forward to his descendants living in the land God had promised. (The book of Exodus tells us how God made it happen for the Israelites.)

We've seen God's promises come true with Jesus, but we still have something to look forward to.

GET ON WITH IT

What are you looking forward to? The weekend? A party? End of exams? University? New job? How about seeing Jesus face-to-face? Spend some time thinking about how incredible that will be — use the eye-opening chapters 21 and 22 of Revelation to help you focus.

THE BOTTOM LINE

Christians can look forward to being with Jesus for ever.

LUKE

The big finale

During this issue of *Engage 365*, we've been weaving our way slowly through the Gospel of Luke. Now it's time for the big finale...

THE STORY SO FAR

Luke 1 to 9 showed us Jesus demonstrating in a whole load of dramatic ways exactly who He is. The miracles pointed us to His identity — He's the Christ. He's the one and only Son of God. And He's the Saviour of the world. And Jesus showed what response was needed: complete trust in Him and His promises.

A YEAR WITH JESUS

Luke 9 to 18 switched from action to teaching. Jesus' disciples were slow to understand who He really was, so Jesus had plenty to teach them. Those ten chapters cover about a year as Jesus heads for Jerusalem.

One thing He taught clearly was that He had to die to save His people.

THE FINAL CHAPTER

Which brings us neatly to Luke 19–24. These six chapters cover the last week before Jesus' death. And some time after. In them we see both God's plan at work and the plan to have Jesus killed. We see God in charge of events and Jesus prepared to endure them, no matter how painful. And good old Luke explains the meaning behind it all.

In writing this book, Luke set out to help His friend Theophilus become more sure of his faith. The closing chapters do the same for us, too.

246 | Luke 19 v 1–10

223 Cancelling debt

Zacchaeus. Short guy. Tax collector. You probably know the story. But don't snooze and miss out on the good stuff. Especially the punchline at the end.

👁 Read Luke 19 v 1–10

ENGAGE YOUR BRAIN

▷ *What did people say about Jesus visiting Zacchaeus? (v7)*

▷ *What surprising thing did Zacchaeus do? (v8)*

▷ *What did Jesus say had happened? (v9)*

▷ *What did Jesus mean by calling Zacchaeus "a son of Abraham"?*

Jews hated tax collectors because they worked for their Roman rulers and cheated people out of cash. Jesus didn't hate Zacchaeus. In fact, He'll welcome anyone who turns to Him.

Zacchaeus showed that he had repented of his sinful ways by paying people back far more than he'd stolen. People who have accepted Jesus show it in the way they live. Their lives are transformed — they're living for God now, not themselves.

Zacchaeus had become one of God's people ("a son of Abraham"). Not by giving his money away, but because he trusted in Jesus.

▷ *What was Jesus' mission? (v10)*

Verse 10 is the punchline of the story. It's one of the greatest verses in the Bible. Despite all our sin, Jesus came looking for us! It doesn't matter what a person's background is or how hated they are — Jesus came for all.

GET ON WITH IT

▷ *If you're not a Christian, what will you do about it?*

▷ *If you are a Christian, how does your life need to show it?*

PRAY ABOUT IT

Ask God to help you share this amazing message with friends who are "lost".

224 | Return of the king

Are you sitting comfortably? It's story time. Well, you won't be sitting comfortably for long because the story Jesus tells isn't an easy one to listen to.

👁 Read Luke 19 v 11–19

ENGAGE YOUR BRAIN

▶ Why did Jesus tell the story?

▶ So what's it about?

▶ How did some people feel about the king? (v14)

▶ How did he treat those who used the money wisely?

The story's about Jesus. Soon after He told the story He would go away (to heaven). One day He will return as King. He'll want to know what we've done with what He's given us (His message, our abilities). He'll reward those who've lived His way and brought others to know Him.

👁 Read verses 20–27

▶ What had this guy done with the money?

▶ What should he have done?

▶ What happened to the king's enemies? (v27)

When Jesus returns, He will find servants and enemies — people who have lived His way, and people who couldn't care less about Him. The outcome for both groups is clear.

GET ON WITH IT

What we do as we wait for Jesus to return really matters.

▶ Are you using what God has given you to serve Him?

▶ How can you better use the abilities God's given you?

▶ How can you warn people who don't know Jesus as their King?

PRAY ABOUT IT

Loads to pray about today.

The King will return. Will He be happy with what you've done for Him?

225 Royal arrival

Luke tells us about a royal visit. But there's no limo, only a donkey. No red carpet, just cloaks and dust. What sort of king is this? Let's follow the procession.

👁 Read Luke 19 v 28–40

ENGAGE YOUR BRAIN

▶ What weird things happened? (v28–36)

▶ What did the people sing? (v38)

Old Testament prophet Zechariah said the one riding into Jerusalem on a donkey would be God's chosen King and Saviour of the world.

People treated Jesus as a king. The Pharisees hated this (v39), but Jesus said that the message that He was King had to be announced — there was no stopping it (v40). God appointed Jesus as King over everything. And everyone must hear about it.

👁 Read verses 41–44

▶ Why was Jesus in tears? (v41–42)

▶ What had the Jewish people failed to understand? (v42, v44)

Jesus predicted the future destruction of Jerusalem. It happened 40 years later when the Romans trashed the whole city.

THINK IT THROUGH

▶ What kind of king is Jesus?

▶ Do you treat Him as King, with authority over your life?

PRAY ABOUT IT

If you can, ask His help to live serving Him, not yourself. If you're not sure whether Jesus is worthy of being your King, read back through Luke's Gospel before you make a decision. Ask God to show you clearly who Jesus is as we read about His death and resurrection.

THE BOTTOM LINE

Jesus is King.

226 Trick question

"Why is the sky blue?" What's the trickiest question you've been asked recently? In today's Bible bit, Jesus faces a crafty question. But first, temple trouble…

◉ Read Luke 19 v 45–48

ENGAGE YOUR BRAIN

▶ *Why did Jesus get angry? (v46)*

▶ *What effect did it have? (v47)*

The temple, built by King Solomon and now being restored by King Herod, was more than a big mansion. It symbolised the place where God met with His people. Yet many people were mistreating God's house. The temple authorities robbed people of their money and, as a result, robbed God of the love of the people. Jesus rightly showed His authority in God's place, the temple. This gave the Jewish leaders murderous motives.

◉ Read Luke 20 v 1–8

▶ *What were the Jewish leaders trying to get Jesus to say? (v2)*

▶ *What was genius about Jesus' reply? (v3–6)*

The religious bigwigs must have been pleased with their question. If Jesus answered "I'm doing this by God's authority" they would probably have killed Him. And if He'd said "No one has given me authority to do it" He would have been proven to be a liar. So Jesus asked them a tricky question instead. Clever, eh?

The plotters fell into their own trap. If they said John the Baptist's work was from God, they'd be admitting Jesus came from God too. But if they said John hadn't been doing God's work, then they feared the people would turn against them.

PRAY ABOUT IT

These guys didn't realise who Jesus really was. Be honest — who do *you* think Jesus is? Will you thank Him for who He is and what He's done?

227 | Another vine mess

Time for a parable — a simple story that has a BIG meaning. See if you can work out what this violent vineyard vignette is all about.

👁 Read Luke 20 v 9–16

The vineyard was an Old Testament picture of God's people, the Israelites. The owner is God. The servants are God's prophets. The tenants are the Jewish leaders. The son is Jesus. And the story's a speedy history of Israel: verses 10–12 are the *past*, verses 13–15 are the *present*, and verses 15b–16 are the *future*.

ENGAGE YOUR BRAIN

▶ *How had the Jews treated God's messengers in the past?*

▶ *How were they treating Jesus and what would they do to Him?*

▶ *What would happen to them in the future?*

👁 Read verses 17–19

▶ *The stone is Jesus. What does verse 17 tell us about Him?*

▶ *What about those who reject Him? (v18)*

God punished the Jews for rejecting Jesus, and turned to those who would accept Him. In the future, God will punish and destroy those who reject Jesus.

PRAY ABOUT IT

Thank God for sending His own Son Jesus into the world even though He knew He would be murdered. Ask God to help you believe the truth about Jesus and not reject Him. Pick five other people to pray this for too.

THE BOTTOM LINE

Those who reject Jesus will be destroyed. Sad but true.

228 Taxing questions

The Jewish leaders are after Jesus' blood. But every time they hit Him with a trick question, Jesus smashes it back in their faces. Watch and learn.

Read Luke 20 v 20–26

ENGAGE YOUR BRAIN

▶ *What were the spies trying to do? (v20)*

▶ *What two things does Jesus' brilliant answer teach? (v25)*

The Jews didn't like paying taxes to the oppressive Romans who ruled them. A "yes" answer from Jesus would have been very unpopular. But a "no" answer would have sounded like law-breaking rebellion against the Romans. Jesus' answer was perfect.

Jesus says we should stick to the law and pay taxes. More importantly, He tells us to give God what we owe Him. The coin had Caesar's image on it. Genesis tells us we're made in God's image, so we belong to Him.

THINK IT THROUGH

Make a list of what you owe God.

Read verses 27–40

▶ *What were the Sadducees trying to prove?*

▶ *What was Jesus' shock answer? (v35–36)*

▶ *How did He prove the Sadducees wrong? (v37–38)*

The Sadducees only believed that the first five books of the Bible (written by Moses) were true. And they didn't believe in life after death. Jesus cleverly used Moses to show they were wrong. There is life after death. Just like Abraham, Isaac and Jacob, all believers will go to live with God. We'll have brand new bodies and there won't be marriage. There will be something better! Life with Jesus — for ever.

PRAY ABOUT IT

Anything you need to say to God today?

Teaching the teachers

These days, Jesus is often portrayed as being a bit of a hippy wimp. Ridiculous. He said and did things that shocked and offended religious leaders. Jesus didn't pull His punches at all.

The Jewish people were waiting for the Christ to come and rescue them. Jesus claimed to be the Christ. The Jewish Old Testament experts knew the Christ would come from King David's family. So they didn't believe he would be God too.

👁 Read Luke 20 v 41–44

Jesus quotes Psalm 110. By calling the Christ "my Lord", David is saying that the Christ (Jesus) is also God. But the Jewish leaders refused to put these two facts together.

👁 Read verses 45–47

ENGAGE YOUR BRAIN

- ▶ Did Jesus criticise the Jewish teachers behind their backs? (v45)

- ▶ How would you describe their attitude? (v46–47)

- ▶ Why would they be punished so severely?

These men had a privileged position — teaching other people about God's word. But they abused their power by cheating helpless people and seeking attention and praise. They would be strongly punished by God. Instead of bringing people closer to God, they were leading them away from Him.

PRAY ABOUT IT

Pray for people who teach you from God's word. Pray that they will understand it and teach it correctly. Pray that they won't be corrupted by greed or pride. By name, thank God for each of them, and all they teach you.

230 Less is more

Jesus has been giving the religious leaders a hard time. They led people away from God rather than towards Him. And they looked down on people less "important" than themselves.

👁 **Read Luke 21 v 1–4**

ENGAGE YOUR BRAIN

▶ *What was special about what the widow did? (v4)*

▶ *Why did Jesus say she'd given more than the rich types?*

This woman had no earning power — her husband had died and women didn't do paid work back then. She was looked down on and treated as a second-class citizen.

▶ *How does Jesus know she's given everything?*

Jesus watches the heart. The widow gave all she had — showing her love for God and trust for the future (even her next meal). She didn't keep one coin for herself. The teachers were just trying to appear impressive.

THINK IT THROUGH

▶ *In what ways are you tempted to be like these teachers?*

▶ *What do you do to get praise or attention?*

▶ *Do you view your money as belonging to you or to God?*

▶ *How is that shown in how you use it?*

GET ON WITH IT

You'll soon discover how much of a hold money has on you when you start giving it away.

▶ *How will you use your money to serve God?*

PRAY ABOUT IT

Jesus sees everything, including your heart. Talk to God right now. Be honest about stuff you've been foolishly trying to hide from Him. Talk to him about your attitude to money and giving.

231 Sign language

"What will happen before the end of the world?"
"How will we know that Jesus is about to return?"
Big questions. But not the most important questions, says Jesus.

👁 Read Luke 21 v 5–7

ENGAGE YOUR BRAIN

▶ *What's Jesus predicting in verse 6?*

▶ *What questions do the disciples ask? (v7)*

Jesus' fight to the death with the religious leaders continued. Their temple in Jerusalem would be trashed because they failed to welcome Jesus as King. The disciples seemed more interested in the end of the world. Jesus does answer their questions (in v20–24 and v32), but not immediately. Before He does, He gives them some warnings. Maybe their questions aren't as important as they seem.

👁 Read verses 8–11

▶ *What will people claim? (v8)*

▶ *What should be our response to these scary things? (v9)*

Stuff like wars and natural disasters will happen before Jesus returns.

We need to be careful not to get caught up in speculation and worry about when it will happen. And we must be wary of anyone who claims to be Christ returned or who claims it's already happening. It will be very obvious when Jesus returns. We need to concentrate on how we live for Him NOW, rather than worrying about exactly when the world will end. Got that? Good.

SHARE IT

Do you know anyone who worries about the end of the world? How can you use this topic to share Jesus' perspective with them?

PRAY ABOUT IT

Ask God to help you not to worry about seemingly big things that really aren't so vital. Ask Him to help you concentrate on serving Him now and sharing His message.

232 Facing the future

Jesus is talking about the future — both the future destruction of Jerusalem (which happened in 70AD) and the end of the world (yet to happen!). Before both of these events Jesus' followers would face tough times.

👁 **Read Luke 21 v 12–15**

ENGAGE YOUR BRAIN

▶ *What must Christ-followers face while they wait for His return? (v12)*

▶ *What good would come of this? (v13)*

▶ *What's the great news for those who stand up for Jesus? (v15)*

Many of Jesus' disciples were imprisoned, tortured or even murdered for spreading His message. Even today — in countries such as Turkey, Sudan and Algeria — Christians are attacked or arrested. That may not happen to us, but we should be ready to tell anyone about Jesus, whoever they are (v15). God has given His Holy Spirit to all Christians, to help them live for Him. The Spirit helps them to tell others about Jesus. Whether it's kings, judges or friends we're talking to.

👁 **Read verses 16–19**

▶ *What's the terrifying truth for Christians? (v16–17)*

▶ *So how can Jesus say verses 18–19?*

Christians are promised hard times in this life. They will be hated, betrayed and attacked. Sometimes by relatives and friends. So how can Jesus say: "Not a hair of your head will perish"? (v18) Well, Christians may be harmed in this life, but God is with them always, looking after them. And He will give eternal life to everyone who "stands firm" for Him. Ultimately, only God's people won't perish. He will keep them safe eternally.

PRAY ABOUT IT

1. Pray for Christians who are persecuted for their faith.
2. Ask God to give you the words to tell people about Jesus.
3. Thank Him that He's promised to help you do it.
4. Ask the Lord to help you stand firm in the face of persecution.

233 Wait for it...

More powerful predictions from Jesus. First off, Jesus talks again about the destruction of Jerusalem. Then He moves on to the end of the world. It may not be cheery stuff, but it's absolutely essential reading.

👁 Read Luke 21 v 20–24

ENGAGE YOUR BRAIN

▶ What was the sign that Jerusalem would be destroyed? (v20)

40 years after Jesus said these words, they came true when the Romans ransacked Jerusalem. There was time for people to escape if they were fast enough. But there will be no escaping when Jesus returns...

👁 Read verses 25–33

▶ How will Jesus return? (v27)

▶ Will anyone miss it?

▶ How should Christians react? (v28)

▶ What's the big news for people who don't believe the warnings?

When Jesus returns, everyone will see and know that He's the King of kings. It will be terrifying and yet Christians look up in hope and joy because Jesus will rescue believers and take them to live with Him.

Jesus could return at any time, so we need to be ready...

👁 Read verses 34–38

▶ What's the warning? (v34)

▶ What will you do to be ready for Jesus' return? (v36)

▶ What do you need to stop doing/ start doing?

▶ What weighs you down in life and makes you forget Jesus is returning?

PRAY ABOUT IT

▶ What do you need to thank and praise God for?

▶ What do you need to admit?

▶ What do you need His help with?

THE BOTTOM LINE

Jesus is coming back. Make sure you're ready.

234 Acts – To be continued

Earlier in Acts, we saw that the gospel has no ethnic boundaries and now we see it spreading to every section of society. But God has enemies who are keen to stop people hearing about Jesus.

👁 Read Acts 13 v 1–12

ENGAGE YOUR BRAIN

▷ *What do the prophets and teachers in Antioch have in common? (v1)*

Trick question! In some ways nothing but in another, everything! Look at the names for a minute. Barnabas we know about. Simeon, from his nickname, was probably a black African, as most likely was Lucius from Cyrene in North Africa. Manaen was an aristocrat from Herod's court, and then we have Saul, the former Pharisee and persecutor of the church. Very different people, but all chosen by God, all saved by the death of His Son and all brothers in Christ.

PRAY ABOUT IT

God shows His power when diverse people become family. Thank Him for the Christian brothers and sisters He's given you, and pray for His help to love them.

▷ *Who wants to speak to Saul and Barnabas? (v7)*

▷ *Who tries to stop them? (v8–10)*

▷ *Does Bar-Jesus/Elymas succeed?*

▷ *What happens to him?*

▷ *What happens to the proconsul?*

Behind every person who opposes the spread of the gospel is the devil. Does that shock you? The last thing the devil wants is people to turn to Jesus and have their sins forgiven. But God's enemies will never succeed. They can be obstructive and they can do real damage but they're ultimately doomed.

THE BOTTOM LINE

God's gospel will go out no matter what.

235 Plan A

People sometimes think what happened in Acts was something new, God's Plan B. But as we see in these verses, God's plan to bring salvation to the world has been His Plan A, right from the beginning.

👁 **Read Acts 13 v 13-31**

ENGAGE YOUR BRAIN

▶ Where do Saul/Paul and his companions start as usual? (v14)

▶ What key events in Israel's history does Paul refer to? List them below:

-
-
-
-
-
-
-
-
-
-
-

▶ Who did God start His plan with? (v17, 26)

▶ Did anything catch God by surprise? (v27)

▶ How did God show that sin and death really were defeated? (v30)

▶ What evidence do we have? (v31)

GET ON WITH IT

Faith isn't some vague thing — it's believing the message of trustworthy witnesses. Christianity isn't just another religion that might be "true for you" but not for everyone. It's God's plan from the beginning; predicted by the prophets and demonstrated through the life and death of Jesus Christ. Can you explain something of this to a friend?

THE BOTTOM LINE

God has a plan.

236 A promise and a choice

Not only has God had His Plan A from the beginning, He's pointed to it all through Israel's history. Jesus' arrival should have been a major "Eureka!" moment for the Jewish people.

👁 Read Acts 13 v 32–41

ENGAGE YOUR BRAIN

- ▶ How did God fulfil His promises to the Israelites? (v32–33)

- ▶ How did God fulfil His promises to David? (v34–37)

- ▶ What wonderful blessing does Jesus' death and resurrection accomplish? (v38–39)

- ▶ Who is forgiveness offered to? (v39)

- ▶ What is the warning the Old Testament also offers? (v40–41)

The choice is clear and very very serious. Choose to believe Jesus or not. Forgiveness is offered to everyone who trusts in Jesus' death in their place. They are *justified* — it's just as if they'd never sinned. Only faith in Jesus brings forgiveness. Relying on yourself or keeping rules won't do it. Failure to trust in Jesus means you'll perish (v41) — you face eternal death.

PRAY ABOUT IT

Thank God that Jesus is the King who lives for ever. Thank Him that everyone who believes in Jesus can be forgiven and justified before God. Spend some time thanking God for bringing that saving message to you.

THE BOTTOM LINE

Jesus lives for ever!

237 Share and beware

Paul and Barnabas took the message of Jesus to the Jews first. Their history and heritage were shouting out that Jesus is the promised King. Surely they would respond with gratitude and joy. Sadly, not many did...

👁 **Read Acts 13 v 42–52**

ENGAGE YOUR BRAIN

▶ *What are the positive signs at first? (v42–44)*

▶ *What do some of the Jews do, and why? (v45)*

▶ *What do Paul and Barnabas do next?*

▶ *Is this their plan or God's? (v46–47)*

▶ *How do the Gentiles respond? (v48)*

You might have thought from everything Paul and Barnabas had said so far that the good news was just for the Jewish people, but here we see God's grace to the whole world — part of His plan all along (v47).

▶ *What impact does the news about Jesus have? (v49)*

▶ *What else? (v50)*

TALK IT OVER

Have you noticed how evangelism often goes hand in hand with persecution? A friend becomes a Christian and her family dismiss her as a religious fanatic. You invite a friend to church and they laugh at you. Chat to another Christian about how you can get your expectations in line with what the Bible teaches in verses 48–50, and pray together to have the courage to share this life-changing message despite any opposition.

PRAY ABOUT IT

Read verse 52 again. Ask God to do the same for you as you live for Jesus and seek to share Him with others.

THE BOTTOM LINE

Expect opposition, but also expect the gospel to save people.

238 Gospel united

Amazing unity between Gentiles and Jews — it can only be the gospel. But it's not just believers who are brought together by the message of Jesus.

👁 Read Acts 14 v 1–7

ENGAGE YOUR BRAIN

▶ Where in Iconium did Paul and Barnabas start (as usual)?

▶ What were the results — good and bad? (v1–2)

▶ How does Luke (the author of Acts) describe the gospel message here? (v3)

We've had loads of descriptions of the gospel message in Acts so far; the good news about the Lord Jesus, the word of the Lord, and now the message of His grace.

▶ Why is this last one such a good way to describe the gospel?

▶ Does verse 5 remind you of anything?

The last time we saw Jews and Gentiles collaborating in a plot like this it led to Jesus' execution. The gospel brings unity; for those who are being saved, a wonderful brotherhood — but for those who reject Christ, it creates new alliances with other enemies of the gospel.

▶ Did all this opposition stop the gospel spreading? (v6–7)

PRAY ABOUT IT

Ask for God's power and courage to keep talking about Jesus when things get tough.

SHARE IT

Can you explain the good news about Jesus without using any jargon, any Christian-y language? Practise it now and pray for a chance to do it soon.

THE BOTTOM LINE

The gospel brings unity of all kinds.

239 Heard it all before

Ever get a feeling of déjà-vu, as if something's happened before? There's some of that today. Ever get a feeling of déjà-vu, as if something's happened before? There's some of that today. Ever get a feeling...

👁 Read Acts 14 v 8–20

Read through the three incidents in these verses and fill in the table below:

Verses	What happens?	Reminds us of...	Similarities/differences?
8–10		Acts 3 v 1–10 Luke 7 v 11–15 Mark 2 v 1–12	
11–18		Acts 12 v 21–23	
19–20		Acts 14 v 5	

▷ *In verses 11–18, how are Paul and Barnabas different to Herod?*

▷ *Why do you think this is?*

Did you notice the way Paul and Barnabas speak to the pagan Lystranites? They still share the good news about Jesus but they start in a very different place from their synagogue routine with all its Old Testament references.
Look at verses 15–17.

▷ *Do you speak about Jesus in a way your friends will understand?*

PRAY ABOUT IT

Ask God to help you talk bravely and understandably about Jesus.

THE BOTTOM LINE

Different places, different people. Same God, same plan.

240 Return journey

After all the travelling and the excitement of people becoming Christians, it's time for some encouragement and a bit of reporting back to base — phew!

👁 Read Acts 14 v 21–28

ENGAGE YOUR BRAIN

▷ What was the outcome of the Derbe visit (v21)?

▷ How did they make sure the disciples in Lystra, Iconium and Antioch were OK before they left? List what they said and did below (v22–23):

-
-
-
-
-

▷ Look at each of the points you've just listed. Why is each one so important?

PRAY ABOUT IT

We often attach a great deal of importance to our church or youth group leaders or older Christians, and to some extent that is right, as God has made them leaders of His people. But ultimately, it's God who will take care of us. See verse 23 and thank God that whatever happens, He will care for you if you've put your trust in Him.

▷ On returning to Antioch, what are we reminded about:

a) how the work started? (v26)

b) how the work was accomplished? (v27)

THE BOTTOM LINE

God saves us, keeps us and works through us by His grace.

241 The great debate

"Unless you do X, you can't be saved." Sadly, throughout history, people have tried to add something extra to the saving message of the gospel. What happened when this reared its head in the early church?

👁 Read Acts 15 v 1–11

ENGAGE YOUR BRAIN

▷ What do the Jewish believers suggest is necessary to be saved? (v1, v5)

▷ Do Paul and Barnabas agree? (v2)

▷ How serious could this dispute become? What might the consequences be?

▷ What solution does the church propose? (v2)

▷ What do all the believers agree about? (v3b)

Before you write this off as a blatantly ridiculous historical argument, think about the following: Have you ever heard or thought: "You can't be a Christian if you smoke / don't go to the right sort of church"?

▷ What does Peter remind everyone about:

a) God's choice? (v7)

b) God's gift? (v8)

c) God's work? (v9)

d) God's salvation? (v11)

▷ How is anyone saved? (v11)

PRAY ABOUT IT

Thank God for His grace and ask Him to forgive you for the times when you have thought that you or other people needed to do anything to contribute to their salvation. Only Jesus' death can rescue us — we can't earn it.

THE BOTTOM LINE

We are saved by God's grace through Jesus, and nothing else.

242 The great debate part II

So how will the "mother church" in Jerusalem handle this Jewish/Gentile debate? Peter has reminded them that everyone is saved by faith in Christ and not by obeying the Law of Moses. So what will the official line be?

👁 Read Acts 15 v 12–21

ENGAGE YOUR BRAIN

▷ *What do Barnabas and Paul remind the assembly is happening? (v12)*

▷ *How does James explain that this has always been part of God's plan? (v13–18)*

▷ *What is his recommendation? (v19–21)*

Notice that James' concern is that they shouldn't make things difficult for the Gentile believers. He gives them a kind of diet version of the Law of Moses — to keep themselves unpolluted by other gods/idols, sex outside marriage or eating violently-killed food.

👁 Read verses 22–35

▷ *How does the church in Jerusalem decide to get this decision out? (v22–29)*

▷ *Who do they say is behind their letter? (v28)*

▷ *How do the Gentile believers respond? (v31)*

▷ *What else do Judas, Silas, Paul and Barnabas do? (v32–35)*

This may seem like a little thing to us, but the inclusion of the Gentiles into the people of God was a massive thing back then and, even though we take it for granted, still is today.

PRAY ABOUT IT

Read 1 Peter 2 v 9–10 and then spend some time thanking God for His mercy to you, whether you're from a Gentile or Jewish background.

THE BOTTOM LINE

God does not want to make things difficult for His children.

243 | Barna' split

After all the positives of the last few chapters, it's really sad to see Paul and Barnabas falling out here. They, like us, were human and imperfect. But God still used them (and uses us!).

👁 Read Acts 15 v 36–41

ENGAGE YOUR BRAIN

▶ *What does Paul want to do? (v36)*

▶ *Is that a good plan?*

▶ *Where does the disagreement lie? (v37–38)*

We're not told whether Paul or Barnabas is in the right here, but the outcome is surely not that great (v39).

▶ *Nevertheless, what do Paul and Barnabas continue to do, despite going their separate ways?*

▶ *What will keep Paul and Silas (and us) going? (v40)*

PRAY ABOUT IT

We are saved by God's grace, but we also live by God's grace. We need to depend on His undeserved kindness every day if we are to live for Him. Ask for that help now.

GET ON WITH IT

Are you annoyed with another Christian at the moment? You might be in the right or the wrong, but what really matters is your attitude.

👁 Read Matthew 5 v 23–24
👁 Read Philippians 2 v 1–8

Pray as you read them.

Then put them into practice!

THE BOTTOM LINE

God's grace keeps us going, despite our weakness.

244 | Psalms – Living with God

"Who gets to live with God?"
How would you answer that question?

👁 Read Psalm 15

ENGAGE YOUR BRAIN

The "sacred tent" and "holy mountain" were the places that represented God's presence among His people. So who, according to David, gets to live with God? Or to phrase it better, what sort of people does God require us to be?

▶ *In the space on the right, put each part of verses 2–5 in your own words.*

This is the kind of person God expects you to be. Think how you shape up alongside each of those qualities.

GET ON WITH IT

▶ *Which do you particularly need to work on?*

It's impossible for us to live up to God's standards shown in verses 2–5. God's people today thank Jesus for making it possible for them to live with God for eternity. Jesus lived a perfect, sinless life, and died in our place to remove God's punishment from us. Because of Him, we're good enough for God!

PRAY ABOUT IT

Does this psalm stir you into action? Ask God to help you love Him and long for His perfection. And thank Him for working in your life to make you more like Jesus.

THE BOTTOM LINE

We're not good enough to live with God. But Jesus has made it possible.

245 | Security firm

What makes you happy in life?
What gives you security and makes you feel safe?
Let's ask David the same questions.

👁 Read Psalm 16 v 1–4

ENGAGE YOUR BRAIN

▶ *Where does David find his security and happiness (v1–2)*

▶ *What will happen to people who follow other gods? (v4)*

▶ *What "gods" are you tempted to chase after? Money? Sport? Relationships? Something else?*

People around David were worshipping other gods — even offering them blood sacrifices (v4). But false gods these days are far more subtle: anything we give more importance to than God becomes a god to us. But David looked to God to bring him happiness and security.

👁 Read verses 5–11

▶ *How does David respond to God's protection?*

▶ *Will this security only last for this life? (v10–11)*

David knows that God will keep him safe, and he can't keep quiet about how happy this makes him. David even seems happy at the prospect of death, because he knows God won't abandon him. Superb.

The New Testament tells us the "holy/faithful one" (v10) is Jesus. David trusted that God would give him eternal life because he knew that one day God would provide a king who'd reign for ever and conquer sin and death.

PRAY ABOUT IT

Thank God that believers are totally safe with Him. For ever. And ask Him to help you ditch any other gods you chase after.

THE BOTTOM LINE

Find total security with God.

EXODUS

Exit strategy

Welcome to the second book of the Bible. Exodus means "exit" or "departure". It's all about God getting His people out of Egypt. In spectacular style.

WAY OUT?

In Genesis we saw God put His man Joseph in Egypt so that God's people would be able to get food and survive years of crippling drought. But how would they get out of Egypt — where they were treated like dirt by the locals — and get to the land God had promised them?

EXIT SIGNS

Step forward Moses, the reluctant hero of Exodus, who God would use in amazing ways to show the Israelites the way to the exit.

HISTORY LESSON

So it's all just ancient history, right? Wrong — Christians today have been rescued by God too, through Jesus' death and resurrection. So we'll see how Exodus sets the scene for what Jesus did.

This poses the big question: if you've been rescued by God, are you living His way right now?

246 Exterminate!

Sometimes things just seem to go from bad to worse. The Israelites were stuck in Egypt, ruled over cruelly by the Egyptians. But things would get much worse before they got better.

👁 Read Exodus 1 v 1–14

ENGAGE YOUR BRAIN

ⓓ *What was going well for the Israelites? (v7)*

ⓓ *What did the Egyptians fear?(v10)*

ⓓ *How did they react? (v14)*

God had chosen a bunch of people — the Israelites — to be His special people. He'd promised Abraham that He'd look after them, give them loads of kids, a homeland in Israel and that through these people the whole world would be blessed (Genesis 12 v 1–3).

And to help them survive a famine, God engineered it so that they ended up in Egypt, where He'd placed His man Joseph to organise food supplies. Clever!

The Israelites were growing rapidly, just as God had promised. This panicked the Egyptians, who tried to grind them down with forced labour. But it didn't seem to work — they just kept growing (v12). So Pharaoh took desperate measures.

👁 Read verses 15–22

ⓓ *What did Pharaoh order? (v16)*

ⓓ *But what happened?*

ⓓ *What's Exodus already teaching us about God? (v20–21)*

God had a plan for His people and, despite the Egyptians extreme cruelty, God's plans would not be stopped. We can already see a glimpse of His rescue, His love and His compassion for His people.

PRAY ABOUT IT

Ask God to show you His awe-inspiring love, compassion and rescue as you read Exodus.

THE BOTTOM LINE

God looks out for His people.

247 | Water baby

God's people, the Israelites, are living in harsh conditions in Egypt. Pharaoh is worried about them getting out of control so he's ordered every Israelite baby to be thrown into the River Nile as soon as it's born.

👁 Read Exodus 2 v 1–4

ENGAGE YOUR BRAIN

▶ *What desperate measures did the baby's mother take?*

This couple were Levites, one of the twelve Israelite tribes. When the woman gave birth to a boy they must have been devastated, knowing he'd have to die. She tried to keep him hidden, but in the end sent him to float down the river in a watertight basket.

👁 Read verses 5–10

▶ *Who rescued the tot?*

▶ *Flick back to Exodus 1 v 22. What might she have done with him?*

▶ *What else worked out brilliantly? (Exodus 2 v 7–9)*

Unbelievably, baby Moses was protected by an Egyptian! Pharaoh's daughter took pity on the little mite, even though he was a Hebrew (Israelite). God had big plans for Moses: He kept Moses alive, got his own mother to look after him, and he was brought up as an Egyptian. This boy was special, and God would use him in surprising ways.

Throughout the Bible we read about God's enemies attacking and trying to destroy God's people. But God is in control, and He will never be wiped out. In fact, they will survive to live eternally with God.

PRAY ABOUT IT

Thank God that He's with His people even through the toughest of times. Thank Him that no one can destroy His people.

THE BOTTOM LINE

God's people will not be destroyed.

248 On the run

Imagine being born in one country but growing up in a totally different one. Where would your loyalties lie? Moses had Hebrew parents but was brought up as an Egyptian. Let's see where his heart was...

👁 Read Exodus 2 v 11–15

ENGAGE YOUR BRAIN

🔹 *Who did Moses side with?*

🔹 *What do you think about his actions and motives? (v12)*

🔹 *What were the consequences? (v14-15)*

Despite being brought up in Pharaoh's family, Moses knew who his people were (v11). When he saw how cruelly the Egyptians treated Hebrews, he snapped. His murderous anger caused him to have to flee Egypt in a hurry. How could God possibly use this runaway killer?

👁 Read verses 16–22

🔹 *How did things work out for Moses?*

Moses ran for his life into the desert. But God was looking after him and led him to a friendly family, and even a wife and son.

THINK IT THROUGH

🔹 *Do you believe God can use you?*

🔹 *Do you think you're too sinful to serve God?*

God often uses weak, sinful people in His plans. Moses had killed a man, yet God kept him safe and would still use him to rescue His people.

Don't limit God. He can do anything, including using seemingly useless people like us. He can use us to spread the gospel and to serve other Christians. The question is, are you ready to let Him use you?

PRAY ABOUT IT

If you actually mean it, ask God to use you in His big plans. But be warned, He will!

THE BOTTOM LINE

God uses the least likely people.

249 Cry for help

Family illness. Depression. Natural disasters. Suffering. It's often in the darkest times that people turn to God for help.

👁 Read Exodus 2 v 23–25

ENGAGE YOUR BRAIN

▷ *What are we told about the Israelites?*

▷ *What do we learn about God?*

▷ *What did God remember?*

The Israelites in Egypt were being treated brutally by the Egyptians — living in slavery, forced to do back-breaking work, and many of their children were drowned at birth. In this moment of great suffering, they cried out to God for help.

👁 Read Genesis 17 v 6–8

▷ *What did God promise Abraham?*

v6:

v7:

v8:

When the Israelites groaned to God, He remembered His covenant agreement with Abraham. God had promised to make Abraham's family into a great nation, giving them the land of Canaan. He would be their God.

The Israelites were God's people — He loved them and would keep His promises as always. He would rescue them from slavery.

PRAY ABOUT IT

God promises to be with all of His people. He hears our prayers too and is concerned for us.

Use Exodus 2 v 24–25 to thank God for what He's like.

THE BOTTOM LINE

God hears His people's cries.

250 Warning: bush fire

The Israelites cried out to God to free them from slavery. By now, Moses was pushing 80 years old, minding his own business, looking after sheep in Midian. He wouldn't have expected to get the big call-up from God.

👁 **Read Exodus 3 v 1–6**

ENGAGE YOUR BRAIN

▶ *What was Moses required to do in God's presence? (v5)*

▶ *How did God introduce Himself? (v6)*

▶ *How did Moses react to that?*

God grabbed Moses' attention in a bizarre way — a bush on fire that didn't burn up. It worked. God let Moses know exactly who was speaking to Him: the God of his ancestors.

No wonder Moses was terrified. He took off his sandals to show respect for God in His presence. And he hid his face, completely humbled by the perfect, holy God of all history.

👁 **Read verses 7–10**

▶ *How would verse 7 have encouraged Moses?*

▶ *But what was the shock news for Moses? (v10)*

The Lord promised a great future for His people — freed from slavery and taken into a land overflowing with the good life (v8). Moses must have been thrilled. Until God gave him the job of rescuer. Panic attack time. We'll look at Moses' reaction tomorrow.

TALK IT THROUGH

▶ *Do you show God enough respect?*

▶ *What do you need to change about the way you talk to God or talk about God?*

PRAY ABOUT IT

If you're a Christian, God has called you too — to spread the word about Jesus and to serve Him throughout your life. Ask God to help you do what He wants you to do.

251 | I AM WHO I AM

Things are starting to kick off. The Israelites cried out to God to rescue them. God appeared to Moses in a burning bush, telling him to bring God's people out of Egypt. But Moses wasn't too excited about the job...

👁 **Read Exodus 3 v 11–12**

ENGAGE YOUR BRAIN

▷ *What was Moses' first excuse?*

▷ *What did God say to reassure him?*

Moses didn't think he was the right man for the job. But God said: *I'll be with you, so trust me.*

Only once the Israelites were out of Egypt would Moses fully realise it was the work of God (v12).

👁 **Read verses 13–15**

▷ *What was Moses' second excuse?*

▷ *What fantastic truth was Moses to tell the people? (v14–15)*

The awesome name for God: I AM. The one who is, for ever. The God of His people — past, present and future (v15). He was Abraham, Isaac and Jacob's God, and He would always be the God of the Israelites. Astonishing stuff.

The God of the Israelites is our God too. He has always existed. He is perfect and will never change. And He will rule His people for ever.

PRAY ABOUT IT

Take time out to praise God for what His name means.

THE BOTTOM LINE

God is, was and always will be. He's the God of the past, present and future, who will always be with His people. Wow.

252 Back to the future

Calendars are usually filled with scribbles detailing all your future plans. Today in Exodus we get to see what God has planned for the Israelites. Not only the events, but the results too!

👁 **Read Exodus 3 v 16–22**

ENGAGE YOUR BRAIN

▷ *How would all this info encourage Moses?*

▷ *Describe the series of events:*

v16–18:

v18–19:

v20:

v21–22:

What an amazing response to the Israelites' cries for help. God promised to rescue them in a spectacular way. God even told Moses exactly how

He would do it, so they could look back and see how God had kept His promises. To the letter.

Yesterday we read how God is the great I AM: He has always existed, He never changes and He'll rule for ever. God knows everything that has happened and everything that will happen. So He could tell Moses what would happen to the Israelites.

GET ON WITH IT

Ever tempted by horoscopes or fortune-telling to find out about the future? Throw them out of your life — they're pointless. God knows all about you. He knows what plans He has for you in the future. We don't need horoscopes — we have a perfect God in control of our future.

PRAY ABOUT IT

Thank God that your future is safe in His hands. Ask Him to use you to serve Him loads in the future.

253 Excuse me

Are you a willing volunteer who's happy to get stuck into anything, or do you prefer to hide in the background? God had promised to use Moses to free the Israelites from slavery, but Moses was full of excuses.

👁 Read Exodus 4 v 1–9

ENGAGE YOUR BRAIN

▶ *What was Moses' excuse?*

▶ *What three signs would God give him as proof?*

Moses was trying to wriggle out of his responsibilities. But God was patient with Moses and gave him proof to show the leaders that he really had met God. But Moses was desperate to get out of it...

👁 Read verses 10–17

▶ *What were Moses' two last desperate excuses? (v10, 13)*

▶ *How did God respond to Moses' lack of trust? (v14–16)*

Moses let his doubts in his own abilities lead to him not trusting God. The Lord can do anything (v11). Of course he could use cowardly Moses. God was angry with Moses' lack of trust, yet still showed incredible patience and reassured Moses by getting his bro Aaron to help him.

GET ON WITH IT

▶ *What responsibilities are you avoiding at the mo?*

▶ *What excuses are you using for not fully serving God?*

▶ *Do you let self-doubt stop you obeying God?*

PRAY ABOUT IT

Bring these things before God right now. Ask Him to help you trust Him to give you the strength and abilities to serve Him.

THE BOTTOM LINE

Stop making excuses with God.

254 | The wanderer returns

Years ago, Moses had fled from Egypt after killing an Egyptian. Finally, he was about to return — this time to rescue God's people from slavery. But would the Israelites trust God and follow Moses?

Read Exodus 4 v 18–23

ENGAGE YOUR BRAIN

- *What was the good news for Moses? (v19)*

- *What was the bad news? (v21)*

- *What did God call the Israelites? (v22)*

God encouraged Moses that it was safe for him to go back to Egypt, so Moses grabbed his family and left. The bad news was that despite Moses performing miracles in front of Pharaoh, he would still refuse to let God's people go. But the Israelites were God's chosen people and God would care for them (v22) and punish Pharaoh for his unbelief (v23).

Read verses 24–26

What a bizarre story. It seems that Moses hadn't circumcised his son (as God had commanded His people to do in Genesis 17 v 9–14) and faced God's punishment. Zipporah saved the day by doing the deed herself and associating Moses with it (v25).

Read verses 27–31

- *How did the Israelite elders respond to Moses and Aaron?*

- *Had Moses been right to worry and try to get out of it?*

Aaron was now onboard to help Moses. And so were the Israelite leaders. When they realised that God had heard their prayers, they bowed down in worship

PRAY ABOUT IT

- *Have you seen God answer your prayers?*

- *Do you know that He loves you?*

- *So what will you say to Him right now?*

255 The final straw

Moses has returned to Egypt to free God's people from slavery. The Israelite leaders are behind him. So far. But now Moses is going to face up to hard-hearted Pharaoh (Amenhotep II) for the first time.

👁 Read Exodus 5 v 1–9

ENGAGE YOUR BRAIN

▶ What did God (through Moses) demand from Pharaoh? (v1)

▶ What was Pharaoh's response? (v2, v4–5)

▶ How was he even more "unfair-oh"? (v6–9)

The Israelites must have got their hopes up. They'd seen Moses and Aaron perform miracles in front of their eyes. Now these two were going to meet Pharaoh and lead God's people out of Egypt! But it wouldn't be that easy. In fact, Pharaoh was going to make it as difficult as he could, making their hard work impossible to do. Make bricks without straw? No chance!

👁 Read verses 10–21

▶ What effect did Pharaoh's cruel work rules have?

▶ What was the Israelites' attitude towards Moses and Aaron now?

Pharaoh's clever ruse to turn God's people against Moses and Aaron had the desired effect. The Israelite leaders were dejected and they blamed M & A. Their trust in God to free them disappeared. *Tomorrow we'll see God's response.*

God didn't promise that Moses' task would be easy. In fact, it now seemed impossible, yet God's promise to rescue the Israelites stood. But it wasn't down to Moses. Despite this impossible situation, God would keep His promises and everyone would see His power.

PRAY ABOUT IT

Ask God to help you trust Him even when things are going badly. And pray for Christian leaders who face opposition despite serving God.

256 Powerful promises

Have you ever got angry with God? Pointed the finger of blame at Him? What causes you to doubt God and His promises? Moses felt useless and rejected and let down by God.

👁 Read Exodus 5 v 22–23

ENGAGE YOUR BRAIN

▶ How would you describe Moses' attitude to God?

▶ What had he forgotten about God?

👁 Read Exodus 6 v 1–5

▶ How did God reassure Moses? (v1)

▶ What reminders did God give to encourage him? (v2–5)

Incredibly encouraging words from God. The Lord would rescue His people (v1). Maybe not immediately, but He would do it. God would keep the promises He made to Moses' ancestors, giving the Israelites a land of their own (v4). Amazingly, God had revealed more of His character to Moses than He had to Abraham and the rest (v3).

👁 Read verses 6–12

▶ What dramatic promises did God make? (v6–8)

▶ How would these things happen?

▶ How did the people respond?

God's promises to His people were phenomenal. But they were so caught up in their current sadness they refused to believe God. And this got Moses down and he doubted God again. Oh dear.

SHARE IT

▶ Who do you know who has stopped trusting God?

▶ What examples of God's faithfulness in the past can you point them to?

PRAY ABOUT IT

Thank God that He keeps His promises. Thank Him for things He's done in the past that show He's totally faithful.

257 Feeling listless

How are you with lists? Or family trees? Do they get you strangely excited or does your brain collapse through boredom? Try to work out if this list of names in Exodus has any relevance at all.

👁 Read Exodus 6 v 13–27

ENGAGE YOUR BRAIN

▷ *What did this list tell people about Aaron and Moses? (v26–7)*

This family roll call told people exactly who A & M were. They were just ordinary Israelites who God would use to do sensational things. And it's a nice reminder that God got these guys in position long before the Exodus. It was all part of God's perfect plans.

👁 Read Exodus 6 v 28 – 7 v 7

▷ *What was Moses to do? (v1–2)*

▷ *What would Pharaoh do? (v4)*

▷ *What would God do? (v5)*

In Old Testament times, God spoke to His people through prophets. In the same way, Moses would give God's message to Pharaoh via the lips of Aaron, acting as a prophet.

God commanded Moses and Aaron to deliver His message to Pharaoh even though they knew Pharaoh wouldn't listen to them. Sometimes telling people about Jesus can be tough like that. They refuse to listen to us. But that's no reason to give up. They still need to hear the message of Jesus and God wants us to keep plugging away.

SHARE IT

▷ *Who do you find it hard to share the gospel with?*

▷ *Who will you resolve to talk to about Jesus again?*

PRAY ABOUT IT

Talk to God about how tough it is, and ask Him to help you not give up.

THE BOTTOM LINE

Keep delivering God's message.

258 Flood of blood

Ever had a conversation (or maybe a full-blooded argument) where you just can't seem to get your point across? The other person refuses to agree with a word you say and you end up so frustrated. Aaaaarrrrrrghhh!

👁 Read Exodus 7 v 8–13

ENGAGE YOUR BRAIN

▶ *What did Aaron do as proof he was sent by God?*

▶ *Were Pharaoh's wise guys more powerful? (v12)*

Aaron's staff transformed into a snake — it was a sign to Pharaoh that Aaron and Moses had been sent by God. It was also a sign of God's great power.

For a moment, it looked as if the magicians were just as powerful — until Aaron's snake munched theirs! Despite this, Pharaoh wouldn't listen to them, just as God had said he wouldn't.

👁 Read verses 14–25

▶ *What should this plague have taught Pharaoh? (v16–17)*

▶ *What was Pharaoh's reaction? (v22–23)*

Try to imagine the whole revolting scene. The Egyptians worshipped the River Nile as a god. But God's men, Moses and Aaron, turned it to blood. In fact, all the water (even in buckets and jars) became bloody and undrinkable. It was a sign that God was in charge, not Pharaoh. But the magicians performed a similar trick and Pharaoh refused to believe in God or release the Israelites.

SHARE IT

▶ *Who refuses to listen when you talk about Jesus?*

▶ *Do you pray for them regularly, and keep taking God's message to them?*

PRAY ABOUT IT

Talk to God about people you know who refuse to accept the truth about Jesus. Ask Him to soften their hearts and to give you the strength and courage to keep talking to them.

259 Hopping mad

Pharaoh refused to let the Israelites go into the desert to worship God. The Lord turned all the water in Egypt to blood, but Pharaoh wouldn't give in. It's now a week later.

Read Exodus 8 v 1–8

ENGAGE YOUR BRAIN

▶ What did Moses ask Pharaoh again? (v1)

▶ What was Pharaoh's surprise reply to the frog infestation? (v8)

The Egyptians worshipped many false gods. One of the popular ones was Hekhet, who was supposedly a woman with a frog's head. By sending the plagues, The Lord was showing that He was the one true God — the only one deserving worship.

Pharaoh was sick of frogs overrunning his palace, so he asked Moses and Aaron to ask God to get rid of them. In return, Pharaoh promised to let the Israelites worship God in the desert.

Read verses 9–15

▶ Why did Moses tell Pharaoh to chose the time of the de-frogging? (v9–10)

▶ So what did Pharaoh do after God got rid of the frogs?

Moses let Pharaoh choose the time so no one could claim it was a coincidence when the frogs suddenly all died. It was obvious that God was behind it (v10). But as soon as the frogs left, Pharaoh hardened his heart and went back on his promise.

We can be just the same. In the middle of a crisis, we'll turn to God, begging Him to help us. Maybe even making promises to Him. But when the crisis is over and life gets back to normal, God is forgotten about and the promises are broken.

PRAY ABOUT IT

Ask God to help you talk to Him more often, not just when you need stuff. How can you start changing the way you pray RIGHT NOW?

260 No flies on Moses

How good are you with bugs and flying things? How about if your house was infested with them — getting in your bed and landing on your cornflakes? How long before it would drive you mad?

👁 Read Exodus 8 v 16–19

ENGAGE YOUR BRAIN

▷ *Could the magicians do a gnatty trick?*

▷ *What did they recognise about this plague?*

Pharaoh's sorcerers couldn't conjure up a cloud of gnats, so they admitted that a power far greater than theirs must be in control. But, yet again, Pharaoh ignored the obvious and refused to listen.

👁 Read verses 20-32

▷ *Why did God keep His people fly-free? (v22)*

▷ *What compromise did Pharaoh offer? (v25)*

▷ *Why wouldn't Moses accept the deal? (v26–27)*

▷ *Pharaoh's response this time? (v32)*

Pharaoh tried to stay in control by offering to let the Israelites sacrifice to God... on his terms. Moses rightly stuck to his guns and said: *"God's way or no way"*. Moses refused to compromise when it came to God's commands. Pharaoh gave in, but yet again changed his mind later.

God made a distinction between His people and His enemies — there were no flies on God's chosen people.

Today, God's people are living under the same conditions as everyone else. But Christians are God's chosen people and one day will live in perfection with Him, far away from pain and misery and punishment.

PRAY ABOUT IT

Thank God that Christians are His chosen people and that, because of Jesus, He will separate them from sickness and misery and evil for ever.

261 Boiling point

If you saw a sign that said: WARNING: VICIOUS BEASTS! would you just carry on strolling, ignoring it? Pharaoh kept ignoring God's painful warnings. Let's see how he does with warning number five.

👁 Read Exodus 9 v 1–7

ENGAGE YOUR BRAIN

▶ *What distinction did God make between His people and the Egyptians? (v4, v7)*

▶ *Describe Pharaoh, in your own words.*

God wasn't exactly being subtle. Pharaoh couldn't have missed the warnings. The Nile turned to blood; his palace was overrun with frogs, gnats and flies; and now all the livestock in Egypt dropped dead. But Pharaoh was stubborn and refused to acknowledge that God was all-powerful and in control.

👁 Read verses 8–12

▶ *How did the magicians cope with this one?*

▶ *And Pharaoh? (v12)*

The magicians had given up trying to copy A & M's miracles — they couldn't even stand up any more. But God made Pharaoh's heart hard, exactly as Pharaoh wanted it — and he refused to listen to God.

GET ON WITH IT

▶ *How do you respond when God speaks to you through the Bible or at church?*

▶ *Do you take any notice?*

▶ *Do you listen to God and do what He says?*

PRAY ABOUT IT

Pray for people you know who refuse to listen to warnings and keep their hearts closed to God. And ask the Lord to help you listen to Him and do what He commands.

THE BOTTOM LINE

Follow the warning signs.

262 | Luke: The big finale

Luke is taking us through Jesus' last week on earth. Today he shows us two big plans — one's a plot to murder Jesus. The other plan is much much bigger than that.

👁 Read Luke 22 v 1–13

ENGAGE YOUR BRAIN

▶ What were the motives behind the murder plot? (v2)

▶ Who was really behind it? (v3)

It was too risky for the Jewish leaders to murder Jesus with so many people packed into Jerusalem for the Passover feast. But then Judas offered them a way of arresting Jesus quietly. This wasn't just a human plot — Satan himself was at work. But there was a bigger plan at work, about to be revealed by Jesus…

👁 Read verses 14–23

You can read about the original Passover in Exodus. The Israelites put the blood of a lamb on their doorposts to escape God's punishment of the ungodly Egyptians. Since then, the Jews had celebrated the Passover feast every year, to remember God's rescue.

▶ How did Jesus use the meal to teach something new?

▶ What are the disciples to remember from now on? (v19–20)

▶ Who's in control of both the plot and the plan? (v22)

Jesus is saying His death is far more important than that first rescue from Egypt. Jesus would rescue people, not from a land, but from their greatest problem (sin) and its effects (God's punishment).

God's new covenant agreement (v20): He will rescue anyone who relies on Jesus' death. That's the only way to eternal life.

PRAY ABOUT IT

The Son of God was killed to put people right with God. Yes, you too.

▶ What do you want to say to Him?

263 | Serving suggestion

Why are people so self-centred? Jesus has told the disciples of His imminent death (far more important than the Passover rescue) and His betrayal. But what do the disciples choose to talk about? Themselves.

👁 Read Luke 22 v 24–30

ENGAGE YOUR BRAIN

▶ *What was on the disciples' minds? (v24)*

▶ *How did people with power usually act? (v25)*

▶ *But what should Jesus' followers be like? (v26)*

▶ *Why? (v27)*

▶ *What was the brilliant news for the disciples? (v27–30)*

Get the message? It's not hard to understand, as Jesus puts it very simply. Unlike earthly kings, Jesus came to serve others. He did this by dying on the cross in our place to take the punishment for our sins. Incredible. So Jesus expects His followers to serve others. That's the sign of true greatness. Stop focusing on yourself and making yourself look good — get down to serving people!

GET ON WITH IT

▶ *Write down three ways you can serve people this week:*

1.

2.

3.

Despite their selfishness, Jesus told His disciples they would rule with Him in His kingdom! Jesus always gives His followers far more than they deserve.

PRAY ABOUT IT

Thank God for sending His Son to serve us by taking our place and facing our punishment. And ask Him to help you actually do the three serving suggestions you wrote down.

THE BOTTOM LINE

Don't be self-centred, put others first.

264 Tough times ahead

Cockerels, sandals, purses and swords — what is Jesus talking about??? It's not a list of birthday presents. Jesus is making a point about standing up for Him — and the opposition His followers will face.

👁 Read Luke 22 v 31–34

ENGAGE YOUR BRAIN

▷ *Who would test Simon Peter? (v31)*

▷ *Was Peter right to be confident in himself? (v34)*

▷ *How did Jesus encourage him? (v32)*

👁 Read verses 35–38

▷ *What was Jesus' surprising instruction to His disciples? (v36)*

▷ *How was Old Testament prophecy (v37) about to come true?*

▷ *What did the disciples think Jesus meant? (v38)*

The disciples relied on other people's hospitality as they travelled around. But Jesus would soon be arrested and taken away from them. Then they would be in great danger, with many people out to get them (you can read about this happening in Acts).

Yet again, the disciples misunderstood Jesus. He wasn't suggesting they get violent, as we'll see in two days' time. The truth is, followers of Jesus are not promised an easy ride. People find His message offensive. Christians will be teased, hassled, shunned and sometimes far worse. Jesus is praying for them that they will have the strength to stand up for Him (Romans 8 v 34).

PRAY ABOUT IT

Ask God to give you the strength and courage to be bold about your beliefs. Pray for particular people who persecute you.

THE BOTTOM LINE

Tough times are ahead for Christians.

265 Prayer in pain

Do real men cry? Do real men eat vegetarian pizza? Do real men admit they need help? Find out the answers to none of those questions but far more important stuff about Jesus.

👁 Read Luke 22 v 39–44

ENGAGE YOUR BRAIN

Answer true or false to these statements, and find which verse gives the answer.

▷ *Jesus could cope alone with what was to come.   T/F*
Verse:

▷ *Jesus faced His death with superhuman ease.   T/F*
Verse:

▷ *Jesus wanted to avoid going to the cross.   T/F*
Verse:

Sinless Jesus would soon become full of sin. He would take our sin upon Himself and be punished painfully. He would face anger and isolation from His Father. "The cup" is an Old Testament phrase meaning God's fierce punishment of sin. Jesus wanted to avoid all this, if that was possible. But He also wanted to see God's great plan completed, so He

was willing to go through these terrible things for His Father.

PRAY ABOUT IT

There was no other way of rescuing sinners. Read 1 Peter 2 v 24 and spend time thanking God that Jesus was willing to do this for you.

👁 Read Luke 22 v 45–46

PRAY ABOUT IT AGAIN

When we face heavy situations or temptation, we need to turn to God in prayer. And make sure we ask what God wants, not just what we want. Talk to the Lord now about what's buzzing around your head.

THE BOTTOM LINE

Jesus followed God's plan right to the end.

266 In denial

When you hear Jesus attacked in conversation, do you stand and fight for your beliefs? Or, like a coward, do you claim to have nothing to do with Him? Peter did both.

Read Luke 22 v 47–53
ENGAGE YOUR BRAIN

▶ What did the disciples do when Jesus was surrounded? (v49–50)

▶ What was Jesus' response? (v51)

▶ What do you think Jesus meant by verse 53?

Jesus stopped the disciples fighting and allowed Himself to be arrested. His enemies thought Jesus was playing into their hands, but He was sticking to God's big rescue plan. He chose to go with His enemies to His death. To save us.

Read verses 54–62

▶ What were the three accusers saying about Peter? (v56, v58–59)

▶ What was Peter's reply?

▶ What made Peter remember His earlier words? (v61)

▶ How did he then react, and why?

Peter had claimed he would stick with Jesus even if it meant prison or death (v33–34). But when it came to the crunch, he denied knowing Jesus.

THINK IT THROUGH

I'm just like Peter when I…

I let God down when I…

I failed to keep promises to God when I…

Read verses 31–32

Jesus knew what was happening and He would still use Peter in amazing ways once he "turned back" to Jesus (it's all in the book of Acts).

PRAY ABOUT IT

▶ Is it time for you to admit things to Jesus?

▶ Is it time to turn back?

267 Jesus on trial

Luke is leading us to the cross. Jesus has said He's a king who will suffer and die. Now it's about to happen. But Luke doesn't describe it timidly. He points the finger, accusing those responsible for this illegal execution.

Read Luke 22 v 63–71

ENGAGE YOUR BRAIN

- What did Jewish leaders want Jesus to say? (v67, v70)

- But who would ultimately be judging who? (v69)

Jesus was being treated like a criminal, yet He would rule in heaven with God and judge these men for rejecting Him. Finally Jesus admitted to being the Son of God (v70). Now they could charge Him with blasphemy — claiming to be God. They failed to recognise that it was the truth.

Read Luke 23 v 1–12

- How would you describe the Jewish leaders' claims? (v2)

- What did Pilate think of their claims? (v4)

- What was Herod most interested in? (v8)

Read verses 13–25

- What was Pilate's verdict this time? (v14–16)

- Why did Pilate change his mind? (v23)

The Jewish bigwigs used an illegal court with false evidence to convict Jesus. Herod was more interested in magic than justice. Pilate knew Jesus was innocent, but gave in to the crowd and sent Jesus to His death. It's easy to point a finger at these crooked people and blame them for Jesus' death. But the Bible says we're responsible too. Our sin, our rebellion, put Him there. Jesus died for our sin.

PRAY ABOUT IT

Thank Jesus for going through so much pain and humiliation for you. Then read 22 v 69, and praise Jesus for His power and authority.

268 Cross purposes

Jesus is on His way to die. Luke paints a very vivid picture of Jesus' final few hours. Take your time with today's Bible bit — take in the sights, sounds and smells. Hear Jesus' emotive words.

👁 Read Luke 23 v 26–31

ENGAGE YOUR BRAIN

- ▶ *What did the women do when they saw Jesus? (v27)*

- ▶ *Who did Jesus say they should really weep for? (v28)*

- ▶ *Why? (v29–31)*

See Simon struggling with the heavy cross… Jesus bruised and beaten… hear women screaming… the clink of soldiers' armour… the bloodthirsty mockers… the smell of death.

Jesus told the women they shouldn't cry for Him but for the people of Jerusalem, because they would be punished for rejecting Him. Verse 31 sounds weird, but the "green tree" means Jesus. He was saying that if an innocent man like Him was killed, then the guilty people of Jerusalem would suffer an even worse fate.

PRAY ABOUT IT

Have you rejected Jesus, or do you live for Him? If we know people who have rejected Jesus, what's our responsibility? Spend time now talking to God about your answers.

👁 Read verses 32–34

- ▶ *What amazing and surprising thing did Jesus say?*

THINK IT THROUGH

Only Jesus can offer forgiveness to sinners. We deserve punishment for rejecting Jesus, but He offers us forgiveness if we accept Him. It's not a decision we can put off. Will you be weeping with the people of Jerusalem or celebrating with Jesus in eternity?

THE BOTTOM LINE

Will you reject or accept Jesus?

269 The criminal and the King

Think of three people you know, who are very different from each other. If you asked each of them their opinion of Jesus, what do you think they'd say? People react to Jesus in different ways...

👁 Read Luke 23 v 35–38

ENGAGE YOUR BRAIN

- ▶ *What did the sign on the cross say? (v38)*

- ▶ *What did these bystanders think of Jesus?*

- ▶ *How did they want Him to prove Himself?*

The sign was meant as a joke, but it was the truth. The Jewish people were mocking, torturing and murdering their King. Jesus was not only their King, He was the King of the universe. But they wouldn't believe it unless Jesus miraculously saved Himself. They refused to believe He was God's Son and didn't realise He had to die to save people.

👁 Read verses 39–43

- ▶ *What did the second criminal recognise about Jesus?*

- ▶ *And about himself? (v41–42)*

- ▶ *What was Jesus able to promise him? (v43)*

This criminal realised he deserved to be killed for his crimes. We all do — we've sinned against God and deserve death. Yet this guy knew that Jesus was King and could rescue him, even as Jesus was dying on the cross. He trusted Jesus to forgive him, and Jesus promised him instant eternal life! Jesus' offer of forgiveness and eternity with Him is available to everyone.

PRAY ABOUT IT

Thank Jesus for this incredible offer. Pray for the people you thought of earlier. Ask God to open their eyes to the truth about Jesus.

THE BOTTOM LINE

Everyone deserves death.
Jesus offers life.

270 | The King is dead

Darkness at midday. A torn curtain in the temple. A good man dying the death of a criminal. People weeping uncontrollably. It sounds like the end of a tragic story. But this was actually the high point in history.

👁 Read Luke 23 v 44–46

ENGAGE YOUR BRAIN

▶ *What was Jesus' attitude as He died?*

The darkness was a miraculous act of God (eclipses don't last 3 hours). The Old Testament speaks of the time when God would judge His people and darkness would come (Amos 8 v 9). Here it is.

In God's temple, people (after various sacrifices) met with God. A huge curtain separated the centre of the temple — the most holy place — from the rest of it. Only the priest could go in there. People couldn't just stroll into God's presence. God is holy; humans aren't. We need someone to deal with our sin first.

▶ *By tearing the curtain, what was God saying is now possible?*

▶ *What does that tell us about Jesus' death?*

👁 Read verses 47–49

▶ *Explain the reactions of…*
the centurion (v47).
the crowds (v48).
Jesus' followers (v49).

Quietly, Luke's Gospel has reached a high point. Jesus has done it. He really is the Saviour of the world. His sacrificial death opened up a way back to God. We can now approach God directly, at any time. It's right that we should be upset when we think about the suffering Jesus went through. But we should also be excited by what Jesus has done for us. He died to rescue us!

PRAY ABOUT IT

Read verses 44–49 again and then talk openly and honestly with God.

THE BOTTOM LINE

Jesus' death opened up the way back to God.

271 Making a stand

On a scale from 1 to 10, how brave would you say you are? What about when it comes to standing out as a Christian? Does your score get higher or lower?

👁 Read Luke 23 v 50–54

ENGAGE YOUR BRAIN

▷ How was Joseph different from many other Jewish leaders? (v50–51)

▷ What was he looking forward to? (v51)

▷ What brave things did he do?

The Council of Jewish leaders (the Sanhedrin) had voted to kill Jesus. To come out as a supporter of Jesus was very dangerous for a member of the Council.

But Joseph was a follower of Jesus, who loved God, and longed to live in God's eternal kingdom. He probably didn't realise what Jesus' death had achieved, but he bravely wanted to do the right thing.

GET ON WITH IT

▷ Are you afraid to be associated with Jesus?

▷ How can you take a stand as a Christian?

👁 Read verses 55–56

▷ What did these women do?

Joseph did something no one else did — he took Jesus' body and gave it a proper burial. These women did what no one else did — they secretly followed Joseph and then prepared spices and perfumes to put on Jesus' body.

GET ON WITH IT

Write down some things you can do for Jesus that not many others can (eg: telling a specific friend about Jesus; showing more love and respect to your parents).

PRAY ABOUT IT

Ask God to give you the courage to do these things for Him. If and when you do them, make a new list!

272 Tomb raiders

Amazingly, Luke's story of Jesus doesn't end with His death — there's more. As you read today's verses, find the pieces of evidence that show that Jesus did actually rise from the dead.

👁 Read Luke 24 v 1–8

ENGAGE YOUR BRAIN

🔘 What did the women find? (v2)

🔘 What didn't they find? (v3)

🔘 What did the shiny men (angels) remind them about? (v5–8)

God the Father brought His Son back to life! It was a big surprise for these women. Yet on several occasions, Jesus had told His followers He would die and rise again. They either didn't understand or refused to believe it.

👁 Read verses 9–12

🔘 How did Jesus' disciples react to the great news? (v11)

🔘 What about Peter? (v12)

An empty tomb. Angels with big news. Jesus' promise that He would be raised back to life. All vital pieces of evidence that the disciples had forgotten or ignored. Tomorrow,

we'll see how the risen Jesus helped them remember.

PRAY ABOUT IT

🔘 What in the Bible do you not understand?

🔘 What do you find hard to believe?

Ask God to help you understand and believe His words in the Bible.

GET ON WITH IT

Jesus is alive! There's more than enough evidence for us.

🔘 How does it help you, knowing our faith is based on fact?

🔘 How will it affect you this week, knowing Jesus is alive for ever?

273 | Road to realisation

Two of Jesus' followers were walking and talking. They'd had great hopes that Jesus was the Messiah who would rescue the Jews. Then He was killed. Their hopes were shattered. But they were in for a big surprise...

👁 Read Luke 24 v 13–27

ENGAGE YOUR BRAIN

▶ *What had these two men failed to understand about Jesus?*

▶ *How did Jesus describe them? (v25)*

▶ *What huge fact did Jesus point out to them? (v26)*

▶ *What is the Old Testament all about? (v27)*

Jesus used the Scriptures to show He had to die — it was part of God's great plan. Jesus had "redeemed Israel" (v21). But He didn't rescue people from Roman bullies, but from sin and God's punishment.

👁 Read verses 28–35

▶ *What made them recognise Jesus? (v30–31)*

▶ *What was the great news at Disciple HQ? (v33–34)*

Suddenly the facts came alive because Jesus is alive. The truth hit them and they wanted to tell everyone. The news that Jesus died for us and is alive for ever is the most vital truth there is.

▶ *How is Jesus' death the most important event in history?*

▶ *Why is Jesus' resurrection so exciting?*

PRAY ABOUT IT

Thank Jesus now for His death and resurrection. Ask Him to help you get excited about it.

274 | Good news and goodbye

It's the last bit of Luke's Gospel, but it's not the end of the story. It's a passage full of surprises, starting with... a surprise party. But here it's the group waiting who are surprised, not the one arriving.

👁 Read Luke 24 v 36–43

ENGAGE YOUR BRAIN

▶ *Surprise! But what did Jesus say to them? (v36)*

▶ *How did Jesus prove He was no ghost?*

👁 Read verses 44–49

▶ *What did Jesus help them understand? (v44–47)*

▶ *What task did Jesus set the disciples? (v47–48)*

▶ *What help would they get? (v49)*

In verse 47, Jesus sums up His message in just six words: "repentance for the forgiveness of sins". *Repentance* describes what people must do in response to Jesus' death and resurrection. They must turn away from sin and turn to Jesus. *Forgiveness of sins* describes what God promises to do. Jesus sent the disciples out to preach this message. It was a tough task, but they would have the Holy Spirit helping them (v49). There's more about that in the book of Acts.

👁 Read verses 50–53

Jesus is in heaven (v51), but His task, with you and me, goes on. And we know God's Spirit lives in us to help us with that job.

▶ *What have you enjoyed about Luke's Gospel?*

▶ *How has it strengthened your faith?*

▶ *What have you learned about Jesus?*

PRAY ABOUT IT

Thank God for specific things you've read and learned in Luke's book. And ask His help to tell Jesus' message to someone else.

That's our job.

ACTS

Paul on tour

In 2005, the Rolling Stones embarked on a 147-date, two-year world tour. At one gig, on Rio de Janeiro beach in Brazil, they played to two million people. By the end of the *A Bigger Bang* tour, they had made £370 million.

That tour record was later broken by U2; then in 2019, Ed Sheeran broke it again. His *Divide* tour was officially the biggest, most attended and highest grossing of all time, lasting 893 days!

Each of these tours may have been the highest grossing ever — but they didn't have the highest impact. That title must belong to the apostle Paul, whose tours took him from Israel through modern-day Turkey and Greece, and eventually all the way to Rome. And at each gig, Paul had a simple message for the thousands who listened: *Jesus died for sins, Jesus has risen in glory, Jesus offers you eternal life.*

Critical reaction to Paul's performances was mixed. Many sneered; lots rioted; and some accepted Jesus as Lord of their lives, and with Paul's help set up churches. Two thousand years later we can still learn a lot from these early Christians about how faith in Jesus shapes life, what good churches and pastors look like, and how God works in and through His people.

So dive into Acts 16 – 20, jump back to AD 49-57, and join Paul on tour!

275 Follow the diversion

Ever been on a car journey and found out the route won't work — there's a big "DIVERSION" sign saying you have to go a different way? Life can be like that, too. Our plans can get seriously diverted.

👁 Read Acts 16 v 1–5

Poor Timothy. He got circumcised (ouch!) to respect Jewish tradition so they could both gain entry to Jewish synagogues as they travelled to preach the gospel. Notice how well it all seems to be going (v5).

👁 Read verses 6–10

ENGAGE YOUR BRAIN

🔸 What was Paul's plan and who put up a diversion sign? (v6)

🔸 What did Paul try to do next? (v7)

🔸 Did it work? Why/why not? (v7)

🔸 What happened next? (v9)

🔸 How did Paul and his companions react? Why? (v10)

THINK IT OVER

🔸 Why had the Spirit put up a couple of diversion signs in verses 6–8?

As we'll see, Paul's time in Macedonia proved to be a great success for the gospel. Lots of churches were set up, and loads of people became Christians. Being diverted there was a great idea of God's!

🔸 What does this section show about how God works in people's lives?

PRAY ABOUT IT

Ask the Spirit to guide and change your plans, and to help you trust Him as He directs your life.

THE BOTTOM LINE

God sometimes puts up diversion signs to get us to just where He wants us to be.

276 | My job, God's job

In (American) football, different players have different jobs. Some are purely blockers; others are runners; one guy is the quarterback. When they all do their job, the results are great! Evangelism's a bit like that...

👁 Read Acts 16 v 11–14

ENGAGE YOUR BRAIN

- ▶ Where do Paul and his group get to? (v12)
- ▶ Where do they go to speak to people about Jesus? (v13)
- ▶ What happens to Lydia? (v14)

THINK IT THROUGH

- ▶ Who told Lydia about Jesus?
- ▶ Who converted Lydia to being a follower of Jesus? (end of v14)
- ▶ When it comes to people becoming Christians, what is our part in it?
- ▶ What is God's role?
- ▶ How is this encouraging for us (especially if we find it hard)?

PRAY ABOUT IT

- ▶ What should we be asking God to help us to do, and what should we be asking God to do?

Pray in that way for some of the people you know well who aren't yet Christians.

👁 Read verse 15

Here we see two signs of someone who's truly become a "believer in the Lord." Lydia is baptised, to show she's a member of God's family; and she invites Paul and his friends to stay at her house, showing she wants to look out for God's family.

THE BOTTOM LINE

God works in people's hearts as His people tell them about His Son.

277 Points of view

Today, you're going to walk in the shoes of the people we meet.

THE SLAVE GIRL

👁 **Read Acts 16 v 16–24**

▶ *What was your problem? (v16)*

▶ *What did you know about Paul and Silas? (v17)*

▶ *What happened, and why? (v18)*

▶ *Why is knowing Jesus good news for you?*

THE JAILER

👁 **Read verses 25–34**

▶ *What was your problem? (v25-27)*

If your prisoners escape, you get executed. So you're face to face with your own death. But Paul and the other prisoners haven't run away...

▶ *What do you want to know? (v30)*

You've come close to dying — and you don't like it. You know these guys are telling people "the way to be saved", but what is it? What do you

need, to be saved from eternal death?

▶ *What does Paul tell you? (v31)*

▶ *How do you react? (v33–34)*

▶ *Why is knowing Jesus good news for you?*

Knowing Jesus brings release from the power of evil; and release from the fear of death.

PAUL AND SILAS

▶ *What happened to you? (v22–24)*

▶ *How did you react? (v25)*

After all they'd been through, Paul and Silas were still praising God and looking to tell others about His Son! They didn't see prison as a problem; they saw it as a possibility to tell more people the good news.

(Read verses 35–40 to see how the story ends.)

▶ *How does Paul and Silas' example encourage & challenge you today?*

278 Be a Berean

Ever heard of the Bereans? No?
Well, it's time to see what they were like; because every
Christian should aim to be a Berean.

👁 Read Acts 17 v 1–9

ENGAGE YOUR BRAIN

▶ *Where does Paul get to? (v1)*

▶ *What does Paul get on with doing? (v2)*

▶ *What's his main message? (v3)*

▶ *What effects does his Bible teaching have? (v4–5)*

So Paul moves on to Berea (v10).

👁 Read verses 10–15

▶ *What makes the Bereans of "noble character"? (v11)*

▶ *When Paul said something, what did they do? (v11)*

▶ *What effects did Paul's Bible teaching have here? (v12)*

It didn't last. Though the Bereans were up for Paul's Bible teaching, many Thessalonians weren't. Look what they did in verses 13–15.

THINK IT THROUGH

▶ *When people examine the Bible, what do they see about Jesus? (v2–3)*

▶ *How can we check whether what a preacher says is true? (v11)*

GET ON WITH IT

▶ *What can you learn from the Bereans?*

▶ *What can you change to be a better "Berean"?*

THE BOTTOM LINE

Be a Berean.

279 Idol capital

What upsets you most in life?
What gets you really worked up?
What do you do to stop it upsetting you?

👁 Read Acts 17 v 16

ENGAGE YOUR BRAIN

▶ *Where had Paul reached now? (v16)*

▶ *How was Paul feeling? (v16)*

▶ *What made Paul feel like that? (v16)*

This was the Roman Empire's capital of ideas. Its people loved to think and talk about religion, and God, and life and death (v21). An idol is something which people treat as God instead of Him. And Athens was the capital of idols.

In those days, idols were often statues; today we may not treat statues as God but we still have idols; money, popularity, sex, career, family, anything that we love and serve and respect as our "god", as the thing which is most important to us.

▶ *Why do you think these idols made Paul feel this way?*

▶ *How much respect was the one true God getting in this city?*

If we love God, we'll hate seeing others refusing to even recognise His existence.

👁 Read verses 17–21

▶ *What did Paul do? (v17)*

▶ *What was his basic message? (end v18)*

THINK ABOUT IT

▶ *How distressed are you when people around you treat something else as their god and ignore Jesus?*

▶ *Does this prompt you to talk to them about Jesus' resurrection?*

THE BOTTOM LINE

Idols should distress us; distress should prompt us to talk about Jesus.

280 Knowing and needing

Who is God? What is He like?
The Athenians knew that they didn't know.
And Paul knew that he did know.
Let's listen in and learn.

👁 Read Acts 17 v 22–28

The Athenians accepted that they didn't really know who God was (v23). So Paul said he'd explain God to them.

ENGAGE YOUR BRAIN

▶ Why should this be good news to the Athenians?

▶ From verses 24–26, fill in the list:

God doesn't…

God has…

▶ What should be people's response to this God? (v27)

THINK IT THROUGH

▶ Does God need anything from you? Why/why not?

▶ Do you need God? Why/why not?

If God needed us to do stuff for Him, then He'd owe us; we'd be able to be in charge of Him and His actions. But as we need God to do stuff for us, then we owe Him; He's in charge of us and should direct our actions.

The Athenians needed to realise that it wasn't for them to say what God is like; it's for God to reveal what He's like.

How do you think the Athenians will react to what Paul's told them? (remember that Athens is full of temples). We'll find out tomorrow.

PRAY ABOUT IT

Dear God, thank you for all that you've done for me and continue to do for me. Help me to remember that I need you, and you don't need me. Make my life revolve around you, and stop me from thinking that you should revolve around me. Amen.

281 A day in God's diary

If someone said: "What does Jesus rising from the dead mean?", what would you say? Paul gives a clear — and surprising — answer to that question as he tells the Athenians about the God who can be known.

Read Acts 17 v 29–34

ENGAGE YOUR BRAIN

▷ Who are humans created by? (v29)

▷ How is Paul pointing out the stupidity of worshipping an idol (something made by man)?

▷ What does God now tell all people to do? (v30)

Repent means to turn around. All people everywhere have worshipped an idol — something that becomes more important to them than God. They need to start treating their Creator as their God.

▷ Because of humanity's idolatry, what kind of day has God put in his diary? (v31)

▷ Who'll do the judging? How do we know that? (v31)

▷ What does Jesus rising from the dead prove? (v31)

THINK IT THROUGH

The only way to escape Jesus' judgment of idolatry in the future is to turn away from idols and towards Jesus as God right now.

▷ Have you ever done that?

▷ In which areas of your life do you struggle to love and serve and obey Jesus as God, instead of something else?

SHARE IT

▷ Think of some friends you'd love to tell about Jesus. What are they treating as God instead of Him?

▷ How can you tell them that Jesus is better than those things, and that judgment is coming?

282 — Me? A minister?

Who do you know who's a minister?
Actually; what is a minister?
That's easy — it's someone who works for a church...
Isn't it?

👁 **Read Acts 18 v 1–4**

ENGAGE YOUR BRAIN

▶ Where's next on Paul's tour?

▶ Paul went to stay with a couple of friends (v2). What did he do with them? (v3)

▶ So, what was Paul doing from Monday to Friday?

▶ What did Paul do at the weekends?

THINK IT THROUGH

▶ What was Paul's ministry?

▶ Was it his full-time job?

▶ What does this show us about who can do ministry?

▶ Is having a full-time job an excuse for not having a ministry?

God calls members of His people to different ministries. Some have a preaching ministry; others are evangelists (like Paul here); some teach children the Bible; others meet with individual Christians to encourage them.

It's easy to think that only "proper" ministers who work full-time for a church will be asked by God to do these things; but Paul's example shows us that a full-time job and ministry can go hand-in-hand.

GET ON WITH IT

▶ What ministry do you think God might want you to help?

▶ Are there times when you're not working (at school, college, uni or job) when you won't take time for yourself but instead use it to serve God's people?

283 Paul's panic

It's so easy to think that Paul just breezed into a city, talked about Jesus, and everyone thought he was great and became Christians. But it wasn't quite like that...

👁 Read Acts 18 v 5–6

ENGAGE YOUR BRAIN

▶ *Who did Paul preach to about the Christ, God's eternal king? (v5)*

Sensible idea: they were God's ancient people, and knew their Old Testaments. They'll be thrilled to hear that Christ has come into the world!

▶ *How did it go? (v6)*

Ever been attacked for being a Christian? You've got something in common with Paul.

👁 Read verses 7–8

▶ *How did Paul react? (v7)*

Strange result: God's ancient people don't want to know about Jesus, so Paul's going to preach to outsiders.

▶ *How did it go? (v8)*

👁 Read verses 9–17

▶ *How was Paul feeling about talking about Jesus in Corinth? (v9)*

▶ *But he didn't need to feel like this — why not? (v10)*

Stunning truth: Jesus has chosen lots of people in Corinth to be His followers; and He's going to use Paul to reach them.

THINK ABOUT IT

▶ *Are Jesus' people always the ones we'd expect to become Christians? (Think about verses 5–8.)*

▶ *How does Jesus reach His people to make them Christians? (Think about verses 10–11.)*

▶ *How is this an encouragement to you as a Christian?*

THE BOTTOM LINE

Jesus uses His people to reach more of His people; and often His people are surprising people.

284 Apeing Apollos

**Acts 17 encouraged us to "be a Berean";
Acts 18 wants us to "ape Apollos", to learn from and
follow his example.**

👁 Read Acts 18 v 18–23

ENGAGE YOUR BRAIN

Paul's time in Corinth has finished and he's moved on. Meanwhile…

👁 Read verses 24–28

▶ Who do we meet in v24, and how's he described? (v24–25)

"He knew only the baptism of John." In other words, he knew that John the Baptist had said Jesus was God's promised King. But there were some important gaps in his understanding. He knew that he needed to repent — turn from sin and back to God. But he didn't fully understand about Jesus' death and resurrection.

▶ When they hear him speak, what do Paul's friends Priscilla and Aquila do? (v26)

▶ Apollos clearly listened to them, and decided to go to another town to serve God there. What did he do? (v27–28)

THINK IT THROUGH

God gives us these little pictures of churches and Christians for us to hold up alongside ourselves and ask how we might live for God better — both as individuals and churches. Here, God wants us to "ape Apollos".

▶ What can we learn from Apollos:

– when it comes to the Bible? (v24, 28)

– when it comes to talking about Jesus? (v25, 28)

– when it comes to being shown a mistake? (v26)

▶ In which of these three areas will you try to ape Apollos?

285 Psalms – Hope and glory

David's in a tight spot again — his enemies are closing in on him, hungry for his blood. No prizes for guessing what David does when all seems lost...

👁 Read Psalm 17 v 1–12

ENGAGE YOUR BRAIN

▶ *Why did David cry out to God? (v11–12)*

▶ *What did he know about God that made him confident? (v6–7)*

▶ *What great things did David ask for? (8–9)*

David was surrounded by vicious enemies, so he called to God for rescue. David knew that God would hear his prayer and he knew God saves and protects His people (v7). David could honestly say to God that his motives for asking were pure (v1–5). Can we always say that?

👁 Read verses 13–15

▶ *What did David ask for? (v13)*

▶ *What was his incredible hope for the future? (v15)*

David knew that those who went against God and His people would have nothing beyond this life to enjoy. In contrast, David was confident that one day he'd be rewarded with seeing God face to face!

That's true for all God's people. God will bring His rescued people to be with Him for ever — to see Him face to face (v15). In the meantime, He'll protect and care for us as His treasured possession (v8).

GET ON WITH IT

Why not try to memorise verse 6? Or verse 8? Or verse 15? You choose.

PRAY ABOUT IT

Use the verse you've chosen to praise God right now. Thank God that His people will get to see His face.

THE BOTTOM LINE

God's people are the apple of His eye.

286 Cheers for the years

King David's looking back on his life and all that God has done for him. God had taken him from shepherd boy to King of Israel, defeating many violent enemies along the way.

👁 Read Psalm 18 v 1–19

ENGAGE YOUR BRAIN

▷ How does David describe God? (v2)

▷ What picture of God do we get from v7–15?

▷ Yet what did this terrifying God do for David? (v16–19)

What an amazing picture of God. David had faced death, but the Lord answered his prayers and rescued him. This terrifying, all-powerful God stepped in and showed great love and care for David. No wonder David's praising the Lord!

▷ How have you seen God's power?

▷ How have you seen His care?

👁 Read verses 20–36

▷ How does God treat people?(v26)

▷ What had He done for David? (v32–36)

David had messed up sometimes, but he'd devoted his life to God, and God helped him along the way (v32).

👁 Read verses 37–50

▷ Who was behind David's victories? (v39)

As God's people today, Christians celebrate what God has done for them through King Jesus. He gained a far greater victory than David — defeating sin, death and the devil.

PRAY ABOUT IT

Like David, will you show your gratitude to God? Maybe you could write your own psalm to Him.

287 Exodus – Hail to the king

Story so far: God's people, the Israelites, were slaves in Egypt. God chose Moses to lead them out of captivity but Pharaoh refused to let them go. So far, God has sent six plagues on Egypt, but Pharaoh won't budge.

👁 Read Exodus 9 v 13–26

ENGAGE YOUR BRAIN

▶ What was the threat to Pharaoh and Egypt? (v14)

▶ Why didn't God just quickly destroy the Egyptians? (v15–16)

▶ What happened to the people who ignored God's warning? (v21, v25)

▶ Where did it not hail? (v26)

God could have easily wiped out the Egyptians to free the Israelites. But He showed His compassion by continuing to give Pharaoh another chance. The Lord was also using the Egyptians as an example to the whole world. Everyone would see His power and how He rescued His people (v16). Notice that, yet again, the Israelites were unharmed.

👁 Read verses 27–35

▶ What surprising things did Pharaoh say? (v27–28)

▶ But what did Moses know? (v30)

▶ Was he right? (v34–35)

▶ What did God show by stopping the hail storm? (v29)

God hit Egypt with its worse hail storm in history — barley, flax, animals and slaves were destroyed. It was so terrible that Pharaoh admitted he was in the wrong and promised to release God's people. But Moses knew that as soon as the hail stopped, Pharaoh's heart would harden again.

PRAY ABOUT IT

By commanding a huge hail storm, God showed how powerful He is — He's in charge of the whole earth. Bow down before our all-powerful God right now. Praise Him for being in control and thank Him for the amazing world He's created and rules.

288 Day of the locust

Pharaoh remained stubborn, refusing to let the Israelites go to worship God in the desert. To bring the Egyptians to their knees again God would now send a plague of... er... locusts? That doesn't sound very scary.

👁 Read Exodus 10 v 1–6

ENGAGE YOUR BRAIN

▶ Why did God allow Pharaoh's heart to be hardened? (v1–2)

▶ What did Pharaoh refuse to do? (v3)

▶ What did God promise as punishment this time?

Pharaoh refused to let the Israelites worship God and so was rightly punished. And through the way God dealt with the Egyptians, people everywhere would hear of God's power and know that He is the one true God.

Despite all the plagues, Pharaoh refused to admit that God was in charge, and he brought more pain and terror on his people.

👁 Read verses 7–20

▶ What offer did Pharaoh make? (v11)

▶ How did Pharaoh react to the locust infestation? (v16–17)

▶ What happened again? (v20)

Pharaoh's officials begged him to let the Israelites worship God in the desert. But Pharaoh was stubborn and proud and would only let the men go. He still refused to obey God. Then after the locusts had done their damage, Pharaoh admitted his sin. But as soon as the locusts had gone, he refused to release God's people.

THINK IT THROUGH

▶ Do you ever say sorry to God but not really mean it?

▶ Or promise to change your ways but not do it?

PRAY ABOUT IT

Talk to God honestly about these things. Ask Him to help you truly change your ways for the better.

314 | Exodus 10 v 21–29

289 | In the dark

Close your eyes. Keep them shut and try walking to the bathroom. Not easy, is it? Imagine living in total darkness for three whole days. Pharaoh didn't enjoy it...

👁 Read Exodus 10 v 21–29

ENGAGE YOUR BRAIN

- ▶ What deal did Pharaoh offer this time? (v24)

- ▶ But how did Moses respond? (v25–26)

- ▶ What was the predictable outcome? (v27–29)

The Egyptians were terrified about being thrown into total darkness for three days. But Pharaoh still refused to bow down to God. He still wanted things his way. He soon learned that you can't bargain with God.

Moses rightly stood up to Pharaoh and didn't give in to his demands. He insisted on obeying all of God's commands and not just part of them. Moses actually commanded the king of Egypt, telling him what to do! (v25) He knew that God was much more powerful than Pharaoh.

THINK IT THROUGH

- ▶ Do you ever compromise with your faith?

- ▶ What wrong things do you refuse to cut out of your life?

- ▶ When do you give God half measures rather than full obedience?

PRAY ABOUT IT

Talk openly with God. Ask Him to help you not to compromise when it comes to obeying Him. Thank Him that He's more powerful than anything or anyone, and can help you in huge ways.

THE BOTTOM LINE

Don't compromise when it comes to obeying God.

290 Final warning

Pharaoh and the Egyptians have had nine warnings from God already. God would give them one more chance to let His people go before hitting them with the most devastating plague of all.

Read Exodus 11 v 1–8

ENGAGE YOUR BRAIN

▶ What did God say would happen? (v1)

▶ What else had God done for His people? (v3)

▶ What was the very bad news for the Egyptians? (v5–6)

▶ How would things be different for the Israelites? (v7–8)

Why would God do such a horrific thing as that? It was punishment for Pharaoh and the Egyptians for enslaving God's people, treating them cruelly (remember Pharaoh slaughtering baby Israelite boys?) and refusing to let them go.

It would show Pharaoh once and for all that God was in charge, not him. And only something as awful as this final plague would make Pharaoh finally let God's people go.

Read verses 9–10

▶ How does v10 sum up chapters 7–11 of Exodus?

Pharaoh refused to change. He refused to obey God and brought disaster on his people. "The Lord hardened Pharaoh's heart" doesn't mean Pharaoh had no choice in the matter. He had already chosen to reject God (Exodus 8 v 15). So God made Pharaoh what he had chosen to be. Pharaoh got the punishment he deserved.

PRAY ABOUT IT

Pray for people you know who refuse to live God's way. Ask the Lord to soften their hearts so that they turn to Him, and live for Him, not themselves.

291 | Making a meal of it

It's getting to the crunch point in Egypt. God would send a final plague, killing the eldest son in each Egyptian family. But what about Israelite families? And what have lambs got to do with it?

👁 Read Exodus 12 v 1–11

ENGAGE YOUR BRAIN

▶ *In your own words, describe what the Israelites had to do.*

▶ *Why did they have to eat in a hurry, with their walking clothes on? (v11)*

God gave His people specific instructions for the Passover. They had to do these things to be rescued by God. And they had to be ready for Him to rescue them.

👁 Read verses 12–13

▶ *What would God do to Egypt?*

▶ *How would the lambs' blood save the Israelites?*

The lamb was killed instead of the firstborn son in each Israelite family. The blood of the lamb was protection. If there was lamb's blood on the door frame, the Lord would pass over that house. The eldest son could say: "That lamb died in my place".

The lamb's death is a picture of what Jesus would do 1500 years later. He would die on the cross to take the punishment we deserve for our sins against God. Christians can look to Jesus and say: "He died in my place".

SHARE IT

▶ *Who can you explain the whole Passover thing to?*

▶ *How can you link it to what Jesus has done for you?*

PRAY ABOUT IT

If you're a Christian, thank God for sending Jesus to die in your place. Praise Him that on the Day of Judgment, He will pass over you and not punish you, because of Jesus' death.

292 Feast first

It's the night of God's final plague on Egypt. Time to eat some strange bread and tasty lamb. One of the most important meals ever.

👁 Read Exodus 12 v 14–20

ENGAGE YOUR BRAIN

▶ *What did the Israelites have to do? (v15–16)*

▶ *Why? (v17)*

▶ *What would happen to anyone who disobeyed God? (v19)*

God was about to rescue them from slavery in Egypt — it would be a day to remember for ever. They would commemorate it by having a special feast week, by not eating food with yeast in it, and by resting from work. Celebrating the feast every year would remind the Israelites of God's great rescue.

Anyone who disobeyed God's command would be cut off from His people. That's how seriously God treats sin. Anyone who refuses to obey Him will be cut off from Him for ever.

👁 Read verses 21–28

▶ *Why did they have to put blood on their door frames and stay indoors? (v23)*

The lamb's blood would save them from God's punishment. And that goes for us too. We've all disobeyed God and all deserve to be cut off from Him. But God sent Jesus to rescue people. Jesus, the Lamb of God, died so that those who trust His blood (death) to rescue them will not be punished by God. Incredible.

PRAY ABOUT IT

You're on your own today.

▶ *What do you want to say to God?*

▶ *What do you need to say to Him?*

THE BOTTOM LINE

Remember God rescuing His people.

293 Time to go

It's the big one — the tenth and final plague.
The Israelites have eaten their lamb, put the blood on
their door-posts, got their yeastless dough and are ready
to leave...

👁 Read Exodus 12 v 29–32

ENGAGE YOUR BRAIN

▶ *How did Pharaoh and the Egyptians react to this final plague? (v30)*

▶ *What did Pharaoh do, at last?*

Pharaoh had repeatedly refused to obey God and release the Israelites. God kept His promise and the eldest son in each Egyptian family died. Only after this final horrific plague did Pharaoh finally obey God and let the Israelites go.

👁 Read verses 33–42

▶ *What did the Egyptian people do? (v33, v36)*

▶ *How were the Israelites able to escape Egypt? (v37)*

▶ *How did they remember it for years to come? (v42)*

The Egyptians were so terrified of God, they wanted the Israelites to

leave! They even gave them gold and silver, as God had said they would (Exodus 3 v 21–22).

Feel the relief — centuries of slavery in a foreign land, then God's dramatic rescue during a midnight slaughter. The New Testament tells us this rescue is a picture of a far greater one, when Jesus died on the cross to rescue His people from slavery to sin.

PRAY ABOUT IT

Read through this story again, thanking God for this amazing rescue. Then reflect on Jesus' death on the cross. Praise God for this ultimate rescue.

THE BOTTOM LINE

God rescues His people.

294 God's people

"ALL ABSEILERS MUST WEAR A HELMET"
To do certain things, you have to follow important rules.
Like wearing a helmet before throwing yourself off a cliff
face. No helmet? No abseiling.

The Israelites had to obey special rules to take part in the Passover feast.

Read Exodus 12 v 43–51

ENGAGE YOUR BRAIN

▶ *Who couldn't eat the Passover meal? (v43, v45, v48)*

▶ *What did you have to do to qualify? (v44, v48)*

Every male wanting to take part had to be an Israelite, one of God's people. The mark of this was being circumcised — having part of the skin around the penis cut off. Ouch. It was a sign that a man or boy belonged to God's people.

Since Jesus died on the cross for us, we don't have to be circumcised to show that we are part of God's family. So what do you need to become one of God's people, a Christian?

Read John 3 v 3

When you believe that Jesus died for you, God forgives your sin and changes you. It's like being born again. You start living for God instead of yourself.

SHARE IT

If someone asked you: "How do you become a Christian?" how would you answer them?

PRAY ABOUT IT

Are you part of God's people? If so, get praising God. If not, what are you going to do about it?

295 | Remember remember

How do you remember stuff, like facts for tests? Do you write them out loads of times, or maybe make up bizarre songs to help you remember? Check out the Israelites' weird way of remembering God's rescue.

👁 Read Exodus 13 v 1–10

ENGAGE YOUR BRAIN

▷ *How did the Israelites celebrate the day God rescued them from Egypt? (v6–7)*

▷ *What would it remind them of? (v8–9)*

▷ *What did God promise His people? (v5)*

For centuries, God had promised to give His people their own land — Canaan. When they eventually arrived there, they were to hold this feast and remember God rescuing them. It would also remind them of God's awesome power and their need to live His way — keeping His law on their lips.

👁 Read verses 11–16

▷ *Why did they dedicate all their firstborn to God? (v14–16)*

Dedicating each firstborn child to God reminded the Israelites that they were God's "firstborn" — His chosen people, rescued by Him.

Christians have been rescued by God from the punishment they deserve for their sin. We were all ruled by the sin in our lives, but Jesus died on the cross to pay the price and buy us back (redeem us).

PRAY ABOUT IT

Thank God for His amazing rescue. Ask Him to help you take His Word — in the Bible — to heart, so that His law is on your lips and you live to please Him.

296 | God's guidance

The Israelites are on the run from Egypt and they're not safe yet. The Egyptian army is behind them and the Philistine army is in front of them. Will they fight or run?

👁 Read Exodus 13 v 17–22

ENGAGE YOUR BRAIN

▶ *Why did God lead His people away from the Philistines? (v17)*

▶ *How did God lead them? (v21)*

God knew the Israelites would freak out and give up if they faced the mighty Philistine army. So He took them the long way round, leading them in a spectacular way — in a pillar of cloud by day and a pillar of fire at night. He didn't leave His people for one second; He was guiding them all the way (v22).

👁 Read verse 19

▶ *Why was Moses carrying Joseph's bones around with him???*

Talk about having a skeleton in your closet! Remember Joseph from the book of Genesis (Day 208)? God had promised Joseph's family that He would give them the country of Canaan to live in. Even though

Joseph lived and died in Egypt, he trusted God's promise to take the Israelites to Canaan. He showed his great faith in God by asking for his bones to be carried to Canaan and buried there (Genesis 50 v 24–26).

GET ON WITH IT

▶ *Are you letting God lead you through life?*

▶ *How can you follow Him more?*

▶ *Which of God's promises in the Bible can you hold on to?*

PRAY ABOUT IT

Thank God that He guides His people through life and never leaves them. And thank God that He always keeps His promises.

THE BOTTOM LINE

God sticks with His people.

297 | In a tight spot

How do you react when you're in a tight spot? Curl up into a ball? Come out fighting? Blame God? Trust Him to get you through?

👁 Read Exodus 14 v 1–9

ENGAGE YOUR BRAIN

▶ *What was God's plan? (v1–4)*

▶ *What would it achieve? (v4)*

▶ *What did Pharaoh and the Egyptians do?*

It seemed like a weird plan that would trap the Israelites — turning around and heading back towards Egypt. Crazy. But God was in complete control. He would rescue His people. He would punish the evil Egyptians. And everyone would know that He was the Lord (v4)!

👁 Read verses 10–14

▶ *What ridiculous claims did the Israelites make? (v11–12)*

▶ *How much were they trusting God?*

▶ *What was Moses' brilliant, inspiring answer?*

The Israelites were so terrified of the Egyptian army they lost all faith in God to protect them. But Moses knew God was in control and would keep His promise to crush the Egyptians and rescue His people. He knew that it wasn't down to their strength — it was all down to God (v14). They just had to sit still; God would fight for them.

PRAY ABOUT IT

Say sorry to God for specific times you've doubted Him. Ask Him to help you trust Him more.

THE BOTTOM LINE

Trust in the Lord.

298 Walking through water

The Israelites were terrified. The huge Egyptian army was hot on their heels and they seemed to be trapped against the banks of the Red Sea. Many of them doubted that God would really rescue them.

👁 Read Exodus 14 v 15–22

ENGAGE YOUR BRAIN

▶ What did God say He would do? (v16–17)

▶ Why? (v18)

▶ What else did He do for His people? (v20)

God promised to rescue His people and keep His word. He put the pillar of cloud between them and the Egyptians, plunging the Egyptians into darkness. He then parted the Red Sea so the Israelites could walk through on dry ground. Amazing.

God wants everyone to know that He is in control of everything. To know that He is the only God and worship Him.

👁 Read verses 23–31

▶ How did God punish Pharaoh and the Egyptians for sinning against Him?

▶ What happened to God's people and how did they respond? (v31)

▶ How has their attitude changed since verses 10–12?

God's enemies got the punishment they deserved. Ultimately, God will punish everyone who refuses to obey Him. And He will rescue His people. When the Israelites saw what He had done, they feared God and put their trust in Him. Finally.

PRAY ABOUT IT

Does this incredible rescue inspire you to trust God and shout thanks to Him? As you praise God for this fantastic rescue mission, thank Him for the ultimate rescue — achieved by Jesus on the cross.

THE BOTTOM LINE

God rescues His people and punishes His enemies.

299 Sing when you're winning

Is there anything that always gets you singing? Maybe you can't resist a bit of karaoke. Or joining in with your team's chants. Moses and the Israelites couldn't stop themselves from singing to God...

👁 Read Exodus 15 v 1–2

ENGAGE YOUR BRAIN

▶ *What were they excitedly singing about God?*

▶ *Which lines can you echo?*

God had rescued His people from slavery and defeated their enemies in spectacular style. And now they wanted to sing about it and praise Him. The great thing is that all Christians can sing and shout verse 2. God has saved them from sin. He is their source of strength. He's the one they want to sing and shout about.

▶ *Is this true for you?*

👁 Read verses 3–12

▶ *How many different phrases do they use to describe God defeating the Egyptians?*

▶ *What do they conclude about God? (v12)*

They had seen God's awesome power right in front of their eyes. He destroyed the massive, terrifying Egyptian army easily. No one can go against God and win. No one is more majestic, more holy, more awesome, more glorious, more wonderful than the Lord.

SHARE IT

▶ *How can you "sing" about God — tell others how incredible and powerful He is?*

PRAY ABOUT IT

Put verses 2 and 12 into your own words as you praise our amazing God right now.

THE BOTTOM LINE

The Lord is my strength and my salvation.

300 Raise the praise

God has rescued His people from slavery. He has brought them out of Egypt and drowned the Egyptian army. Moses and the Israelites can't stop singing and worshipping their awesome God.

👁 Read Exodus 15 v 13–18

ENGAGE YOUR BRAIN

▶ *What did the future hold for God's people? (v13, v17)*

▶ *What will happen to their enemies? (v14–16)*

▶ *What did they recognise about God? (v18)*

Suddenly, the future looked much brighter for the Israelites. There were many enemies ahead of them, but God had already done the hard part — of course He'd protect them against other nations. And give them the land He'd promised (v17). Because of His love for His people, God would lead them and even live with them (v13).

👁 Read verses 19–21

▶ *Who else joined in with the singing and dancing?*

Everyone was overjoyed that God was with them, leading them. Christians can be just as confident in God as Moses and Miriam were. God has already done so much for them — rescuing them from sin and judgment. They know that no enemy is more powerful than God, and one day He will take them to live with Him for ever. The Lord will reign for ever!

PRAY ABOUT IT

Read slowly through the verses again, taking time to praise and thank God for all He's done. Nothing can defeat Him. He's the eternal King who rules for ever.

THE BOTTOM LINE

God will reign for ever!

301 Three days later...

God had led His people through the Red Sea and had destroyed the Egyptian army. The Israelites were thrilled — praising God and trusting Him to lead them. But would it last?

👁 **Read Exodus 15 v 22–24**

ENGAGE YOUR BRAIN

▸ *How did the people react to the first bad situation they found themselves in?*

They were in the desert with no clean water to drink, so it's not surprising they grumbled. But they had already forgotten that God had done amazing things for them and He was with them all the way.

We can sometimes be very quick to forget God and all that He's done for us, and start complaining. God had a good reason for not giving them fresh water right away. He was testing the Israelites to see if they still trusted Him.

👁 **Read verses 25–27**

▸ *What did God do? (v25)*

▸ *What did God require of His people? (v26)*

Despite their grumbling, God made the stagnant water sweet and drinkable. And He made His point: *"You've seen all that I've done for you, so trust me and obey me."*

PRAY ABOUT IT

God says the same to us: *"Remember all I've done for you; trust me through the tough times; obey my commands and live my way."*

Ask the Lord to help you do these things.

THE BOTTOM LINE

Trust and obey.

REVELATION

Revealing Jesus

Beasts with seven heads. Angels sending plagues. Horses with snakes' tails. The moon turned blood red. The number 666. Armageddon. Dragons. Welcome to Revelation.

Are you excited about reading it? Or worried? Relax. To understand Revelation, all you need is God's help and your Bible. *Engage* will simply show you how the Old Testament helps us unwrap Revelation — all the weird, noisy, fiery, surreal bits too.

Above all, this book is a revelation of Jesus. It teaches us that Jesus has already won the great battle over everything that opposes God and His people. Amazingly, dying on the cross was Jesus' decisive victory. And because Jesus has won, His task when He returns is to get rid of His enemies once and for all.

Before that time, Revelation warns that life will most likely be rough, painful and puzzling. Particularly for Christians. But Jesus has won. So stick with Him and hang in there.

Revelation is full of pictures, symbols and numbers. Take them literally and you're in for a nightmare. But the rest of the Bible helps us understand many of them. The most used numbers in Revelation are these:

3 = repetition for emphasis
4 = the whole of creation
6 = the human number
7 = completion/perfection
12 = God's true people

We'll explain why they're understood like this as we go along. Other numbers and many symbols are mentioned, and we'll explain them too!

302 Let's get started

Revelation is a letter written by John, the disciple of Jesus, about a vision God gave him. It's also a prophecy — teaching us about the future, as well as the past and the present. Most of all it's a revelation of who Jesus is.

👁 Read Revelation 1 v 1–3

ENGAGE YOUR BRAIN

▶ *How does John describe this book? (v1)*

▶ *What must we do to really benefit from Revelation? (v3)*

Revelation contains loads of pictures, visions and weird stuff. But, ultimately, it's revealing Jesus to us. As He really is now. So read it, make sure you really hear what God's saying, and take it to heart.

👁 Read verses 4–8

▶ *How is God the Father described? (v4, 8)*

▶ *How about Jesus? (v5)*

▶ *What has He done for us? (v5–6)*

▶ *What will happen when He returns? (v7)*

The number seven appears immediately. In Revelation, seven stands for perfection and completeness. John sent this letter to seven churches — but it's for the whole church, all Christians. The "seven spirits" (v4) means the Holy Spirit, who is completely perfect.

Verses 5–6 vividly describe Jesus and His relationship with us. He faithfully witnessed to the truth and was killed. He was raised from death as the first of many God will raise (all believers, when Jesus returns!). He is now in heaven as the Ruler of everything.

PRAY ABOUT IT

Jesus loves us and died on the cross to free all believers from their sins. In fact, He's made them into a kingdom and priests who will live with and serve God for ever. Get thanking and praising Him right now!

303 | Son shining

The Christian life is often tough. But however rough, God is in control. It's easy to forget that it's Jesus Christ who has ultimate authority in this world of ours.

👁 Read Revelation 1 v 9–11

ENGAGE YOUR BRAIN

▶ *What were John and these Christians sharing in? (v9)*

▶ *What did the voice tell John to do? (v11)*

John told people about Jesus and so was chased away and forced to live on the island of Patmos. He reminds us in verse 9 that the Christian life isn't easy; in this world we must stick together as we face suffering and tough times, waiting for Jesus' return.

👁 Read verses 12–16

▶ *How is this incredible person described?*

▶ *Where was He standing and what was in His hands? (v13, 16)*

The name "son of man" (v13) is from the book of Daniel, and describes someone who was given worldwide, eternal authority by God.

👁 Read verses 17–20

▶ *How does this person describe Himself? (v18)*

▶ *What must John write? (v19)*

▶ *So what's Revelation about?*

▶ *What's the deal with the stars and the lampstands? (v20)*

This is Jesus. Read through verses 12–18 again and see how He's not the weak, cuddly character many people see Him as, but the all-powerful ruler of the universe!

THINK IT OVER

At that time, Christians were in real danger of losing their lives for their faith. If ever we are, then what encouragement is there in this passage that we won't be losers?

PRAY ABOUT IT

Jesus has all authority. Thank God for Jesus right now.

304 | Church news letter

There are seven letters to seven churches. Since seven in Revelation is the complete number, these letters are to the whole church, all over the world. So what Jesus said to these churches, He's saying to you and your church.

👁 Read Revelation 2 v 1–7

ENGAGE YOUR BRAIN

▶ What good things does Jesus say about these Christians? (v2–3)

▶ What criticisms did He have? (v4)

▶ So what should they do? (v5)

▶ What's the threat? (v5)

▶ What's the reward? (v7)

These guys worked hard for the gospel and hung in there during hard times. They got rid of false teachers who were trying to drag them down. But they'd lost their first love — it seems their initial enthusiasm for Jesus and living His way had tailed off dramatically. They'd be in serious trouble unless they sorted this out. And what a great reward for those who love and serve Jesus — eternal life with Him (v7).

👁 Read verses 8–11

▶ What problems did the church in Smyrna have? (v9)

▶ How did Jesus encourage them? (v10)

▶ What's the great promise? (v11)

Jargon buster: "synagogue of Satan" = Jews who persecuted Christians; "ten days" = a limited time; "second death" = being punished at God's final judgment. Anyway, these guys were being terribly persecuted for their faith. BUT... they were truly rich for suffering for Jesus and would be given the crown of eternal life!

PRAY ABOUT IT

Have you lost your love for Jesus? What will you do about it? What will you say to Him and ask Him right now? Pray that you'll keep going through the dark times, looking forward to glorious eternity.

305 Good news, bad news

In John's incredible vision, Jesus told him to write to seven churches. Let's see what Jesus said to churches 3 and 4. Remember, this message is for the whole church — that means all Christians.

👁 Read Revelation 2 v 12–17

ENGAGE YOUR BRAIN

▶ How was Pergamum described? (v13)

▶ What was good about this church? (v13)

▶ What was not so good? (v14-15)

▶ What's the warning? (v16)

Pergamum was a tough place to be a Christian. Roman emperors and gods were worshipped and Christians were persecuted or even killed (v13). So these believers were commended for not giving up on Jesus. However, they'd listened to false teachers and were involved in idol worship and sexual sin. Jesus told them to repent and turn back to Him.

👁 Read verse 18–29

▶ What had these Christians got right? (v19)

▶ What was wrong here? (v20)

▶ What was the bad news for the woman who was leading them astray? (v21–23)

The church in Thyatira was doing great things (v19); but some of them were involved in idol worship and sexual sin. A female prophet in the church was behind most of it and was rightly punished for it. Yet for those who kept obeying Jesus, they would share in His rule and authority. What an amazing promise — one day believers will rule with Jesus!

GET ON WITH IT

▶ What do you "worship" more than God?

▶ How do you disobey God when it comes to sex stuff?

▶ What do you need to do about these things?

PRAY ABOUT IT

Talk to God about this stuff.

306 | Poking and perking

We all need a poke in the ribs sometimes — that's what the Christians in Sardis receive here. We also need encouragement and a pat on the back too, just as the church in Philadelphia did.

👁 Read Revelation 3 v 1–6

ENGAGE YOUR BRAIN

▶ *What did people think of this church? What was the truth? (v1)*

▶ *What must they do? (v2)*

▶ *How? (v3)*

▶ *What if they didn't? (v3)*

▶ *What's the evidence that there were some who had a real relationship with Jesus? (v4)*

▶ *What's promised to them? (v4–5)*

👁 Read verse 7–13

▶ *How does Jesus encourage this church? (v8–9)*

▶ *How else? (v10)*

▶ *So what should they do in the meantime? (v11)*

▶ *What do you think v12 means?*

There were only a small number of Christians in Philadelphia, a city with many Jews who were saying: "You Christians aren't the true people of God. We are. It's us who belong in the temple and city of God, not you!" Life was tough for Christians there, and they were feeling weak. But God would protect them and one day they'd be strong (like pillars, v12) and would be with God for ever.

THINK IT OVER

▶ *What would Jesus challenge you about?*

▶ *What would He urge you to change?*

▶ *How has He encouraged you through His words in Revelation?*

PRAY ABOUT IT

Talk these issues over with God. And pray for any Christians you know who are in the minority and feeling weak.

307 | Lukewarm Laodicea

Laodicea was a wealthy city with loads of successful industries. The last of Jesus' seven letters was written to the Christians who lived there. And it was a huge wake-up call for them.

👁 Read Revelation 3 v 14

ENGAGE YOUR BRAIN

▶ What do these descriptions of Jesus tell us about Him?

"Amen" is the Hebrew word for "truth". Jesus is the truth and speaks the truth. He's totally faithful and we can trust everything He says. He rules all of God's creation. Listen to Him.

👁 Read verses 15–18

▶ What was the problem? (v14–15)

▶ How did they view themselves? (v17)

▶ What didn't they realise? (v17)

▶ What must they do? (v18)

These Christians were lukewarm — not having the guts to live for Jesus wholeheartedly. Laodicea was famous for its wealth, fabrics and eye ointment ("salve"). Jesus told them their wealth was worth nothing; they needed true riches

from Jesus. They needed to cover their shamefulness. And to see they must turn away from selfish living and start obeying God.

👁 Read verses 19–22

▶ What should these guys do? (v19)

▶ What's the great offer? (v20)

▶ What's the reward for those who accept Jesus' offer? (v21)

Money and possessions may make us feel secure, but only trusting in Jesus can bring us eternal security.

PRAY ABOUT IT

Pray for friends (maybe yourself too) who rely on money and possessions but really need the security of life with Jesus.

THE BOTTOM LINE

True riches are only found in Jesus.

308 | Heavenly view

**The scene now switches from earth to heaven.
John is given a front-row view right inside.
Come and sit on his shoulders to see.**

👁 **Read Revelation 4 v 1–6**

ENGAGE YOUR BRAIN

▶ *What does John see at the centre of heaven? (v2)*

▶ *What do you think v3–5 tells us about the person on the throne?*

Verses 3–6 are full of Old Testament references (eg: the rainbow recalls God's promise to Noah and His power shown in the flood). John's telling us exactly who's on the throne — it's the God of Noah, of Moses, the God who gave His law at Mount Sinai with thunder and lightning. He's on the throne, in control of the universe.

Notice the 24 thrones around the main one. There were 12 tribes of Israel and 12 disciples of Jesus: these 24 elders symbolise all God's people.

👁 **Read verses 6–11**

▶ *What were these weird creatures doing? (v8)*

▶ *And the elders? (v9–10)*

▶ *What are the reasons for bowing down to God? (v11)*

The four fantastic creatures symbolise the world that God has created. One day, the whole world — everything God has made — will worship Him.

THINK IT OVER

In this amazing vision, John is shown the world from the perspective of heaven: God's in complete control. Think how this would have encouraged Christians in the seven churches who were under attack for their beliefs.

▶ *How is it an encouragement to you too?*

THE BOTTOM LINE

God's on His throne. King for ever.

309 Lion or lamb?

Ready for more of John's vision of the heavenly throne room? It involves a hard-to-open scroll, a lion, a lamb, and all those animals and elders again. Remember, Revelation is revealing the real Jesus to us.

👁 Read Revelation 5 v 1–5

ENGAGE YOUR BRAIN

▶ *Why is John weeping? (v4)*

▶ *What stopped his tears? (v5)*

The scroll contains God's plan for world history. Until it's opened, God's plan to act in rescue and judgment remains unknown and uncompleted. But the Lion of Judah (Jesus) can open it. So get ready for this roaring lion…

👁 Read verses 6–10

▶ *What does John see instead of a lion? (v6)*

▶ *What happened when He took the scroll? (v8)*

▶ *How would you summarise their new song? (v9–10)*

Jesus is pictured as both the lion (to show His total authority) and the lamb (to show He laid down His life for people in sacrificial service). Jesus' death is central to everything.

👁 Read verses 11–14

Thousands and thousands of angels giving Jesus the praise He deserves for dying in our place.

PRAY ABOUT IT

If you agree with the angels' words, make a point of honouring Jesus in your own words right now.

THE BOTTOM LINE

Jesus' death is central to the whole of history.

310 Dark riders

Now we get to the juicy stuff you've been waiting for: the four horsemen of the apocolypse, souls of the dead, earthquakes, the moon turning blood red, stars falling from the sky. Terrifying, but essential stuff.

👁 Read Revelation 6 v 1–8

We've now reached the first series of events describing history between Christ's resurrection and return.

ENGAGE YOUR BRAIN

▶ *What picture do we get?*

The white horse = aggressive military regimes; red horse = war; black horse = famine that follows war; pale horse = death that follows famine and war.

▶ *What shows that these things are in Jesus' control? (v2, v4, v8)*

▶ *How is this truth supported by verses 1, 3, 5 and 7?*

👁 Read verses 9–11

▶ *What extra suffering will some believers face? (v9)*

▶ *What will they ask? (v10)*

▶ *What will they be told? (v11)*

👁 Read verses 12–17

▶ *How would you sum up the events described here?*

The first five seals are about human history before Jesus returns. The sixth seal brings God's judgment on the cruel, persecuting rulers we've been reading about in verses 1–11. The big question is in verse 17: "The great day of their wrath has come, and who can withstand it?" We'll discover the answer tomorrow.

PRAY ABOUT IT

Thank God that He's in control of our world, even when it doesn't seem like it. Thank Him that He looks after His people and their future with Him is totally secure.

311 | Making a stand

Yesterday we read about the terrifying things that would happen in the world before Jesus returns. It ended with the question: "The great day of their wrath has come, and who can withstand it?" Well, here's the answer...

👁 Read Revelation 7 v 1–10

▶ *Who will be safe? (v3)*

▶ *How are they described? (v9)*

▶ *And what did they recognise? (v10)*

Don't get hung up on the number 144,000. It's not to be taken literally — there are more Christians than that! From John's perspective, they're a huge crowd, too large to count (v9). From God's perspective, they total 144,000. That's best understood as representing the complete people of God (12 tribes of Israel x 12 apostles x 1000, the superlative number). The important fact is that God's people are all safe because Jesus has rescued them (v10).

👁 Read verses 11–17

▶ *How does John describe the huge crowd? (v14)*

▶ *What made their robes white?*

▶ *What's the great future for these people? (v15–16)*

▶ *Why and how? (v17)*

The "great tribulation" is a time of great suffering and persecution. These believers know from the pain of their sufferings that rescue is only found in God. They only have victory because of the blood of Jesus. Yes, Christians suffer in this life. But it's only for a very short time compared to an eternity living with God, under His protection. There will be no more hunger, thirst, tears or suffering.

THINK IT OVER

▶ *What encouragement is there for Christians when life gets hard?*

▶ *What future is there?*

PRAY ABOUT IT

What do you want to say to God today?

312 Incensed and fiery

More weird images and names now. But get the truths behind them. And remember that chapters 8–11 view the same period of history as chapters 6–7 (the time between Jesus' resurrection and His return), but from a new angle.

👁 **Read Revelation 8 v 1–6**

ENGAGE YOUR BRAIN

▷ *What happened during the silence? (v3)*

A censer was filled with sweet-smelling incense, used during special ceremonies. But here it was filled with the prayers of Christians ("saints"). The angel was helping deliver these prayers. It's a great reminder that our prayers are never merely our own — the Holy Spirit helps us pray (Romans 8 v 26–27).

The prayers here were dramatically answered as the angel threw down fire on the earth: God is about to act in judgment…

👁 **Read verses 7–13**

▷ *What effect do these judgments have on the world?*

v7:

v8–9:

v11:

v12:

▷ *And what was the warning? (v13)*

The first four trumpets bring disaster on the world. But this time it's nature that's affected — the earth, sea, rivers and skies. It seems as if human sin is the cause of this punishment, which is terrifying yet only partial — one third of the world affected. The worrying thing is that the next few trumpets will bring worse judgments (v13). But that comes tomorrow.

PRAY ABOUT IT

It's humans who have brought God's judgment on the world. What specific sins do you need to admit to God and repent of right now? Thank Him that He hasn't destroyed us and our world, even though we deserve it.

313 | Scorpion attack

So, four of the seven angels have blown trumpets and the world has been struck with natural disasters. Now for judgments five and six, which affect humans more directly. Hope you're not scared of bugs.

👁 Read Revelation 9 v 1–12

ENGAGE YOUR BRAIN

▶ Any ideas who the fallen star is? (v1, 11)

▶ Who was singled out for torture? (v4)

▶ How bad was it? (v5–6)

The fallen star (also called Abaddon and Apollyon, which mean Destroyer) seems to be Satan. Yet any power he has is limited (v4–5) — God is the one in control. So the devil and evil forces will torment non-Christians for a while ("five months") but even that is limited.

👁 Read verses 13–21

▶ What tragedy did the sixth trumpet announce? (v15)

▶ Yet what effect did it have on mankind? (v20–21)

This time the evil armies do kill people — many people. Surely this would be recognised as punishment from God! But no, people continue to worship idols, steal, murder and sin sexually. People never seem to learn. The situation seems hopeless. But this isn't the end. We've had six of the seven angelic trumpets — so one remains. But you'll have to wait for that.

GET ON WITH IT

▶ Who do you know who refuses to turn to God?

▶ How can you explain to them the seriousness of their decision?

▶ Which sins do you keep going back to despite what Jesus has done for you?

▶ How can you (with God's help) attack these sins in a new way?

PRAY ABOUT IT

Whatever is on your heart and mind, take it to God right now.

314 Sweet and sour

The first six trumpets brought God's judgment on the world, yet people ignored the warnings and carried on sinning. There's now a pause before the seventh and final trumpet is sounded.

👁 Read Revelation 10 v 1–4

ENGAGE YOUR BRAIN

▶ *How is this new angel described? (v1, 3)*

▶ *What was he holding? (v2)*

▶ *What's the surprising instruction to John? (v4)*

This angel's appearance and voice reminds us of God, so he seems to be speaking God's words, on His behalf. Yet John is told not to write them down. We'll never know what they were. If God has decided we shouldn't hear them, then it's best that we don't!

👁 Read verses 5–11

▶ *What was John told to do next? (v8)*

▶ *In what contrasting ways is the scroll described? (v9)*

▶ *What else is John commanded to do? (v11)*

The sixth trumpet has sounded, the end of the world and judgment are just around the corner, but before then there is a job to do. The giant angel has been carrying a little scroll, which John is told to eat. It tastes sweet in his mouth but disagrees with his stomach.

The word of God is sweet — great news to many. But it also has a bitter quality that many don't want to hear. The gospel includes the bitter truth of punishment for rejecting God as well as the sweet news of rescue for those who trust Jesus.

THINK IT OVER

▶ *What experience have you had of the joy of the gospel?*

▶ *When has the gospel brought you rejection?*

▶ *How does chapter 10 encourage us to hang in there, in telling our friends about the gospel?*

315 Expert witness

Yesterday we read about the gospel message being both sweet and bitter. Well, today we'll discover just how hard to swallow some people find it. Get ready for more crazy imagery too.

👁 Read Revelation 11 v 1–6

ENGAGE YOUR BRAIN

▷ *What was John's task? (v1)*

▷ *What would happen to God's city? (v2)*

▷ *How will God make sure His message is heard? (v3, 5, 6)*

God's people would be trampled for a while (v2). The two witnesses stand for Christians who spread the message of Jesus. God will protect them and their message and it will have a powerful effect. Although this wouldn't last for ever.

👁 Read verses 7–14

▷ *What would happen to the witnesses? (v7)*

▷ *Whose side is the world on? (v8–10)*

▷ *But what would happen to them? (v13)*

▷ *What about the witnesses? (v11–12)*

This all seems to be pointing to a time in history when the Christian message is ignored and appears to be defeated by Satan (v7). Many people see the message of Jesus as irritating and tormenting them and they'd love to see it defeated (v10). But when Jesus returns, His witnesses will be raised to live with Him and the gospel will be shown to be the truth. Christians can be killed but they can't be destroyed. They'll live for ever with Jesus.

👁 Read verses 15–19

▷ *What's the great news when Jesus returns? (v15)*

▷ *What'll happen when He does? (v18)*

PRAY ABOUT IT

Pray that you and your church will faithfully share gospel truth.

316 | Acts – Paul on tour

Paul's still touring around, telling people about Jesus and helping start up new churches. Next, he reaches Ephesus, a city known worldwide for its huge temple to the goddess Artemis.

👁 Read Acts 19 v 1–10

ENGAGE YOUR BRAIN

▷ *Who haven't these disciples heard of? (v2)*

▷ *Which type of baptism have they had? (v3)*

These guys knew about John the Baptist (Jesus' cousin who was the support act who paved the way for Jesus), but they didn't know much about Jesus Himself.

▷ *What had John told people to do? (v4)*

▷ *What do they do as a visible sign they now believe in Jesus? (v5)*

▷ *What amazing things happen? (v6)*

The Holy Spirit doesn't enable everyone to speak different languages or prophesy. But He does make a difference to everyone He lives in, just in different ways.

THINK IT THROUGH

▷ *Who does the Holy Spirit live in? (v4–6)*

Sometimes Christians worry they need something extra to really have the Holy Spirit living in them; a special experience, baptism or service. But if you believe in Jesus as your Lord, then the Spirit lives in you! Christians get baptised as a sign that Jesus has turned their lives around. That's the consistent message of the apostles; look back to Peter's words in Acts 2 v 38.

317 | Man, not machine

What does Jesus mean to you?
How would you describe Him in one sentence?
How do you treat Him?

👁 Read Acts 19 v 11–16

ENGAGE YOUR BRAIN

▶ *How did God show that Paul was His servant? (v11–12)*

▶ *Describe what happens in verses 13–16 in your own words.*

▶ *What did these guys think saying "the name of Jesus" would do? (v13)*

They thought that Jesus was like a machine, to be used as they wanted. If they said: "In the name of Jesus, come out", hey presto, the demons would come out. But Jesus isn't a machine; He's someone we need to know and relate to as a person.

THINK IT THROUGH

We may not try to use Jesus to get rid of evil spirits; but we can try to use Him as a machine in other ways, as a mechanism who'll do what we want. We need to treat Jesus as the person He is; speak to Him, hear from Him, relate to Him as a someone, not as a something. These guys got it wrong; let's see some other guys getting it right.

👁 Read verses 17–22

▶ *How did these men show they truly respected Jesus? (v18-19)*

They completely turned away from the fake things they'd been trusting in, despite the cost.

PRAY ABOUT IT

Talk to Jesus now. If recently you've not been spending much time talking and listening to Jesus, ask Him to forgive you and make sure you get back into the habit.

THE BOTTOM LINE

Treat Jesus as a person to relate to, not a machine to be used.

318 I predict a riot

You may have noticed that when Paul talks about Christianity, it often ends in a riot. We've seen that in Ephesus lots of people had put their trust in Christ — but today the riot kicks off.

👁 Read Acts 19 v 23–27

ENGAGE YOUR BRAIN

▶ *What's Demetrius' job? (v24)*

▶ *What's his problem with what Paul's been saying? (v25–26)*

▶ *What does he think the result of this will be? (v27)*

THINK IT THROUGH

▶ *Why are they opposed to Paul's message?*

▶ *What does this suggest about why people might oppose Christianity today?*

It's not because they think it's not true, but because they see it will change things and perhaps make life tougher for them.

👁 Read verses 28–34

▶ *How do Demetrius' buddies react? (v28)*

▶ *What happens? (v29–34)*

Notice they're not explaining why they think Paul's wrong. They're opposing him not with reasoned argument, but with ranting and aggression. Some of them don't even really know why they're there! (v32)

👁 Read verses 35–41

One guy, the city clerk, doesn't get carried away. He calms the crowd and sends them home before much damage is done.

PRAY ABOUT IT

Ask God to help you keep talking about Jesus even when you face opposition. Ask God to remind you that gospel success provokes gospel opposition. Pray for Christians who live in countries where talking openly about Jesus provokes aggression — that God would give them the courage to keep sharing the gospel.

319 Is Paul the real deal?

You listened to this guy Paul... you put your trust in Jesus... and since then there's been rioting and threats against you. Was it really a good idea to listen to Paul?

👁 Read Acts 20 v 1-5

Paul sails to Macedonia to encourage the Christians there (v2).

👁 Read verses 6-12

▶ *In Troas, how does one guy react to Paul's epic talk? (v9)*

If you've ever nodded off in a Bible talk, you're not the first! At least you didn't die!

▶ *What does Paul do? (v10-11)*

What on earth's going on here?! To get this episode's significance, let's rewind 1,000 years, to the time when Elijah was God's chief messenger.

👁 Read 1 Kings 17 v 17-24

Elijah's staying with a widow. When her son dies, she thinks Elijah's presence has brought only trouble.

▶ *What happens next? (v19-23)*

▶ *What does she realise about Elijah because of what she's seen? (v24)*

The widow needed reassuring that Elijah really was God's messenger, and that it was worth listening to him. God reassured her by acting powerfully through Elijah to bring life to the dead.

THINK IT THROUGH

The Christians of Troas needed reassuring that Paul really was God's messenger, and that it was worth listening to him. God did this in a spectacular way.

Paul's the real deal. And the centre of Paul's message was that through Jesus, God can give life to the dead.

▶ *How do these Christians feel? (Acts 20 v 12)*

THE BOTTOM LINE

Paul is God's chosen messenger; we can trust what he says.

320 Crucial qualities

Most churches have a pastor; some have several. What's the job description for a pastor? Pretty funny, friendly, remembers names? Or is there more to it than that? What would be your top three criteria for a church pastor?

👁 Read Acts 20 v 13–17

Paul's on his way to Jerusalem. He's in a hurry, but stops off at Ephesus to speak to the leaders of the church he set up there.

👁 Read verses 18–21

Quality #1

▶ What did Paul do as their pastor? (v19)

▶ Was this easy for him to do? Why, or why not? (end of v19)

Quality #2

▶ What did pastor Paul preach, and where did he do it? (v20)

"Helpful" is an interesting word. Pastor Paul didn't only tell people what they wanted to hear, but what was helpful — what they needed. And he didn't only do it on Sundays.

Quality #3

▶ What else did Paul spend his time in Ephesus doing? (v21)

THINK IT THROUGH

▶ Sum up pastor Paul's three crucial qualities in your own words:

1.

2.

3.

PRAY ABOUT IT

It's pretty hard being a pastor. There are testing setbacks; there's lots of work to do; there's rarely much thanks. So pray for the pastor (or pastors) at your church now; and commit to praying every week for them, that they'd be like pastor Paul in what they do.

THE BOTTOM LINE

Pastors serve Jesus; preach helpfully; and share the gospel.

321 | Racing through life

How much do you value your life? Is there anything worth more to you than enjoying a good life?

👁 Read Acts 20 v 22–24

ENGAGE YOUR BRAIN

▶ Where's Paul going, and why?

▶ What does Paul know will happen when he gets there? (v23)

Paul's not being over-the-top here. In the last few cities he's been to, he's been caught up in riots, imprisoned, flogged, arrested and mocked. Paul certainly didn't have an easy life. Here's a question: Why didn't he stop? Why go to Jerusalem when he knew what kind of things were facing him there? He's done loads for Jesus — why not retire?

▶ Why won't Paul settle for a comfortable life? (v24)

▶ What two things matter to him more than his life? (v24)

THINK IT THROUGH

▶ Do you think Paul is right to have this view of things?

▶ Why, or why not?

▶ How much do you value your life?

▶ Is serving Jesus worth more to you?

▶ How is Paul's attitude a challenge to you?

PRAY ABOUT IT

None of us find it easy to look at life the way Paul did. We need God's help to have this attitude — why not ask Him for it now, if you can do so and genuinely mean it?

THE BOTTOM LINE

"I consider my life worth nothing to me; my only aim is to finish the race and complete the task the Lord Jesus has given me."

322 How to be a good shepherd

Sheep are simple animals. Basically, they need two things: grass to eat, and protection from wolves who'll eat them.

👁 Read Acts 20 v 25–28

ENGAGE YOUR BRAIN

Paul calls the members of a church a "flock": so their overseers, or leaders, are "shepherds".

▶ Why's the church so precious? (end of v28)

▶ If you're a Christian, how does it make you feel to be described like this?

Sheep need feeding...

▶ What had Paul preached and proclaimed to them? (v25–27)

▶ What food do Christians need?

Sheep need protecting...

👁 Read verses 29–31

▶ What's going to happen to this flock? (v29)

▶ What does Paul mean by this? (v30)

▶ What should the shepherds, and the sheep, do? (v28, v31)

GET ON WITH IT

Paul's talking to the leaders of a church; telling them to copy him in feeding the flock with all of God's truth, and protecting the flock by opposing people who want to distort God's truth. Maybe you're a leader of a group at your church (Sunday school, youth group, etc); Paul's talking to you. Are you feeding and protecting?

Maybe you're not a shepherd — but if you're a Christian, you're a sheep! Make it easier for your shepherd to look after you: get to church regularly, be eager to hear all of God's truth (even the difficult bits), and watch out for anyone who tries to change what God says in the Bible.

PRAY ABOUT IT

Pray for your pastor(s) again.

323 Keep going!

Paul brought the message about Jesus to Ephesus; he set up the church in Ephesus; he's taught the Bible to the Christians of Ephesus. How on earth will they keep going now that he's leaving? Can they manage without Paul?

Read Acts 20 v 32–35

ENGAGE YOUR BRAIN

▶ *Under whose care does Paul know these Christians are? (v32)*

▶ *How will God keep caring for them? (v32)*

In His undeserved kindness (grace), God will build them up and one day they will live with Him in perfection.

THINK ABOUT IT

▶ *Why would this be of great comfort to Paul as he left?*

▶ *Why would this humble Paul as he left?*

▶ *Why would this encourage the Ephesian Christians as he left?*

▶ *Do they need Paul?*

▶ *What is the one thing that they do need to keep going?*

Read verses 36–38

▶ *What do Paul and his Christian friends make sure they do before he leaves?*

We're not told what they said; but we can guess from verses 32–35. Surely they thanked God for His grace to them, and asked God that in His grace He'd keep building them up in their faith and get them to their eternal inheritance with Him.

PRAY ABOUT IT

Spend some time praying for God's ongoing grace for yourself. Then pray for His ongoing grace for particular Christian friends of yours.

THE BOTTOM LINE

God's grace keeps His people going.

324 Psalms – Brilliance above

As the prisoner flees across the yard, the security system is triggered. Nothing escapes the glare of the floodlights and he's exposed — no cover, no excuses, he makes himself as small as possible...

Keep that picture in mind as you...

👁 Read Psalm 19 v 1–6

ENGAGE YOUR BRAIN

▶ *The sky has a message. What is it?*

▶ *Where and when can it be heard?*

THINK IT OVER

Do you know anyone who has dismissed faith in God due to a lack of evidence? According to David, they're just not listening. We're living under a permanent, international demonstration of the wonder of God. Just look around you!

👁 Read verses 7–14

▶ *Write down the descriptions of God's commands and words.*

▶ *Faced with such perfection, what two types of sin does David become aware of? (v 12–13)*

Not only does the sun beat down a daily reminder of God's power, God has given us His perfect and precious commands. What can match the insight and plain-talking truth of the Bible? Quite simply, everything that comes from God is beyond brilliant.

PRAY ABOUT IT

As you come face to face with the God of obvious power and unbeatable wisdom, make verse 14 the words of your own prayer.

GET ON WITH IT

Find five minutes today to spend with Psalm 19 in the open air. Don't forget to look up!

325 | Winning mentality

It's great for a sports team to expect victory and be full of confidence. It's another thing all together to advance-order crates of champagne and an open-top bus for the victory parade. Just how confident should a Christian be?

👁 Read Psalm 20 v 1–5

ENGAGE YOUR BRAIN

David's prayer was to be used when the nation's on the brink of war.

▶ *What help and protection can they expect? (v1–2)*

▶ *What scene are they imagining when it's all over? (v5)*

THINK IT OVER

Approaching a tough challenge, you can find your knees shaking. Knowing you're backed up by a huge bank balance, crowds of fans and years of experience can add a sense of security — but what if you've nothing on your side but God?

👁 Read verses 6–9

▶ *What's the result of trusting in military might? (v7–8)*

▶ *What's the result of depending on God?*

Bold words. But what makes David so sure that faith works? Check out 1 Samuel 17 v 45–47.

If David is a sneak preview, Jesus is the real thing — the anointed King! Since His epic battle with the enemy is now past, the cross and resurrection history, the result is guaranteed; we can be ultra confident of the coming victory celebration.

THE BOTTOM LINE

"Some trust in _____ and _____ but we trust in the name of our God."

Fill in the blanks with popular alternatives to God-focused living.

PRAY ABOUT IT

Admit to God about times when you rely on yourself and not Him. Then pray — tell Him everything: don't hold back, and ask Him to help you trust Him more.

326 The secret of success

It's time to collect your Oscar. Having dressed up like royalty, walked the red carpet and wrestled the paparazzi, you step up to receive your reward. As you tentatively approach the microphone, who will you thank?

👁 Read Psalm 21 v 1–13

ENGAGE YOUR BRAIN

Compare the king's victory song (v1–7) with the fate of his enemies (v8–12).

▶ *Who gets what they want? (v2, v11)*

▶ *What is their destiny? (v4, v10)*

▶ *What will they get when they meet God? (v6, v9)*

THINK IT OVER

But why is God on the king's side? Because he's all about God's glory (v1). These are God's military campaigns fought with heaven's muscle. (See what happens with David's own hairbrained scheme in 1 Chronicles 21 v 13–14.)

👁 Read Psalm 21 v 4–7

▶ *Why might his hopes in verses 4 and 6 sound like an exaggeration?*

With his feet still rooted to the earth, David's speaking as if he's in heaven already — it sounds a bit odd. But try putting these words in the mouth of Jesus. They fit perfectly. Jesus is the everlasting king, and here we get a snapshot of His passion and purpose.

GET ON WITH IT

The point of life is not to big yourself up, but to show that Jesus is the best. Get a sticky note, and write on it the goal of your existence, in your own words. Attach it to the ceiling, above your bed, or whatever is the first thing you see each day.

PRAY ABOUT IT

In John 17 v 20–23, Jesus prays for us! Read it and put yourself in the picture. Ask God that together with your church or Christian mates, you'll find ways to let the world know of His outrageous love.

EXODUS

The big clean-up

You've finally left home. And you're about to start sharing a house with your best friends in the whole world, Barry and Flo — it's going to be great! But there are a few issues you need to sort out first...

HOUSE RULES

To begin with, the house is a total mess; in fact it's a disaster zone. There's no way you could live there until some serious cleaning takes place. Barry, bless him, hasn't ever grasped the concept of washing dishes and wouldn't know which end of a vacuum cleaner was which.

And there's also the matter of setting some ground rules, like taking it in turns to buy the milk, how to pay shared bills and who cleans the bathroom. But once things are clean and you've sorted out the house rules, it's going to be awesome living with these guys!

You're probably thinking: *What does this have to do with the second half of Exodus??!*

THE STORY SO FAR

God's people have been rescued from slavery in Egypt with some astounding displays of God's power. But what have they been rescued for? Well, God intends to fulfil all His promises to Abraham — promises of a land to live in, a great nation of people and blessing. As God starts to do that, one big part of the blessing is that He will live among them.

However, just like Barry and Flo, the Israelites have got some serious cleaning up to do before a pure and holy God can live with such a sinful bunch of people. And God is going to give them some ground rules about how it will all work.

So read on to see how this incredible "house share" began.

327 Short-term memory

It's six weeks after Operation Exodus when God rescued His people from slavery in Egypt. Under Moses' leadership, the Israelites are headed for the Promised Land. But it's not going to be a straightforward journey...

👁 **Read Exodus 16 v 1–12**

ENGAGE YOUR BRAIN

▶ *Why are people grumbling? (v3)*

▶ *What are their rose-tinted memories of Egypt? (v3)*

Hang on a minute! Is this the same place we're talking about? The one where you were in terrible slavery, where the country's ruler wanted to kill all your baby boys? Get real!

GET ON WITH IT

Be honest with yourself. Do you ever catch yourself thinking: "Life would be so much easier if I wasn't a Christian. I could get drunk, date that guy/girl or sleep with them, spend my money on whatever I wanted, sleep in on Sunday mornings..."? Missing your old sinful ways? Don't fool yourself — life without God is slavery and it ends in death. Don't slip into that way of thinking; it's very dangerous.

▶ *Who are the Israelites grumbling about? (v2)*

▶ *Are you sure? (v8)*

▶ *What might you expect God's reaction to be?*

▶ *What is His reaction? (v4, v12)*

How amazing is that? Instead of blasting them into oblivion, God kindly provides them with bread and meat.

▶ *What does He want the Israelites to remember? (v12)*

PRAY ABOUT IT

Do you know that the LORD is your God? Really know it? Think about who He is — kind and gracious, compassionate and slow to anger — and then thank Him that trusting in Jesus means He is your God too.

THE BOTTOM LINE

Don't wish for life without God.

328 Birds and bread

All that grumbling must have given the Israelites an appetite. Just as He promised, God provides quail — a posh sort of pheasant — and supernatural bread from heaven. Dig in!

👁 Read Exodus 16 v 13–36

ENGAGE YOUR BRAIN

▶ What food does God provide in the evening? And the morning?

▶ What instructions does Moses give about collecting the manna?

v16:

v19:

v22–23:

▶ What happens when the people don't follow those instructions?

▶ What is God trying to teach His people about Himself? (v28-29)

▶ How long will it take them to learn that? (v32, v35)

We might think that the Israelites were incredibly slow on the uptake — of course God knew what they needed and of course He would provide for them as He'd promised. Why on earth didn't they trust Him?

PRAY ABOUT IT

Take a minute to ask yourself the same question and answer it honestly. Why don't *you* always trust God?

Talk to God about your answer and ask Him to help you trust Him more.

GET ON WITH IT

Is there something in your life that you know God wants you to do or stop doing? Will you take Him seriously and obey Him?

THE BOTTOM LINE

Trusting God means doing what He says.

329 Rock on!

Imagine the situation. You've seen God do amazing miracles to rescue you. He's guiding you personally by day and night and is providing wonderful supernatural food for you every day. Then you get a bit thirsty...

👁 Read Exodus 17 v 1–7

ENGAGE YOUR BRAIN

▷ *Read verse 1 again. What should the people have done?*

▷ *What did they do? (v2)*

▷ *Again, who are they really having a go at? (v2, v7)*

▷ *Why is verse 7 so shocking?*

▷ *What is Moses' response to the situation? (v4)*

Pray or pout? Turn to God or turn against Him? Every time they encounter a difficulty, the Israelites just moan. That's not to say there wasn't a real need, but their response was all wrong. Moses gets it right — he takes his problems straight to God. And notice he's not doing so in a calm and super spiritual manner — he's complaining too. BUT Moses addresses his complaints to the One who can do something about them!

PRAY ABOUT IT

Are you tempted to complain rather than pray when things are tough? Spend some time now asking for God's help with the difficulties you face. Say sorry for the times you moan about life.

▷ *Sum up in a word God's response to these grumblers in verses 6–7.*

Incredibly, God once again meets the needs of this bunch of moaners and in a very strange way — did you notice verse 6? In some way God is present there in front of Moses and provides the water they need to live.

THE BOTTOM LINE

If you want to complain — take your complaints to the top, to God.

330 Hands up

The Israelites faced lack of food and water, and God provided for their needs every step of the way. But in these next few verses they face a new threat.

👁 Read Exodus 17 v 8–16

ENGAGE YOUR BRAIN

▶ *What danger does Israel face in verse 8?*

The Amalekites were a nasty bunch — one of their preferred strategies was to lurk behind straggling travellers and attack the old and weak (Deuteronomy 25 v 17–18).

▶ *What is the outcome of the battle and how does it come about?*

It's not quite clear what Moses is doing with his hands in the air — he could be praying or he could be signalling the troops to advance rather than retreat. Moses mentions that it's the staff of God he's holding, which makes it very clear that he is relying totally on God.

▶ *What is God's promise to Moses about Israel's enemy? (v14)*

▶ *Who does Moses give all the credit to? (v16)*

Moses put his trust firmly in God to rescue His people and defend them. He calls the Lord his banner — maybe our equivalent would be a football scarf or a t-shirt that shows where your loyalties lie.

PRAY ABOUT IT

Ask God for His help to stand firm, trusting in Him for everything today. Thank Him for other Christians you know who help you to stand firm.

THE BOTTOM LINE

Is the Lord your banner?

331 In-laws and outlaws

No major crisis for the Israelites today — phew! At last, they can concentrate on normal stuff like family reunions and daily business.

👁 Read Exodus 18 v 1–12

ENGAGE YOUR BRAIN

▶ Who turns up to see Moses?

▶ What does Moses' choice of names for his kids tell us about:

a) God?

b) Moses' attitude to God?

We don't know much about Jethro's religion, despite him being called the "priest" of Midian. But he certainly ends up worshipping the Lord here.

▶ What is so great about the topic of Moses' and Jethro's conversation (v7-12)?

SHARE IT

Have you ever tried telling others about the amazing things God has done for you both now and in the past? Not just your Christian mates, but all your friends?

👁 Read verses 13–27

▶ Why is Moses' father-in-law so dumbfounded? (v14)

▶ What is Moses doing (v13, v15–16) and why is it so full-on?

▶ What is Jethro's advice? Do you think it sounds sensible?

Sometimes we're not keen to take advice from people — how do we know they're right? What if they're not even Christians? Notice the key thing about Jethro's advice: not only is it sensible (Moses is headed for exhaustion), but it's God-centred (see v19-21, v23).

PRAY ABOUT IT

Thank God for people who look out for you and give you good advice.

THE BOTTOM LINE

God should get the glory in the big things and the small things.

332 Get ready

Chances are you've heard of what happened on Mount Sinai (if not, read on), so we know from verse 2 that something pretty special is coming up, but the build-up alone in this chapter is mind-blowing. Check it out...

👁 Read Exodus 19 v 1–6

ENGAGE YOUR BRAIN

- ▶ What does God remind the Israelites about Himself in verses 4–6?

- ▶ What does He promise them in those verses?

- ▶ How would you describe this relationship?

This is amazing stuff — God is offering these people an incredible privilege, not because they are anything special but because He loves them. That's what the Bible calls *grace* – God's undeserved kindness.

👁 Read verses 7–25

- ▶ How do the people respond? (v8)

- ▶ What strikes you most about the preparations which need to be made for God to communicate with human beings? (v10–24)

God is incomprehensibly holy. He is so perfect that without limits and safety barriers, we would be destroyed by His burning perfection. All of the descriptions used — thunder, lightning, darkness, earthquakes, fire and loud noise serve to highlight how immensely powerful and terrifying God is.

PRAY ABOUT IT

Do you realise that God is like this? Spend some time reflecting on these verses again as you talk to Him.

PRAY ABOUT IT SOME MORE

And yet God wants to communicate with us; this terrifying God is the same one who calls His people His "treasured possession". Thank Him.

THE BOTTOM LINE

God is holy. He's a God of grace. Praise Him.

333 ┆ Starter for ten

We might think we know the Ten Commandments: "Thou shalt not blah, blah, blah". But look again at the way they begin. Everything God expects of His people is based on understanding His character and His relationship with them.

👁 **Read Exodus 20 v 1–6**

ENGAGE YOUR BRAIN

▶ List the three things God says about Himself in verses 2, 5 & 6.

1.

2.

3.

When you see "the LORD" in the Bible, it means the special name of God which He revealed to Moses – "I Am". It means the only God, the eternal God, who is the same yesterday, today and for ever.

▶ What words would you use to define the relationship God has with His people? (v5–6)

▶ What does God forbid them to do?

GET ON WITH IT

Do you have any gods or idols that you worship in the place of the true and living God? Is there something that gets in the way of loving God wholeheartedly? Popularity? Sport? Entertainment? Friends? A boyfriend or girlfriend? Or even your own selfishness? Pray for God's help and get rid of them – ruthlessly.

▶ Why do you think God is so serious about the consequence of not putting Him first? (v5)

The statements that God makes about Himself in verse 5 and verse 6 seem very different. But God is good and holy (not overlooking sin) as well as being compassionate and faithful (showing love to a thousand generations).

PRAY ABOUT IT

Ask for God's help to love Him and keep His commandments — not just these ten but everything that Jesus summed up in these words: "Love the Lord your God with all your heart, soul, mind and strength" and "Love your neighbour as yourself".

334 Remember God

Here's some more guidance on how God wants His people to live. Once again, remembering Him is at the heart of it all.

👁 Read Exodus 20 v 7

ENGAGE YOUR BRAIN

▶ *Why is God's "name" so important?*

We've already seen how God's name told the Israelites about His character — who He was. To misuse it or treat it lightly shows contempt for who He is.

GET ON WITH IT

Hopefully it shocks you or makes you uncomfortable when friends or family use Jesus' name as a swear word. Can you think of something to say that shows how offensive it is to you without sounding judgmental?

👁 Read verses 8–11

▶ *What should the Sabbath be like? (v9–10)*

▶ *Why is the Sabbath special? (v11)*

Interestingly, the command about the Sabbath isn't repeated in the New Testament — but while not all Christians believe we have to have a special day as the Jews did, the principle to have a day of rest and time to meet with other Christians is still a good one.

▶ *Do you work hard?*

▶ *Do you get enough rest?*

▶ *Are you making meeting other believers a priority?*

TALK IT OVER

Why is it so important for Christians to meet together regularly? Chat it through with an older Christian — look at Hebrews 10 v 24–25 as a starting point.

THE BOTTOM LINE

Remember God.

335 The final six

God's top ten countdown is nearing its end.
More of the big ten now...

👁 **Read Exodus 20 v 12–17**

ENGAGE YOUR BRAIN

God's blueprint for how His people were to live covers thoughts, words and deeds.

▷ *Can you spot examples of each in these verses?*

▷ *Do you think Christians have to obey the Ten Commandments today?*

Remember that the Israelites had already been rescued by God. The Ten Commandments and all the other laws that followed were to help them live after they had been rescued. So for us, following these or any other rules won't get us into God's good books — it's trusting Jesus that rescues us. In fact the Ten Commandments often show up how rubbish we are and how much we need the rescue that Jesus offers.

But Jesus didn't abolish these commands, so they are not irrelevant — in fact He took them even further. Take a few moments to read Matthew 5 v 17–48.

▷ *What have the Ten Commandments taught you about God?*

PRAY ABOUT IT

Have these commands of God highlighted any areas of your life where you're not pleasing Him? Pray about that now.

THE BOTTOM LINE

God wants to be God of our thoughts, words and actions.

336 | Powerful God

God has laid out the first part of His blueprint for how His people should live — so how will they respond?

👁 Read Exodus 20 v 18–21

ENGAGE YOUR BRAIN

▶ *What is the Israelites' reaction to what they have seen and heard? (v18–19)*

▶ *What do verses 18, 19 and 21 remind us about God?*

▶ *And about human beings?*

Remind yourself of the end of chapter 19 — to come face to face with God (or anywhere remotely near Him) is a terrifying experience. His holiness shows up our sin.

In a similar way, when Peter witnessed one of Jesus' first miracles he cried: "Go away from me, Lord; I am a sinful man!" (Luke 5 v 8)

PRAY ABOUT IT

Do you sometimes forget how holy and awesomely powerful God is? Spend some time reflecting on that now. Then thank Him that we can speak to Him with confidence because of what Jesus accomplished on the cross.

👁 Read verses 22–26

▶ *What made the Israelites uniquely privileged? (v22)*

▶ *So what does God remind them about? (v23)*

God then gives them some instructions about how they can approach Him. The simple altar meant anyone could make a sacrifice to God to have their sins forgiven, BUT they mustn't get too close (v26) without being properly prepared.

THE BOTTOM LINE

God is perfect and holy and deserves our full respect and worship.

337 | Revelation – Revealing Jesus

Time to rejoin Revelation and the third series of events describing history between Jesus' resurrection and return. We've been shown tyranny (chs. 6–7) and chaos (chs. 8–11). Next up is persecution (chs. 12–14).

Read Revelation 12 v 1–6

ENGAGE YOUR BRAIN

- *What did John see next? (v1–2)*

- *What terrifying thing happened? (v3–4)*

- *How was the dragon foiled? (v5–6)*

The woman represents God's people and she's about to give birth to Jesus. The dragon stands for Satan. All his heads, horns and crowns stand for power and authority. He was hoping to destroy Christ (v4) but his plan failed: Jesus was born and was taken up to heaven (after His death and resurrection) where He rules with God (v5). In the meantime, God's people are in the desert (v6) — God is caring for them on earth before they go to live with Him in heaven.

Read verses 7–12

- *What happened to the devil and his angels? (v7–9)*

- *What is Satan's aim? (v9)*

- *Who defeated Satan? (v10–11)*

Jesus has already defeated Satan! And Christians share in that victory. We overcome the devil by relying on and talking about Jesus' victory at the cross. The bad news is that Satan is furious and is currently taking out his anger on Christians. But his time won't last for long (v12).

Read verses 13–17

Satan is out to get the church — all believers. But he won't succeed because God protects them. The devil will attack us, but if we choose to live God's way, He'll always give us a way to escape.

PRAY ABOUT IT

Thank God that He's already defeated Satan and that He protects Christians.

338 ¦ Simply the beast

Satan's aim is to lead the whole world away from God. He does this using political powers and false prophets. Of course, Revelation paints a wilder, more dramatic picture of this with sea beasts and giant monsters!

👁 Read Revelation 13 v 1–10

ENGAGE YOUR BRAIN

▶ *Where does the beast get his power? (v2)*

▶ *What does this beast do? (v6–7)*

▶ *How does the world react to the beast? (v3–4)*

This sea beast seems to symbolise political regimes which Satan (the dragon) uses to oppress God's people and demand worship from the world. In many nations, political and religious powers speak against Christianity and throw Christians into prison. But these powers won't last for ever.

👁 Read verses 11–18

▶ *What does the second beast do? (v11–12)*

▶ *How does he deceive people? (v13–14)*

▶ *What happens to people under this beast's authority? (v15–17)*

This beast is false religion. It looks like Jesus (the lamb) but speaks for the dragon, Satan (v11). It performs miracles too. But we can see through such fake leaders — if their message is not the gospel of Jesus, the rest is irrelevant however impressive it looks.

When false religion is backed by corrupt political power, Christians suffer (v15). This happens all over the world. Sometimes there will be violent persecution. Quite often though it's simply the loss of economic and social privileges (v17). Christians can't get jobs or miss out on promotion for sticking to their principles.

PRAY ABOUT IT

Pray for Christians you know who are persecuted for their faith. Research two countries where Christians are persecuted. Pray for them regularly.

339 | Angelic messages

We've been warned that the beast is at work. Next, Revelation talks about the church during this time and about the devastating final judgment which will bring the end for God's enemies.

👁 Read Revelation 14 v 1–5

ENGAGE YOUR BRAIN

▷ *What do you think this is all about?*

Back in chapter 7, we learned that this 144,000 stands for all of God's people (and there are actually millions of them). Here they are, safe with Jesus ("the Lamb"). Christians will get a tough time on earth but they can be certain of eternity with Christ. Believers try to stay sexually pure, avoid lies and follow Jesus.

👁 Read verses 6–13

▷ *What's angel 1's message and who is it for? (v6)*

▷ *What's the right response? (v7)*

▷ *What does angel 2 say is the future for Babylon — those who reject God? (v8)*

▷ *Angel 3: What will happen to Satan's followers? (v9–11)*

▷ *What's required of Christians (saints) until Jesus returns? (v12)*

Before the victory is complete, believers have the task of spreading the gospel (the message of the angels). We want people to avoid God's punishment and give Him glory instead. So we've got to tell them about Jesus.

SHARE IT

Spend time thinking how you can share the gospel effectively with the people you most often come into contact with.

PRAY ABOUT IT

Thank God that His people are safe and have a great future ahead of them. Ask Him to help you share the gospel even when it's difficult.

340 Grim reaping

And now for a straightforward and boring part of Revelation... Not really — time for more angels, a devastating harvest, some plagues and some great singing!

👁 Read Revelation 14 v 14–20

ENGAGE YOUR BRAIN

▶ *Who's in charge? (v14)*

▶ *What was it time for? (v15)*

▶ *What terrible image is used for the fate of those who worship the beast? (v19–20)*

Jesus will return as Judge. At this final harvest, those who've trusted Jesus for rescue and forgiveness will be gathered to Him. But those who've rejected Him and ignored God's warnings will be punished.

👁 Read Revelation 15 v 1–4

▶ *What did these angels have with them? (v1)*

▶ *Who else was present? (v2)*

▶ *What were they doing? (v3)*

▶ *What aspects of God's character did they sing about? (v3–4)*

▶ *So how should everyone respond? (v4)*

In Moses' time, God's people sang about the Lord defeating the Egyptians and rescuing His people. When Jesus returns, His people will sing His praises for defeating sin and death and the devil. And for rescuing them, bring them to eternal safety.

More on the angels with plagues coming tomorrow.

PRAY ABOUT IT

Plead with God to rescue friends who are heading for His punishment. Then praise Him, using 15 v 3–4 to focus on His perfect holiness.

THE BOTTOM LINE

God alone is holy. All nations will worship Him.

341 Angels of destruction

It's time for the last of the four series of events which describe history between Jesus' resurrection and return. This time the focus is on destruction and God's final judgment.

👁 Read Revelation 15 v 5 – 16 v 7

▷ What did these angels bring? (15 v 7)

▷ Who gets the full blast of God's anger? (16 v 2)

▷ What happens to the sea? (v3–4)

▷ Why is this fair? (v5–7)

The main targets of God's fair punishment are those who rejected Jesus and so are on the beast's (Satan's) side. The sea is turned to blood and everything in it dies. This is punishing those who have shed the blood of believers.

👁 Read Revelation 16 v 8–16

▷ What other punishment is dished out? (v8, 10, 12)

▷ What two responses did people have? (v9, v11)

Surely people would turn to God and repent. Well, some people do turn to God when faced with suffering. But many curse God and refuse to admit their sin and their need for God.

👁 Read verses 17–21

▷ What was the effect of this final "plague"? (v19–21)

Instead of describing the final battle hinted at in verses 13–16, the scene switches to the final judgment. It's horrific and yet people are still unrepentant and cursing God (v21). And there's more to come, but we'll read about that tomorrow.

PRAY ABOUT IT

Remember people you care about who refuse to listen to God or trust Jesus. Spend longer than usual praying for each of them, that they would admit their sin and turn to Jesus for forgiveness.

342 | Toxic temptation

The message of Revelation 17 is BEWARE! Be very, very ware. The godless lifestyle of this world can be very seductive… but it doesn't deliver what it offers and has a limited future.

👁 Read Revelation 17 v 1–6

ENGAGE YOUR BRAIN

▶ *What impact did the prostitute have on the world? (v2)*

▶ *And on God's people? (v6)*

The prostitute in John's vision represents godless society through the ages — from ancient Babylon and Rome to everywhere and everyone who seduce people away from God with hideous sin (v4). And everyone who persecutes God's people (v6)

👁 Read verses 7–14

▶ *How is the beast described and how will he affect the world? (v8)*

▶ *What's his attitude to Jesus? (v14)*

▶ *Who will win and why? (v14)*

We've met this beast before — he represents cruel rulers. Non-Christians especially are impressed by such leaders (v8). But such evil powers will be destroyed by Jesus (v14).

👁 Read verses 15–18

▶ *What's surprising about the prostitute's downfall? (v16)*

▶ *Who is really in control? (v17)*

The devil's at work behind the godless regimes of this world. But in the end, they self-destruct because God's in control (v17). Chapter 17 shows us the attraction of living life without God. It's tempting, oh so seductive, and so liberating, we think. But a life of materialism or self-serving pleasure contains its own self-destruct button. It won't satisfy or deliver… and it won't give any hope for the future beyond death.

PRAY ABOUT IT

Talk to God honestly about the things that seduce and tempt you away from Him. Thank Him that Jesus is the winner, not the devil. And ask Him to help you choose the winning side and live accordingly.

343 | Babylon bashed

Godless society ("Babylon") has its attractions. Revelation shows it up for what it really is: short-lived and under God's judgment. Before launching His new world (ch 21–22), God destroys all evil in His final judgment (ch 18–20).

👁 Read Revelation 18 v 1–8

ENGAGE YOUR BRAIN

- ▶ *How is Babylon described? (v2–3)*

- ▶ *Why must God's people keep away from Babylon? (v4)*

- ▶ *What will happen to Babylon? (v8)*

There are so many temptations in the world — sex and wealth (v3) are two of the biggest ones. It's easy to think that, as Christians, we're immune to these temptations without noticing they're already seducing us.

👁 Read verses 9–24

- ▶ *How will rulers react to Babylon's downfall? (v9)*

- ▶ *What about salesmen? (v15–16)*

- ▶ *But what about believers? (v20)*

- ▶ *Why will Babylon be destroyed? (v23–24)*

Babylon stands for life without God. Despite all the warnings, many people would rather live for themselves and ignore God completely. Wealth and greed in particular pull people away from God. So many people chase after the "good life" rather than a God life. But Babylon will be destroyed and God's people will celebrate.

GET ON WITH IT

- ▶ *In what ways are you greedy?*

- ▶ *How do sex or relationships pull you away from God?*

- ▶ *What temptations do you need to deal with right now?*

PRAY ABOUT IT

Ask God's help to fight the specific temptations you struggle with. Pray, too, for friends who are being pulled away from God by the world.

344 White wedding

Yesterday we read about Babylon's downfall. Godless living ultimately ends in destruction. Today we're invited to a wedding party. I bet you can't guess who's getting married...

👁 Read Revelation 19 v 1–5

ENGAGE YOUR BRAIN

▷ Why is life with God better than life without Him ("Babylon")? (v1–2)

▷ What's the response once God's enemies have been defeated? (v5)

It's not popular to talk about God's judgment. But we must remember that any punishment from God is totally fair. In fact, God's judgment is a cause for celebration. We can praise and thank God for being true and fair and punishing evil as well as rescuing His people.

👁 Read verses 6–10

▷ What else was worth celebrating? (v7)

▷ Who's getting hitched?

▷ Why was John wrong to worship the angel? (v10)

All heaven celebrates as God's enemies are defeated and God's kingdom is established. Time for a wedding! Jesus (the Lamb) is getting married. But who could possibly be married to Jesus? Well, the rest of the Bible says that the church — God's people — are His bride. Amazing. Believers will be with Christ for ever.

The chapter ends on a strange note with John being told off for worshipping the angel messenger. Only God deserves our worship and devotion. Angels are God's servants just as we are. It's the message of Christ and what He's done for us that matters, not the messenger. So don't be tempted to idolise people who teach you. Save hero worship for God.

PRAY ABOUT IT AGAIN

Use today's verses to help you praise God in prayer right now.

345 Conquering King

At the final judgment, God will destroy all who oppose Him. In a great end-time battle? No, that's already happened. Jesus has won already, on the cross. Now it's time to finish off those enemies...

👁 Read Revelation 19 v 11–16

ENGAGE YOUR BRAIN

▷ *How is this terrifying figure described in v11, v12 & v13?*

▷ *What has He come to do? (v15)*

▷ *Who is He? (v16)*

This is Jesus — and He's not to be messed with. The blood on His robes (v13) probably refers to His death, which brought victory over His enemies (v15). The sharp sword that comes out of His mouth is the word of God and its effect is devastating. There is no doubt who the winner is — Jesus is King of kings and Lord of lords (v16). He is God and He's boss of everything.

👁 Read verses 17–21

▷ *What does the devil (and all who reject God) do? (v19)*

▷ *How do you see that attitude in people around you?*

▷ *What happens to those who rebel against God? (v20–21)*

Yesterday we read about the great wedding feast for all believers. Here, the birds are invited to feast on the bodies of God's defeated enemies (v17–18). Grim. They all think they can defeat God but the battle is over immediately. The beast and false prophet are captured and destroyed. The rest of the evil armies are defeated by God's word (v21).

THINK IT OVER

This is a terrible picture of what happens to those who reject God. We all need to take in the reality of this.

▷ *What motivation is there here for us to tell others about this?*

▷ *How does Jesus in verses 11–16 differ from the usual view of Him?*

▷ *How might your thinking about Jesus need to change?*

346 Satan's doom

The judgment goes on: it's Satan himself who's now in trouble. Then everybody faces God's judgment. Yes, everybody. What's described next is the final judgment and the time leading up to it.

👁 Read Revelation 20 v 1–6

ENGAGE YOUR BRAIN

▶ What happens to Satan? (v1–3)

▶ Who share in Jesus' victory at this time? (v4)

Christians often argue over exactly when this "1000 year" reign will take place. During this time, the devil will be thrown into a bottomless pit (v1) and stopped from deceiving the nations (v3). This isn't the final judgment as Satan will be released again for a short time. The suggestion is that during this "1000 years" Satan's influence will be restricted by the faithfulness of Christians, many prepared to die for the gospel (v4–6).

👁 Read verses 7–10

▶ What will Satan do when he's released? (v8)

▶ But what would happen to the devil and his army? (v10)

Satan is released for a limited time and will gather God's enemies from all the nations. But this mighty-looking rebellion ends as soon as it's begun and the devil will be punished for ever. Notice that Satan suffers the same punishment as all who reject God — he won't be enjoying hell!

👁 Read verses 11–15

▶ Who will face the final judgment? & how will they be judged? (v12)

▶ Who will be punished? (v15)

The enemies of God have been destroyed; now everyone who has ever lived will be judged. No one can avoid it and they'll be judged on what they've done in their lives. Everyone who has trusted in Jesus to save them will be OK. But those who've ignored or dismissed God will be punished.

Thank God for Jesus' victory and the fact all believers share in it. Now pray for three more people you know who refuse to trust in Jesus.

347 The future's bright

Satan is defeated and all God's enemies have been punished. So what will happen to believers and where will they live? It's time for "Jerusalem II — The Comeback".

👁 Read Revelation 21 v 1–4

ENGAGE YOUR BRAIN

▶ What did John see next? (v1–2)

▶ What is the amazing news for God's people? (v3)

▶ What will never happen again? (v4)

The Bible doesn't actually tell us much about eternal life. But what it does tell us is tantalising. Most importantly, God will live with His people — in fact He'll bring heaven down to us! (v2) Heaven and earth will be united: the original relationship between God and humans which existed in the Garden of Eden will be restored. There will be no more sadness or suffering.

👁 Read verses 5–8

▶ How does God describe Himself? (v6)

▶ What will He give to believers?

v6:

v7:

▶ What about everyone else? (v8)

The message for us is: "Keep going!" If we stick at it and keep trusting in Jesus, the future is so bright! The alternative is horrific (v8).

PRAY ABOUT IT

Go through today's reading, verse by verse, using it to prompt your prayers.

THE BOTTOM LINE

"God's dwelling-place is now among the people, and he will dwell with them. They will be his people, and God himself will be with them and be their God." (v3)

348 Bright lights, big city

No tears, no pain, no death. Revelation ends, as it began, with a vision. It's a vision of the new creation, a reality which helps us make sense of all that we experience here and now.

👁 Read Revelation 21 v 9–22

ENGAGE YOUR BRAIN

- 𝕀 *What was the angel going to show John? (v9)*

- 𝕀 *What did John actually see? (v10)*

- 𝕀 *What was it like? (v11–21)*

- 𝕀 *Why was there no temple — a place to worship God? (v22)*

It will be glorious and brilliant. Literally. The bride and the city are pictures of God's people, who will be with Him when He fulfils His promises. The twelve tribes (v12) and twelve apostles (v14) represent the whole of God's people. They'll all be there.

In the Old Testament, the temple symbolised God's presence. In the new Jerusalem, there won't be a need for a temple because God will actually live with His people there.

👁 Read verses 23–27

- 𝕀 *Why no sun or moon? (v23)*

- 𝕀 *What will fill God's city? (v24–26)*

- 𝕀 *What will not be there? (v27)*

- 𝕀 *Who will be there? (v27)*

👁 Read Revelation 22 v 1–5

We've seen that the city is the source of the world's light. Here, the river flowing from it shows us it's also the source of life. The tree of life (last seen in the Garden of Eden in Genesis) is in God's new city to bring healing to people of all nations. There will be no more suffering. God will now live with His people in His perfect city. Incredible.

PRAY ABOUT IT

Thank God that His people will live in a new, perfect place, better than Eden. They'll have a face-to-face relationship with Him that can never be spoiled.

349 The last word

Time to look back. Jesus is at the centre of John's vision and He's won a great victory for His people. So remember: whatever difficulties and opposition you face, Christians are on the winning side. Hang in there.

👁 Read Revelation 22 v 6–11

ENGAGE YOUR BRAIN

▶ *What does Jesus remind us of? (v7)*

▶ *When is the message of Revelation for? (v10)*

▶ *So what's happening now? (v11)*

Revelation is a letter from John and it ends with loads of short bits of info and instruction. Believers should act on what they've heard in Revelation (v7). We must worship only God (v8–9). Jesus reminds us that the book is for now, not just the future (v10), yet life will continue as normal (v11).

👁 Read verses 12–16

▶ *How does Jesus describe Himself? (v13, 16)*

▶ *How would you put verse 14 in your own words? And verse 15?*

All the names that Jesus gives Himself here remind us that He is God. One day (possibly soon) He will return and everyone who trusts in Him will be rewarded. But everyone else will be thrown out of God's presence.

👁 Read verses 17–21

▶ *Who's inviting who to what? (v17)*

▶ *What's the final warning? (v18–19)*

▶ *What should be our attitude after reading Revelation? (v20)*

We've all been invited to take the free gift of eternal life made available through Jesus' death. So life may be tough for Christians, but we should be looking forward to a perfect future with Him.

PRAY ABOUT IT

Having read this incredible book, only you know what you need to talk to God about.

ACTS

Under pressure

Acts has told us the story of Paul, the persecutor of Christians; Paul, the planter of churches; and now, in the last eight chapters, it's the story of Paul, the prisoner in chains.

We're going to follow Paul, who Jesus converted from one of His greatest enemies to one of His greatest workers as Paul walked along a road to Damascus (read about it in Acts 9). We'll see him under pressure — serious pressure. Will he lose his faith in God? Will he shut up about Jesus? As he travels to Jerusalem, and then on to Rome, will loneliness, imprisonment, danger, deceit and shipwreck stop him following Christ?

As we read these words of Luke (who was an eyewitness of many of the events he tells us about), we're not only finding out about Paul, though. We're also finding out about Jesus, the Son of God, who keeps His promises even when His people are under pressure.

And we're finding out about life as a follower of Jesus today. In watching how Paul the prisoner reacts to scrapes, setbacks and sadnesses, we can learn how Jesus wants His followers today to act when we find ourselves under pressure. So let's get back on the road with Paul…

350 | Christian sense

"Better safe than sorry." "Common sense is vital." "Don't take risks." It's all good advice, but are they the final word for the Christian? Is that how believers should live?

ENGAGE YOUR BRAIN

▶ Look back to Acts 19 v 21. Where's Paul decided to visit?

◉ Read Acts 21 v 1–12

▶ List the verses in which Paul is advised not to go to Jerusalem.

▶ Who is speaking to him in each of these verses?

▶ Why do they advise him to change his mind? (v11)

▶ Which words show how concerned they were?

◉ Read verses 13–16

▶ Does Paul change his mind? Why / why not?

▶ How do his friends respond? (v14–15)

THINK IT THROUGH

▶ What would common sense say about Paul's plan to go to Jerusalem?

And that's what his friends say to him. They're not wrong to do this; there's a place for sensible advice — but sensible advice doesn't have the last word for the Christian.

▶ What should our attitude be when we're called to do something risky for Jesus? (v13)

▶ What should be our response when a Christian friend decides to take a risk for Jesus? (v14)

GET ON WITH IT

▶ Is there an area of your life where you're being sensible, but it's stopping you living 100% for Jesus?

▶ How does this section challenge you to change?

351 Bending over backwards

This is quite a tricky section, because Paul seems to do things that he's told others in Acts and his letters not to do — so we'll need to look hard at what we're actually being taught.

👁 Read Acts 21 v 17–26

ENGAGE YOUR BRAIN

▶ *Where's Paul? (v17)*

▶ *How do the Christians there react to him and what God's been doing through him? (v17–20)*

But people have been hearing dangerous things about Paul…

▶ *What have some Jewish Christians been told? (v21)*

The issue here is whether Paul's been telling Jews who've become Christians to turn their backs on their Jewish heritage and culture.

▶ *What's the solution Paul's Christian friends in Jerusalem suggest? (v22–24)*

▶ *What does Paul do?*

▶ *He's not doing this because he has to, to be a Christian — so what's his motivation for doing it?*

👁 Read verses 27–36

Paul's done everything he can to ensure Christianity doesn't have a bad name.

▶ *How do the people respond?*

▶ *What do they want to do? (v 31)*

THINK ABOUT IT

👁 Read Romans 12 v 17–18

Paul's practising what he preached. He's bent over backwards to live at peace with everyone around him — but it isn't possible, because the people around him have rejected his gospel message and are determined to see the worst in him.

GET ON WITH IT

What have you learned about how you should live among friends and family who don't believe the gospel?

352 But seriously...

If you're really serious about God and knowing Him, what will you do? That's what Paul wants the people who are trying to kill him to think about.

👁 Read Acts 21 v 37 – 22 v 2

ENGAGE YOUR BRAIN

🔹 *What does Paul ask the Roman commander? (v39)*

🔹 *Based on what you know of Paul, what do you think Paul will want to talk to them about?*

👁 Read Acts 22 v 3–9

🔹 *How does Paul introduce himself? (v3)*

🔹 *Why, do you think?*

🔹 *What does Paul say about his attitude to God? (end v3)*

"Zealous" means "seriously serious". Paul was serious about the whole God thing: and these people think they are, too.

🔹 *In the past, what did Paul think being zealous for God meant he needed to do? (v4–5)*

🔹 *What was his relationship to Jesus at that time? (v7–8)*

But when Jesus appeared to Paul and spoke to him as he travelled to Damascus, he realised that he'd misunderstood how to be serious about following God.

👁 Read Acts 22 v 10–21

🔹 *If someone's really serious about knowing God, what must they do? (v15–16)*

THE BOTTOM LINE

Taking God seriously means following Christ, not persecuting Him.

GET ON WITH IT

🔹 *Who do you know who says they take God seriously, but pushes Jesus out instead of living for Him?*

🔹 *How can you explain to them how to take God seriously?*

353 So many voices

Ever felt surrounded by so many people talking to and at you that you don't know what to do or who to listen to?

👁 Read Acts 22 v 21–29

ENGAGE YOUR BRAIN

▷ What does Paul tell the crowd Jesus had told him to do? (v21)

▷ How do the crowd react? (v22)

Telling people about Jesus can be met with anger and hostility. The message is: don't tell us about Jesus!

👁 Read Acts 22 v 30 – 23 v 5

Paul is hauled up before the Jewish religious court (Sanhedrin) that had condemned Jesus to death, flogged the disciples Peter and John, and killed the Christian Stephen.

▷ What does Paul say to them? (v1)

In other words: I've done nothing wrong, because my duty to God is to follow Jesus and spread His message.

▷ What does the high priest do in response? (v2)

▷ What's his message to Paul about living for Christ?

👁 Read Acts 23 v 6–11

▷ What does Paul say about why he's on trial? (v6)

▷ How do the Sadducees respond, and why? (v7–10)

▷ What's the Sadducees' message to Paul about believing in the risen Christ?

▷ Who comes and speaks to Paul? (v11)

▷ What's His message to Paul about how he's preaching and living?

PRAY ABOUT IT

Lord Jesus, Help me to listen to your word in the Bible and to ignore people who tell me to stop speaking about you, living for you, or believing in you. Amen.

354 | We'll kill him!

Paul's in serious trouble. The Jewish leaders hate him; the crowd wants to kill him; the Roman authorities don't know what to do with him.

Read Acts 23 v 12–24
ENGAGE YOUR BRAIN

▶ What's shocking about verse 12?

▶ What is their plan? (v13-15)

▶ Why doesn't the plan work? (v16–24)

Read verses 25–35

The commander, Lysias, writes a letter to his boss, Governor Felix, about Paul.

▶ What does the commander miss out of the story? (v27–30: compare it with 22 v 22–29)

▶ Why do you think he changes the details a bit?

THINK IT THROUGH

Paul's protected by a man, who wants to use him to look good, from a bunch of men, who want to kill him to shut him up. No one actually cares about him. It must have been seriously lonely and hugely terrifying.

▶ Look back to 23 v 11. How would this have encouraged Paul?

And behind the scenes of this passage, God is working to ensure that His plan happens.

PRAY ABOUT IT

In our world right now thousands of Christians are being plotted against by those who want to kill them, and are only protected by authorities when it suits them. Pray for these Christians now, that they'd remember that Jesus is in charge, and that He'll look after them until it is time for them to join Him in eternal life.

THE BOTTOM LINE

No matter what those around you are doing, trust in Jesus for your life and your death.

355 Court-ing controversy

**We're in court. The judge: Roman governor Felix.
The prosecution: Jewish religious leaders.
The accused: Christian missionary Paul.
The punishment if found guilty: death.**

👁 Read Acts 24 v 1–9

ENGAGE YOUR BRAIN

▶ *What does the prosecution lawyer accuse Paul of?*

If true, Paul hadn't only broken Jewish religious laws; he'd also broken Roman state laws.

▶ *What do the witnesses say? (v9)*

👁 Read verses 10–21

▶ *How does Paul defend himself from the accusations?*

▶ *What's the one thing he wants to admit publicly? (v14)*

The Way = Christianity.

👁 Read verses 22–27

The governor chickens out! He knows Paul isn't guilty, but he knows the Jews will cause trouble if he says that: so he leaves Paul in prison for two years.

▶ *What happens while Paul's in prison? (v24)*

Drusilla was a stunner. She'd been married to another ruler, but had left him for Felix. It had caused a huge scandal.

▶ *What does Paul tell them about? (v24–25)*

Seriously brave. Paul talked about self-control to a couple who had failed to resist their adulterous urges! Paul talked about the judgment to come to two powerful figures who were facing that judgment. Paul's happy to defend himself against untruth to save his life; but he'll always risk his life to tell people the truth about God's judgment, our sin, and Christ's rescue.

GET ON WITH IT

▶ *Who can you take a risk with to talk to about Jesus?*

356 When being offensive is good

Paul's enemies don't give up easily as they try to kill him... but then, neither does Paul as he tries to talk about Jesus. It's like a deadly staring match, with the Romans as the judge. Who'll blink first?

👁 Read Acts 25 v 1–9

It's another trial; the new Roman governor, Festus, is judge. Again the Jews, who've had another murderous plot foiled (v3–5), bring "many serious charges against him" (v7).

▶ What's the basic message of Paul's defence? (v8)

▶ Is he guilty of wrongdoing under either Jewish or Roman law?

▶ Festus, like the other Romans, wants to use Paul for his own ends — so what does he ask Paul to do? (v9)

▶ Why's this a problem for Paul? (look back to v3)

In the end, Paul ends up heading for Rome, not Jerusalem (v 10–12).

👁 Read verses 13–22

▶ Who appears on the scene? (v13)

▶ What does Festus tell them the whole argument between Paul and the Jews boils down to? (v19)

▶ What has Paul clearly still been talking about loads?

THINK ABOUT IT

Paul's obeyed the law; he's obeyed the leaders of the state; he's obeyed local traditions.

▶ What's the one way he's caused offence?

▶ Will he stop?

GET ON WITH IT

▶ How's this an encouragement and challenge to you?

THE BOTTOM LINE

Whatever happens, keep talking about a "dead man" named Jesus who you know is alive.

357 Christianity on trial

"How can you be a Christian and intelligent?" "What about other religions?" "Why do you have to take it so seriously?" Sound familiar? Let's see how Paul answers.

👁 Read Acts 25 v 23–27

Agrippa II ruled part of Israel. His great-grandfather, Herod, tried to kill Jesus when he was born. His grandfather, Herod Antipas, killed John the Baptist. His father, Herod Agrippa I, beheaded Jesus' apostle James. Not a nice family!

👁 Read Acts 26 v 1–23

▷ What job had Jesus given Paul? (v15–18)

▷ So, had Paul forgotten about the Jewish Scriptures (the Old Testament), and all the promises God had made in them? (v6–7)

▷ What's Paul saying about how the Old Testament links to Jesus?

▷ What does v 22-23 add?

THINK IT THROUGH

▷ How would you explain the gospel to someone who's been brought up as a Jew?

▷ What point does Paul make in verse 8?

▷ What would you say to someone who thinks there might be a God, but thinks Christian belief is stupid?

▷ Jesus had called Paul to live for him (v16–18); how did Paul respond (v19–20)?

▷ What had this resulted in? (v21)

Paul obeyed Jesus. He went and told the world that Jesus had risen, even though he risked death by doing it. When Jesus calls you to follow Him, you can't half-obey; it requires 100% commitment.

PRAY ABOUT IT

Lord Jesus, Thank you that you're the One all God's promises came true through. Thank you that you've called me to be forgiven, be part of your people, and serve you with my life. Amen.

358 Response to a response

There are two responses in today's section: people's response to Paul, and Paul's response to people.

👁 Read Acts 26 v 19–28

ENGAGE YOUR BRAIN

Paul's basic message to the governor and king: God's King, Jesus, suffered, died and rose from the dead to offer the light of eternal life to all (v23).

▶ *How does Festus respond? (v24)*

Paul asks Agrippa if he believes the Old Testament prophets, who Paul says point to Jesus being God's King.

▶ *How does Agrippa respond? (v28)*

The tone here is probably: "You (a prisoner in chains) think you can persuade me (a powerful king) to become a Christian? Ha!"

▶ *Which words best describe Festus and Agrippa's response to Paul's message?*

👁 Read verses 29–32

▶ *What's Paul's response to this sneering king? (v29)*

▶ *What does he have that he wants the king to have?*

Paul's amazing here. You'd think his prayer would be "God, please get me out of here alive"; but in fact it's "God, please give these people faith in your Son".

GET ON WITH IT

▶ *How does your attitude to your life need to change to be more like Paul's?*

PRAY ABOUT IT

Think of someone you know who sneers at you for being a Christian, and commit to praying for them daily.

THE BOTTOM LINE

People often respond to Christianity by sneering; Christians should respond to them by praying.

359 When times get tough

Ever had a day, a week or even a year when everything just goes wrong? What's God doing in those times? How should you react?

When it all goes wrong...

👁 **Read Acts 27 v 1–12**

Paul's going to Rome: but by the end of verse 8 they've only reached Crete, less than halfway.

▶ *What's the problem? (v9)*

▶ *What does Paul advise? (v 9–10)*

▶ *What decision is made? (v12)*

👁 **Read verses 13–20**

▶ *What happens at sea?*

▶ *The ship's crew try everything; but by verse 20, how's everybody feeling?*

Luke says "we" — even Paul's Christian friends felt like this.

... listen to God's promises

👁 **Read verses 21–26**

▶ *What's Paul been told? (v23–24)*

▶ *So what does he tell everyone to do? (v25)*

... and trust in them.

Notice that Paul doesn't just know what God's said: crucially, he trusts God to do what He's said.

THINK ABOUT IT

▶ *What had God promised Paul twice now? (Acts 23 v 11 and 27 v 24)*

▶ *Did God at any stage promise Paul that life would be easy along the way?*

GET ON WITH IT

God hasn't promised all Christians that He'll get them to Rome; but He has promised to get them to eternal life.

▶ *What have you learned about what to do when everything in life seems to be going wrong?*

360 Put your feet up?

Paul is trusting God to keep His promise to get him to Rome. So now Paul can just relax, put his feet up and wait for God to sort it all out, right? Err... wrong, actually.

Read Acts 27 v 27–32

ENGAGE YOUR BRAIN

▶ *What do the sailors do? (v30)*

This would stop anyone getting to Rome!

▶ *What does Paul do? (v31–32)*

Problem solved — the Rome trip's still on!

Read verses 33–38

▶ *What's the problem? (v33)*

▶ *What does Paul do? (v34–36)*

Problem solved — Rome's still on!

Read verses 39–44

▶ *What do the soldiers intend to do? (v42)*

▶ *What does the centurion do, and why? (v43–44)*

Paul hasn't solved this problem directly — and yet the centurion "wanted to spare Paul's life", probably because Paul had been such a help to him during the storm. Anyway, problem solved — Rome's still on!

THINK ABOUT IT

▶ *Does trusting in God's promises mean we don't work hard to keep things on track ourselves?*

▶ *Does working hard mean we don't need to trust in God to make His promises come true?*

After all, God usually works through His people to make His promises come true! Think of one aspect of your life where you need to trust in God's promises and work hard yourself.

THE BOTTOM LINE

Christians trust God will make His promises come true; then get on with working to make them come true.

361 | Can you believe it?

When people don't believe in God, they'll believe in anything.

👁 Read Acts 28 v 1–4

ENGAGE YOUR BRAIN

▶ Where have Paul and the others ended up? (v1)

▶ What happens to Paul? (v2–3)

▶ What do the islanders conclude about Paul, and why? (v4)

▶ What mistake are they making in their beliefs?

👁 Read verses 5–10

▶ What doesn't happen to Paul? (v5–6)

▶ What do the islanders conclude about Paul now, and why? (v6)

▶ What mistake are they making in their beliefs?

▶ What does Paul go on to do? (v8–9)

▶ When confronted with the sick man, what does Paul do first? (v8)

▶ What's he showing about who's in charge?

THINK ABOUT IT

It's easy to look down on the islanders for what they believed about Paul just because of the snake. But are people so different today? How many people believe the stars affect their personal lives? How many people think doing a certain thing will bring them "luck"? How many people treat someone other than Christ — a boyfriend, or a daughter, or even money or career or sex — as their "god", the thing they worship and would do anything for? Maybe we're not so different…

GET ON WITH IT

▶ Are you treating anything other than Jesus as a "god" in your life?

Look out for your friends saying something that shows what they believe — it might give you an opportunity to share how your beliefs are different.

362 | Done Rome-in

Which do you think is the world's most important city? What's the world's most exciting city? For people in Paul's time, those questions were easy to answer — Rome, the capital of the largest empire mankind had ever known.

👁 Read Acts 28 v 11–16

ENGAGE YOUR BRAIN

▷ Where does Paul finally end up? (v14)

It was the end of Paul's journey.

▷ Despite all the difficulties in getting there, should we be surprised by this? (Think back to Acts 23 v 11 and 27 v 23–24.)

▷ What kind of situation did Paul find himself in? (28 v 16)

▷ What have we been reminded about God's promises?

▷ What happened when Paul reached Puteoli?

▷ What happened as he approached Rome?

▷ Remember that Paul is a prisoner who may soon be condemned to death — why is the action of the people in verse 15 surprising?

▷ What does it show about their priorities?

GET ON WITH IT

▷ Do you ever keep quiet when other Christians are sharing the gospel or when your friends are criticising Christianity?

▷ How does this passage encourage you to change?

THE BOTTOM LINE

God's promises always come true. God's people stick up for each other.

363 The end?

We've reached the end of Acts (congratulations!)
Is it a happy ending? Sad ending? Unfinished ending?

👁 Read Acts 28 v 17–24

ENGAGE YOUR BRAIN

▶ *Paul's chained to a Roman guard — what does he still want to do? (v20, v23)*

▶ *What's the response from the Jews (v24)?*

👁 Read verses 25–31

▶ *Who's Paul going to tell about Jesus now?*

▶ *What does he predict? (v28)*

▶ *What's Paul doing as the book ends (v30–31)?*

This is what Paul's always done, whenever, wherever and however he can. It's a happy ending! Yes — Paul's in Rome, telling people about Jesus. Not sad at all, then? Hmmm… Paul's under house arrest, chained to a guard. God's done great things through Paul, but God hasn't given him an easy life.

So, that's it, finished! Not really… Paul's reached Rome, the centre of the Roman Empire. From Rome, the gospel can go to "the ends of the earth", just as Jesus said way back in Acts 1 v 8. And the gospel's still doing that — as you take it to those you live with, work with, go to school with. The Acts of Jesus, reigning in heaven and working through His people, are not finished yet — and if you're a Christian, you're part of it!

PRAY ABOUT IT

Think of three people you see often who aren't Christians. Ask God for chances to tell them about Christ; ask for the courage and the words when those chances come.

364 | Heartcry of a hero

Some songs sound familiar. Perhaps they're just so cleverly crafted that you feel as if you've heard them before... or maybe the lyrics and tune have actually been stolen from another song.

👁 Read Psalm 22 v 1–21

ENGAGE YOUR BRAIN

▶ *Find the verses that sound like quotes from Jesus' crucifixion.*

His cry from the cross:

Mocked by soldiers:

Gambling for His robe:

The nails:

(All these details also feature in Mark 15 v 16–39.)

THINK IT OVER

This is no freaky coincidence. According to Hebrews 2 v 12, we can hear the words of Psalm 22 as Jesus' own. It's mind-boggling that this song, so clearly telling us about Jesus' last hours, was composed hundreds of years before!

👁 Read verses 22–31

▶ *What will He be doing? (v22, v25)*

▶ *What does He call us to do? (v23–24)*

▶ *What will be the world's response now and in the future? (v30–31)*

This psalm is like reading an "interview" with the Saviour of the entire world, even as the rescue takes place! It reveals that through excruciating agony and humiliation, Jesus saw the bigger picture — God being massively honoured as future generations hear His message of ultimate love. As He died, you were on His mind.

PRAY ABOUT IT

Now re-read verses 22–31, and join in worshipping the God who gave His Son for you.

365 Off course?

The GPS/sat nav takes you down a country lane at night. As the tarmac becomes a dirt track, you start to doubt the voice of technology. But how do you know you're on the right track with God?

👁 Read Psalm 23 v 1–3

ENGAGE YOUR BRAIN

▶ *How is the Shepherd's route described? (v3)*

▶ *Why does He lead David along the right path? (v3)*

THINK IT OVER

It might seem surprising that God's main concern in leading David is His own reputation. But then again, since the focus of the entire universe is the fame of heaven's King (look back at Psalm 19), steering our lives in the same direction is a smart choice. If we're being shepherded for God's purposes, what can go wrong?

"If God is for us, who can be against us?" (Romans 8 v 31)

👁 Read verses 4–6

▶ *How does David feel during dark times? (v4)*

▶ *Who's watching at the feast? (v5)*

Just because the path is set by God doesn't make it easy. But even in the darkest place, God's supplies are limitless.

THINK IT OVER

▶ *What's the worst thing you can imagine happening to you?*

Painful as it is, picture it. Can God's love reach you there? Absolutely.

THE BOTTOM LINE

Make it your goal to trust the presence and love of God to take you through great times and hard times.

GET ON WITH IT

Add Habakkuk 3 v 17–18 to your bedroom décor. Adopt it as a defining attitude for life, especially during tough times.

What is the Bible?

One of the main ambitions of *Engage 365* is to encourage you to dive into God's word. So here are four major truths about the Bible and how they affect the way we study it.

1. THE BIBLE IS FROM GOD

Paul tells us that the Bible is "God-breathed" (2 Timothy 3 v 16–17) — it comes directly from God. Behind the human writers, He is the ultimate author. When we read the Bible, we're reading God's words to us! And Paul tells us we should use God's words to teach us, train us and challenge us, so that we can serve God with our lives.

2. THE BIBLE IS TRUE

One of the amazing things about God is that He doesn't lie (Titus 1 v 2). He doesn't make mistakes either, because He knows everything there is to know. If the Bible is God's word, then it follows that the Bible doesn't lie or make mistakes. We can trust everything the Bible says. It will never mislead us. The word of God is the strongest foundation that you can build your life on.

3. WHAT GOD SAYS GOES

Another vital truth to remember as we read the Bible is this: what God says goes. He is the supreme Lord and King of the universe. He is the one in charge. Christians want to live with God in charge of their lives, and in practice that means obeying God's word. As we read the Bible, we should expect to find God saying things we don't like or find difficult (2 Timothy 3 v 16). We should expect to be corrected and trained in living God's right way. You might find it helpful to use the sides of the *Engage 365* pages, or a separate notebook, to jot down what God is teaching you.

4. GOD GIVES US HELP

We're not left alone with God's huge book! The Holy Spirit helps Christians understand the Bible (1 Corinthians 2 v 9–13). Someone who isn't a Christian won't be able to fully understand the Bible, because they don't have the Spirit helping them (1 Corinthians 2 v 14). We should be wary of the "expert" on TV or the latest controversial book about Christianity. It's easy to bow to what seems to be impressive knowledge, but if they haven't got the Spirit of God working in them, then they haven't a hope of grasping the Bible's message. However, Christians can understand the Bible for themselves, since all Christians have the Spirit. All God's children have access to God's truth.

We need to remember that we depend on God to help us understand His word and His ways (2 Timothy 2 v 7). We can't do it alone, so we must ask for God's help. Pray before you open the Bible. Pray when you get stuck and don't understand stuff. Pray when you do understand it — and say thank you!

SO, WHAT IS THE BIBLE?

▶ *The Bible is God's word direct from God to us. It is relevant today as God speaks into our lives.*

▶ *The Bible is totally true and trustworthy.*

▶ *So we must obey it — what God says goes.*

▶ *We're not on our own — the Holy Spirit helps us understand God's word and apply it to our lives.*

What's the point?

Do you ever read a Bible passage and think "What is the point of that?" It's a good question to ask.

WRITING WITH PURPOSE

It sounds obvious when you say it, but the Bible authors wrote their books with a particular purpose in mind. They weren't just scribbling down random things that popped into their heads. We know that, because they often tell us what their aim is.

For instance, near the end of his Gospel, John says: "Jesus performed many other signs in the presence of his disciples, which are not recorded in this book. But these are written that you may believe that Jesus is the Messiah, the Son of God, and that by believing you may have life in his name" (John 20 v 30–31).

There are loads of things that John could have told us about Jesus but hasn't. He has selected his material with the specific aim of showing us that Jesus is the Messiah/Christ, the Son of God, so that we will come to believe in Him and so have eternal life.

Since the writers of the Bible were inspired by God (2 Timothy 3 v 16), their purpose is God's purpose. This means that one of the most helpful questions we can ever ask is "Why did the author write this?"

IT'S OBVIOUS

Sometimes the author bluntly tells us why he is writing his book, in what's sometimes called the "purpose statement". We've already seen one from John's Gospel. Now check out these two:

Luke 1 v 1–4
1 John 5 v 13

SEARCHING FOR CLUES

But what about Bible books that don't obviously state their purpose? Here are a few tips.

1. Get to know the book
Nothing beats reading the whole book several times. Becoming familiar

with a Bible book helps you to notice themes running through it and to work out the writer's purpose.

2. Ask key questions

These questions are especially helpful if you're reading a New Testament letter (like 1 Timothy) or an Old Testament prophet (like Habakkuk). You might need to grab a study Bible or a commentary to find the answers.

▶ *Who is writing and who's he writing to?*

▶ *What is the situation of the author and the original readers?*

▶ *Are there any problems the author says need to be dealt with?*

▶ *Are there any repeated themes, or a single idea that holds everything together?*

3. What's in and what's out?

"Narrative" books are ones that talk us through historical events (like Genesis or Acts). In these books, you can get an idea of the author's purpose from what he chooses to put in and what he leaves out of his account. Sometimes the author hits the accelerator pedal and covers someone's whole life in two verses; at other times he slows down and gives us a few hours in great detail. We should be asking, "Why do we hear so much about this and so little about that?"

In this article, we've shown you the very best tool for understanding the Bible. Whenever you read a Bible passage, ask: "What's the author's purpose for writing this?", "What are the big themes?", "What is the author trying to do?"

In other words, what's the point?

A novel idea

Go grab a novel right now if you can. One you've never read. Flick to a random page and read any sentence. Does it make any sense? Do you have any idea what's happening in the story?

CONTEXT MATTERS

A novel only makes sense if you start at the beginning and follow the story, watching events unfold and characters develop. We should treat the Bible more like a novel and not just separate verses that we read on their own. Not that we have to read the whole thing from beginning to end every time we open it. But we do need to recognise that individual chapters are connected to what comes before and after. It's called *context* — and it matters!

There's a (probably made-up) story of a guy who was wanting guidance in life and so he flicked through his Bible and put his finger on a verse at random, expecting helpful advice. The verse his finger landed on was: "So Judas threw the money into the temple and left. Then he went away and hanged himself". Thinking that couldn't be what God wanted him to do, he quickly flicked again

to another random verse: "Jesus told him, 'Go and do likewise'". This really freaked the guy out, so he quickly put his finger on another random verse and read: "What you are about to do, do quickly".

Obviously, this guy took these verses completely out of context and so came to a conclusion that was far from what those verses were actually saying. He got completely the wrong message as a result.

LOOK ALL AROUND

There are different levels of context. A sentence comes in the context of a paragraph. A paragraph comes in the context of a chapter or section. A chapter comes in the context of a whole Bible book, and the book comes in the context of the whole Bible. It's very important, as we study a part of the Bible, that we ask how it fits in with what comes before and after.

For instance, in Exodus 20 v 3 we read: "You shall have no other gods before me". This is the first of the Ten Commandments. If we read this and the nine others that follow it on their own, we could come up with all kinds of crazy ideas. You could get the impression that you become one of God's people by being good enough; that you can earn your way to eternal life by keeping these ten rules.

But that big misunderstanding is impossible if we start reading just one verse earlier: "I am the LORD your God, who brought you out of Egypt, out of the land of slavery. You shall have no other gods before me".

God gives these commandments to a people He has *already* saved from Egypt — that's clear not only from the preceding verse, but also from the previous nineteen chapters, which have described the rescue in jaw-dropping detail. God *can't* be saying that they have to obey His laws in order to be saved. He's saying that this is how they should behave *now* that they have been saved!

When reading a Bible bit, take time out to look at what's around that verse or section. What has occurred just before, and what happens just after it? And how do the surrounding Bible passages help you understand the bit you're looking at?

Try it next time you open your Bible…

The ideas on pages 394–399 are taken from *Dig Deeper* by Nigel Beynon and Andrew Sach, published by IVP.

thegoodbook
COMPANY

BIBLICAL | RELEVANT | ACCESSIBLE

At The Good Book Company, we are dedicated to helping Christians and local churches grow. We believe that God's growth process always starts with hearing clearly what he has said to us through his timeless word—the Bible.

Ever since we opened our doors in 1991, we have been striving to produce Bible-based resources that bring glory to God. We have grown to become an international provider of user-friendly resources to the Christian community, with believers of all backgrounds and denominations using our books, Bible studies, devotionals, evangelistic resources, and DVD-based courses.

We want to equip ordinary Christians to live for Christ day by day, and churches to grow in their knowledge of God, their love for one another, and the effectiveness of their outreach.

Call us for a discussion of your needs or visit one of our local websites for more information on the resources and services we provide.

Your friends at The Good Book Company

thegoodbook.com | thegoodbook.co.uk
thegoodbook.com.au | thegoodbook.co.nz
thegoodbook.co.in